DATE DUE

Revised

How to
you

ting

Rapaport

McKennitt

 A Jerome Headlands Press Book

Prentice Hall
Upper Saddle River, New Jersey

loging-in-Publication Data

Rapaport, Diane Sward.
　　How to make & sell your own recording : the complete guide to
independent recording / Diane Sward Rapaport.
　　　p. cm.
　　"A Jerome Headlands Press book."
　　Includes index.
　　ISBN 0-13-923947-2 (pbk.)
　　1. Sound recording industry—United States. 2. Popular
music—Writing and publishing. I. Title. II. Title: How to make and
sell your own recording
　　ML3790 .R36 1999
　　781.49'068—dc21

99-21099
CIP

Prentice-Hall, Inc.
Upper Saddle River, NJ 07458

Produced by—
Jerome Headlands Press, Inc.
PO Box N
Jerome, Arizona 86331

Editor—George Glassman
Cover and book design—Sullivan Santamaria Design, Inc.
Cover and interior photography—Peter Williams Photography
Index—James Minkin, James Minkin Indexing Services

Manufactured in the United States of America

10 9 8 7 6 5 4 3 2 1

ISBN 0-13-923947-2

Prentice-Hall International (UK) Limited, London
Prentice-Hall of Australia Pty. Limited, Sydney
Prentice-Hall Canada Inc., Toronto
Prentice-Hall Hispanoamericana, S.A., Mexico
Prentice-Hall of India Private Limited, New Delhi
Prentice-Hall of Japan, Inc., Tokyo
Pearson Education Asia Pte. Ltd., Singapore
Editora Prentice-Hall do Brasil, Ltda., Rio de Janeiro

Page vii constitutes an extension of the copyright page.

contents

permissions
permissions

the author gratefully acknowledges permission to reproduce graphic art or reprint text excerpts from the following books: *Grateful Dead: The Official Book of the Dead Heads* © 1983, Paul Grushkin, Cynthia Bassett, and Jonas Grushkin; *How to Be Your Own Booking Agent* © 1998 The New Music Times, Inc.; *The Musician's Business and Legal Guide* © 1996 Beverly Hills Bar Association; *The Craft and Business of Songwriting* © 1988 John Braheny; *The Billboard Guide to Home Recording* © 1996 Ray Baragary; *Creating Internet Entertainment* © 1997 Jeannie Novak and Pete Markiewicz; *Ladyslipper Catalog* © 1998 Ladyslipper, Inc.; *The Acoustic Musician's Guide to Sound Reinforcement & Live Recording* © 1998 Mike Sokol; *How to Make Money Performing in Schools* © 1996 Silcox Productions; *Bluegrass Music in the Schools* © 1998 International Bluegrass Music Association.

The author also acknowledges permission to use the following articles: "Financing" and "Recording Contracts" both © 1999 by Edward R. Hearn, Esq.; and "Sampling" © 1999 by Gregory T. Victoroff, Esq.

Permission to use selected graphics and other materials was graciously granted by Alesis Corporation; Roland Corporation; Sony Electronics Corporation; and TASCAM/TEAC America, Inc.

NOTICE ABOUT TRADEMARKS

Designations used by companies to distinguish their products are often claimed as trademarks. Rather than list the names of entities that own the trademarks or insert a trademark symbol with each mention of trademarked names, Jerome Headlands Press, Inc. states that it is using the names only for editorial purposes with no intention of infringing upon any trademark.

foreword

foreword

I have long taken the view that I would rather work toward seizing my destiny than have it thrust upon me. Now, many years after I took the first small steps in that direction, I am honored to have been asked to write the foreword for the 20th anniversary edition of *How To Make And Sell Your Own Recording.* As I do so, I find myself looking back on the progress of my own career and the extent to which its direction was shaped by this very book.

Having made my way through some of the the compounds and corridors of the emperor's palace of the music industry, I have discovered that, all too frequently, the emperor has no clothes. As in any field, the music business is only as good as the people you work with. Furthermore, the degree to which you will be able to effect change depends on your capacity for collaboration and your willingness to interface with those people. You will always be in a better position to realize your goals when you are armed with the knowledge of the way things work, and the readiness to play some part in the process.

There is much misinformation and myth about what artists themselves can and should be doing on the "business" side of their careers. In my more cynical moments, I have wondered whether some record companies, managers, agents, lawyers, and promoters have a vested interest in artists remaining ignorant of the forces which directly influence their work. At the end of the day, the ultimate responsibility for any artist's destiny lies with the artist, and we must be prepared to take on that challenge.

People in all professions, from restaurateurs to shop owners, rightly see creativity as a vital ingredient of their work, but would never dream of completely abdicating their business responsibilities and passing them on to somebody else. In my experience, artists do exactly that, far too readily and frequently.

I can understand why many of us are initially daunted by the prospect of becoming more hands-on in the execution or administration of practical matters, including that of creating a recording itself. There are budgets, timelines, and mechanical and technical matters galore, but they are not beyond comprehension, particularly when taken piece by piece at a point in one's career where there is time to learn, and the volume and complexity is not as great as it will be when the pace quickens.

Learning business is not unlike learning music: you start modestly, with simple steps, and as you reach one plateau, you acquire the skills and confidence you need to reach the next level.

Having a map such as this book is vital.

Of course, creating a recording is only part of the equation. Marketing, promotion and distribution are equally deserving of attention. Reaching out more directly to those that might be interested in our work, and maintaining and expanding that connection, is one of the most significant components in developing a strong and lasting career. Fortunately, we are living at a time when technology affords us even more choices and options than ever before. Depending on our resources, we can remain effective in the realm of things such as keeping one's own mailing list and operating through the postal system; exploring the possibilities in the burgeoning on-line world; selling recordings at one's performances, or dealing directly with retailers. As one eventually realizes, distribution, marketing, and promotional arrangements vary widely, and can be assembled relative to one's needs and resources, and even these potentially complex activities need not be insurmountably hard to learn.

A greater understanding of the music business will show that there are certain musical genres and scales of operation that are far more likely to be successful and lucrative outside the boundaries of a major label than within them. The perceived notion that a major label deal is necessary needs constant and vigilant reevaluation: for the vast majority of those that become recording artists, making and selling your own record is, indeed, the way to begin.

The main ingredients in building a solid and successful career, in addition to your talent and vision, are curiosity, tenacity, determination, and a fondness for creative problem solving. It is my sincere hope that as you become more familiar and comfortable with the different facets of the business side of music, you will recognize the value of the effort it takes to realize your potential and protect the integrity of your creative work.

I am thoroughly convinced that this book has played a pioneering role in the long-overdue broadening of the avenues of the music industry. Over the years, Diane's book has worked to reshape the way music is marketed, and has helped to introduce ostensibly "uncommercial," innovative, and truly special artists and their music to receptive audiences. It has been a map to guide thousands of artists that have picked their way through the corridors of the emperor's palace. More importantly, it has helped many of them realize their dreams.

I know that *How To Make And Sell Your Own Recording,* revised and updated, will continue to do what it has done for the last twenty years: bring artist, music, and audience together for all the right reasons.

Here, then, is a good map and true. I wish its readers every success on their journeys.

—Loreena McKennitt

acknowledgments

acknowledgments

researching, writing, and producing a manual for musicians is a collaboration. The first people I want to thank are the musicians that shared their music, graphics, and stories. I've taught, interviewed, and have been written to by thousands of them. This book could not have been written without their tales of struggle and success. Their music, which covers so many different genres, provides continual inspiration and pleasure.

I want to thank Loreena McKennitt for her gracious foreword. Her music has inspired me from the first time I heard a demo sent me in 1985 by my friend, Richard Flohil, a publicist and concert promoter from Toronto, Ontario, Canada. I also want to thank Loreena's office staff, particularly Karen Shook and Jane Boyce at Quinlan Road, Limited.

I want to thank my expert readers. They read entire chapters or segments of chapters to make sure "I got the information right." Dave McAvinchey, Guitar Nine Records; Jim Bosken, founder of QCA Manufacturing; John Braheny, author of *The Craft and Business of Songwriting;* Edward Hearn, attorney; David Litwin, David Litwin Productions; Jeannie Novak and Pete Markiewicz, founders of Kaleidospace and authors of *Creating Internet Entertainment* and *Internet World Guide to Maintaining and Updating*

Dynamic Web Sites; Charlie Pilzer, Air Show Mastering; Micah Solomon, owner, Oasis CD and Cassette Duplication; Walter Rapaport, Rapasound; Douglas Welch, Welchwrite; and Gregory Victoroff, attorney. A special thanks to Paul Foschino, Marketing Director, Sony Electronics, Inc. for letting me preview the four-track MiniDisc recorder.

Next, I want to thank those I interviewed for this edition that were very generous with information and graphics. Mike Anderson, Anomaly Records; Michael Bannister, Burning Sky; Richard Brooks, Capstone Records; Cynthia Connolly, Dischord Records; Dean and Dudley Evenson, Tom Barabas, Pauline Young, and Pat Hayes, Soundings of the Planet; Uli Elser, Alternative Tentacles Records; Hardy Fox, The Cryptic Corporation; Richard Flohil, music publicist and concert promoter; Bobbito Garcia, Fondle 'Em Records; Steven Halpern, Inner Peace Music; Stephen Hill, Hearts of Space; Tracy Hill, Press Network; Bob Feldman, Red House Records; Walt Goodridge, Niche Market Exclusives; Ken Irwin, cofounder, Rounder Records; Jester, Doppler Effects Records; Pete and Maura Kennedy, The Kennedys, Commission Impossible Management; David Lau, Brookwood Studio, Inc.; Katie Lee, Katydid Books & Music;

Jody and Michael McFadin, Ubiquity Records; John McCutcheon; Bill McGee, and Danja Mowf, Funtown Music Media; Don MacInnis, Record Technology Inc.; Priscilla and Barton McLean, McLean Mix; James Marienthal, Silver Wave Records; Pat Martin, Executive Director, the Association For Independent Music (AFIM); Craig Miller, Acoustic Disc Records; Lisa Otey, Owl's Nest Productions; Holger Petersen, Stony Plain Records; Dan Sause, co-owner, Locals Only; Peter Spellman, Music Business Solutions; Dean Shostak; Brian Sheen, Manager, Liberties Bed; Dawn Holstein, Spinner.com; Chris Strachwitz and Tom Diamant, Arhoolie Records; Mike Sokol, author; Julie Sullivan, Keith Gommora, and Aaron Tyler of Green Sky; Sue Trainor, Christina Muir, and Sue Ribaudo, Hot Soup; Edward Wong, owner Sandbox Automatic; Mike Young, DiscMakers; and John Ziegler, Major Lingo.

I also want to acknowledge the many people I met at the National Association of Music Manufacturers (NAMM) Convention held in Anaheim, California in February 1998. The show was particularly helpful about new recording, composing, and performing technologies. Thanks also to the people I met and talked with at the Folk Alliance Conference held in February 1998 in Memphis, Tennessee.

Thank you to Norwell F. (Bud) Therien, Jr., Executive Publisher, Art & Music, College Division, Prentice Hall, and to Christopher Johnson, Senior Acquisitions Editor, Music, Prentice Hall; to Steve Wilson and David McCumiskey of Music Sales for their help getting my book into music and record stores; and to Chuck Madden of Davitt & Hanser for carrying my book in their catalog.

I also want to thank the design and production team of Jerome Headlands Press: Julie Sullivan, Joan Carstensen, and Amy Regez of Sullivan Santamaria Design; Peter Williams for cover photography; Northland Graphics, color separations; Splendid Graphics, graphic scans; George Glassman, Glassman Enterprises, for his excellent editing job; James Minkin for the index; and Henry Vincent, CPA and Norrie Benjamin, bookkeeper, for the fine bean counting!

Sue Tillman, editorial assistant and office manager at Jerome Headlands Press, deserves a special word of appreciation for her attention to detail, her patience, and her commitment to doing a job as perfectly as it can be done—and from saving me, many, many times, from certain chaos.

I am very grateful to my family, friends, and business associates for their continued enthusiasm and support.

Finally, thanks go to the following musicians and companies that provided photographs and other materials for use in the book.

Acoustic Disc
(David Grisman)
PO Box 4143
San Rafael, CA 94913-4143
www.dawgnet.com

Airshow Mastering Inc.
3063 Sterling Circle, Suite 3
Boulder, CO 80301
www.airshowmastering.com

Alesis Corporation
3630 Holdrege Avenue
Los Angeles, CA 90016
www.alesis.com

Alternative Tentacles Records
PO Box 419092
San Francisco, CA 94141-9092
www.alternativetentacles.com

Anomaly Records
PO Box 260
Milton Mills, NH 03852
www.sonicjoyride.com

Appalseed
(John McCutcheon)
1025 Locust Avenue
Charlottesville, VA 22901
www.folkmusic.com

Appleseed Recordings
PO Box 2593
West Chester, PA 19380
www.appleseedrec.com

Arhoolie Records
10341 San Pablo Avenue
El Cerrito, CA 94530
www.arhoolie.com

Azure Records
(Trapezoid)
PO Box 38
Washington, VA 22747

The Brookwood Studio, Inc.
(David Lau)
1155 Rosewood, Suite A
Ann Arbor, MI 48104
www.brookwoodstudio.com

Capstone Records
252 De Kalb Avenue
Brooklyn, NY 11205

Commission Impossible
   Management
(The Kennedys)
PO Box 8461
Reston, VA 20195-2361

The Cryptic Corporation
(The Residents)
604 Mission Street #300
San Francisco, CA 94105
www.residents.com

David Litwin Productions
(David Litwin)
2658 Bridgeway, Suite 101
Sausalito, CA 94965
E-mail—DAVLITWIN@aol.com

Dischord Records
(Fugazi)
3819 Beecher Street, N.W.
Washington, DC 20007-1802
www.dischord.com

Fondle 'Em Records
323 East 9th Street, Basement
New York, NY 10003
www.sandbox.pair.com or
www.fatbeats.com

Funtown Music Media
(Danja Mowf)
PO Box 25696
Richmond, VA 23260
www.flavatown.com

Green Sky
c/o Julie Sullivan
658 North Locust
Flagstaff, AZ 86001
E-mail—julie@ssdzn.com

Guitar Nine Records
(Dan McAvinchey)
8201 Hambledon Court
Raleigh, NC 27615
www.guitar9.com

Hearts of Space
PO Box 31321
San Francisco, CA 94131
www.hos.com

Hidden Waters Music
(Peg Millett)
PO Box 2544
Prescott, AZ 86302

Hot Soup
PO Box 412
Columbia, MD 21045
www.pobox.com/~hotsoup

Inner Peace Music
PO Box 2644
San Anselmo, CA 94979-2644
www.innerpeacemusic.com

Kaleidospace, LLC
PO Box 5458
Santa Monica, CA 90409
www.kspace.com

Katydid Books & Music
(Katie Lee)
PO Box 395
Jerome, AZ 86331
E-mail—katydid@verdenet.com

Ladyslipper
3205 Hillsborough Road
Durham, NC 27705
www.ladyslipper.org

Liberties Bed
WCMA
1355 Palmetto Park Road, Suite
258
Boca Raton, FL 33486

Locals Only
916 West Burnside
Portland, OR 97209
www.localsonline.com

Lyrichord Discs, Inc.
141 Perry Street
New York, NY 10014
www.lyrichord.com

Major Lingo
115 East Pinal Street
Cottonwood, AZ 86326
www.primenet.com/~panguy/lingo

McLean Mix
55 Coon Brook Road
Peterburgh, NY 12138
www.emf.org/people_mclean.html

Music Business Solutions
(Peter Spellman)
PO Box 230266, Astor Station
Boston, MA 02123-0266
www.mbsolutions.com

Oasis CD & Cassette Duplication
659 Zachary Taylor Highway
PO Box 721
Flint Hill, VA 22627
www.oasisCD.com

Owl's Nest Productions
(Lisa Otey)
PO Box 77865
Tucson, AZ 85703
E-mail—owl@azstarnet.com

QCA, Inc.
2832 Spring Grove Avenue
Cincinnati, OH 45225
www.pol.com/qca

Quinlan Road
PO Box 933
Stratford, ON N5A 7M3
Canada
www.quinlanroad.com

Red House Records
501 West Lynnhurst Avenue
St. Paul, MN 55104
www.redhouserecords.com

Roland Corporation U.S.
7200 Dominion Circle
Los Angeles, CA 90040-3696
www.rolandus.com

Rounder Records Group
One Camp Street
Cambridge, MA 02140
www.rounder.com

RTI
Record Technology Inc.
486 Dawson Drive
Camarillo, CA 93012

Rykodisc USA
(Burning Sky)
Shetland Park
27 Congress Street
Salem, MA 01970
www.rykodisc.com

Dean Shostak
PO Box 465
Williamsburg, VA 23187
www.glassmusic.com

Silver Wave Records
PO Box 7943
Boulder, CO 80306
www.silverwave.com

Sony Electronics Inc.
Professional Audio Group
1 Sony Drive
Park Ridge, NJ 07656
www.sony.com/proaudio

Soundings of the Planet
PO Box 4472
Bellingham, WA 98227
www.soundings.com

Stony Plain Records
PO Box 861
Edmonton, AB T5J 2L8
Canada
www.stonyplainmusic.com

TASCAM/TEAC America Inc.
7733 Telegraph Road
Montebello, CA 90640
www.tascam.com

Ubiquity Recordings
54 Washburn Street
San Francisco, CA 94103
www.ubiquityrecords.com

Kate Wolf
PO Box 151208
San Rafael, CA 94915-1208
www.katewolf.com

WorldWind
(James Durst)
PO Box 801
Amherst, NH 03031
www.songs.com/jd

How to Make and Sell Your Own Record

REVISED THIRD EDITION

INCLUDES COMPACT DISCS

HOW TO
MAKE
AND SELL
YOUR OWN
RECORD

75,000 COPIES SOLD

THE COMPLETE GUIDE
TO INDEPENDENT RECORDING

HOW TO MAKE & SELL
YOUR OWN RECORDING
A Guide for the Nineties
DIANE SWARD RAPAPORT

The first edition of this book was
published in 1979. It has been
updated every five years; and has
sold more than 150,000 copies.

introduction

introduction

PHOTO BY PETER WILLIAMS

i first learned of independent record labels in San Francisco in 1976. Some were labels started by artists, such as acoustic guitarist Will Ackerman; singer-songwriter Kate Wolf; new age artist Steven Halpern; stylized avante-garde punk band The Residents; R. Crumb and His Cheap Suit Serenaders; and shakuhachi flute artist, Masayuki Koga. Others were started by entrepreneurs to breathe life into niche genres, such as Arhoolie Records (folk, blues, Cajun, zydeco, Tex-Mex); 1750 Arch Records (classical); Olivia (music for women); Kicking Mule (guitar and banjo music); Bay Records (folk music); and Redwood Records (social protest).

"We were a cottage industry of necessity: and our cause was visibility and empowerment," said Judy Dlugacz, founder of Olivia Records. Her words echoed the sentiments of hundreds of indie labels that mushroomed throughout the United States during the mid-seventies.

Today, indie labels and their artists have succeeded in ways that few dreamed. They have captured over 15% market share from the major labels, according to Sound Scan, Inc., a company that tracks sales of records at retail record outlets. And according to the RIAA, sales of indie records in the United States totaled $2.9 billion dollars in 1998. (When this book was first published in 1979, annual domestic record sales for all labels were only $4.5 billion dollars.)

The actual income generated by indie recordings may be much higher, because Sound Scan statistics do not include mail-order sales or those generated at performances and in non-record retail stores.

This amounts to a revolution made up of tens of thousands of independent recording artists, ranging from artists that put out a CD or cassette and sell only a few recordings at performances in their home towns, to artists recording for labels that release many records annually in particular genres and generate gross incomes to several million dollars annually. The revolution has no leader, no dominant indie label or artist with multiple platinum sales, no recording epicenter, and only sparse exposure on major network radio and television stations.

Their success is due to a synergy of factors: the tenacity, imagination and perseverance of the artists; affordable recording and computing technology; availability of music business and audio education for musicians; continuing growth of alternative promotion and distribution networks that serve niche music genres, including the Internet; and increased memberships and participation in trade organizations, such as the Association For Independent Music (AFIM), Folk Alliance, Gospel Music Association, etc.

The success of the independent recording revolution is not only to be measured by market share and dollars earned.

Independent artists have succeeded in achieving aesthetic and financial freedom. "So maybe I don't make $100,000 bucks and have gold records. But I get the music out. I make a living—I enjoy what I'm doing—and I can do the music the way I feel it," said David Grisman in an interview with me in 1976.

Independent artists have succeeded in overcoming the conditioning, perpetuated by hype, habit, and cliché, which said money matters are best left to business people.

Fueled by the knowledge they could put out their own recordings, musicians sought out opportunities for education and began to take control of their careers. This helped spur the growth of the music business and audio education industry. In 1976, books and schools offering music business information were few. Today, music business and audio technology classes are available in more than 250 colleges and universities, at more than 50 private audio and music schools, such as Berklee in Boston, and at huge music conferences. There are several hundred music business and technology books available.

Independent recording artists are contributing to the rejuvenation of local and regional economies. Most towns with populations of 5000 have a resident artist or band selling their own recordings. Many of the larger indies are not based in major label recording centers of Los Angeles, New York, or Nashville, but are scattered throughout the United States. American Gramophone is based in Omaha, Rounder Records in Boston, Arhoolie in Oakland, Red House in St. Paul, Silver Wave in Boulder, etc.

Most of their artists spend money locally for graphic design, printing, clothing, audio and computing technology, recording studios, education, etc. Their gigs generate money for club owners and promoters. As a band or company expands sales beyond their local community, they return some of these earnings to their home communities, which further increases their economic health.

The income generated and spent by indie artists in making and selling their recordings supports a large decentralized entertainment industry, which runs less visibly, but parallel to the major label companies that continue to homogenize and narrow their focus to only a few musical genres and consolidate themselves into major media conglomerates.

Perhaps the greatest contribution of independent artists is that they have revitalized music in America by enriching the spectrum that is available to the public.

ABOUT THIS BOOK

This book is written to help guide you on all the steps you need to take to make and sell your records or to set up an indie record label. It is written in reverse order—the chapters on promotion and sales come first. This is where your thinking should start: how many records can you reasonably expect to sell during the first year of their release? Too often, artists, in their enthusiasm for making a record, fail to deal with this important question until after they have spent all their money on making the record.

The answer to that question sets the boundaries of your budget for design and printing of promotional materials, recording costs, manufacturing, etc. In the excitement of creating music, it is easy to overlook practical considerations: how to assemble promotional materials and send them to the right people; how to get your records into stores; how to choose printers, manufacturers, graphic designers, engineers; how to promote your music, etc.

One caution: prices given are "average" at the time the book was sent to the printer. Be sure to get up-to-date price information before you finalize your cost projections and plans.

This book won't make your music great or turn you into an overnight success. It will, however, spare you from some of the frustrations that result from ignorance and trial and error. It can help you shape your fantasies, take charge of your career, and share your music.

—Diane Sward Rapaport

THE RADIO SHOW "MUSIC FROM THE HEARTS OF SPACE" GREW OUT OF producer Stephen Hill's fascination with melodic electro-acoustic space music. His show began in the 1970s as a weekly late-night radio program in the San Francisco Bay Area. In 1983, the show was nationally syndicated for public radio. Today it airs on over 275 radio stations, including some in four of the top five U.S. radio markets and some in the majority of the top fifty.

Hill launched the Hearts of Space record label in 1984. The label's recordings began appearing on Billboard's Top Adult Alternatives Albums Chart (New Age and World Music) in 1990.

A second label, Hearts O' Space, was started in 1992 to feature the best in contemporary Celtic music from around the world. In 1995–96, the album *Celtic Twilight 2* was number two on Billboard's World Music album charts. *Celtic Twilight 1* has sold more than half a million copies worldwide. Other imprints owned by Hill and his wife Leyla include Fathom (tribal/electronic/ambient sounds), World Class (world music), and RGB (pop electronica).

PHOTO BY MARI KANE

Stephen Hill
Founder

Since 1984, we've sold more than three and a half million records, which proves the power of niche marketing. But remember, music is a fashion business and unless you're involved in mainstream genres, such as rock 'n' roll, you have to change the focus of your company from time to time or at least deal with multiple niche genres. New Age music was hot in 1986. Now it is just another category. Today Celtic music is hot, but its popularity will also deflate. Some other genre will capture an audience's heart. If it is music we care about, we'll jump into it and put out a quality product. That's what happened when we released Sacred Treasures, *a recording that featured the great choral music of the Russian Orthodox church with compositions by Rachmaninoff and Tchaikovsky.*

—Stephen Hill
www.hos.com

promotion

promotion

the first thing most people do when they receive their recordings from the manufacturer is call their families and friends with the news.

Letting other people know and getting them excited about your recording is called "promotion." Its purpose is to create a demand for your recordings and your performances. You can start with a few devoted fans and end up with your picture on the cover of *Rolling Stone*.

Promotion works by persuading people, whose opinions are respected, to share information and enthusiasm with others. Devoted fans play your recordings for friends, bring them to gigs, and set up fan Web sites. DJs may play cuts, critics may review it, and reporters may interview you. These people acquaint others with your music and stimulate curiosity, interest, and excitement. They assure potential buyers it will be worthwhile to spend money on your recording. These people have credibility because they present opinions, not advertising. Promotion, at its most successful, persuades people to buy your recording and come to your performances, induces media people to give you attention, and gets concert and festival promoters to hire you.

Recording label personnel also define promotion as getting airplay. Promotion people take recordings to radio stations and persuade the appropriate people to play them on the air. An illegal form of persuasion is payola, paying DJs or programmers to play recordings.

In this book, the term promotion means getting free publicity, including airplay, and using media attention and your recording to increase your fan following, get better gigs, and attract business people that can help further your career.

Television appearances, reviews, interviews, and articles seldom happen by chance. Millions of dollars are spent yearly by public relations firms and publicists. They understand that reporters, news directors, reviewers, and critics are waiting for news to be delivered to them in the form of press releases, free recordings, and invitations to performances and parties. They expect to be courted, cajoled, and pleaded with to talk or write about an event or to play a recording. The combination of money, personnel, power, and influence put out by major recording labels for publicity and promotion resembles a military campaign in its complexity, intensity, and sophistication. You will be competing with their efforts for attention.

If you finance, produce, and manufacture your own recording, not doing the necessary promotion is just plain crazy. You are the one who should direct the energy that creates airplay, reviews, and sales, because you care the most. Although you can hire people to do some specific tasks of promotion, the main responsibility rests with you. Remember, it is your efforts and music that will reap the benefits you deserve!

Promotion can be done by anyone willing to persevere and spend a little money. Once you know the techniques and tools involved, diligence and a professional approach will earn results. By adding persistence, imagination, and old-fashioned chutzpah, you will attract the attention you need. When you understand the basics of a successful promotional campaign you can apply the techniques to publicizing any business, be it a recording studio, sound reinforcement company, or publishing venture.

Researching your audience, assembling a media list, looking at Web sites, writing press releases, and putting together a plan costs little more than time. Spend it liberally. The time you use for promotion can cut into the time you spend creating your music and rehearsing, but it

is unrealistic to ignore these responsibilities until you can afford a public relations (PR) person. You should, however, plan your time so you do not have to divide your energy during the critical period of recording.

Successful promotion happens over the long haul. It will take quite awhile before you see tangible results—maybe as long (or longer) as two months to convince an influential reviewer to come and hear you perform; three months to book some good college dates; six months to convince two or three radio stations to play your recording. It may take years and the release of more than one recording to build a successful career.

Meanwhile, you will be doing the seemingly endless work of mailing press release after press release, making phone calls, responding to e-mail, and updating mailing lists and your Web site. Eventually, you will see progress in all areas: increased attendance at gigs, better gigs, reviews, airplay, and more sales.

Money should be budgeted for promotional materials and ongoing business needs for at least a year following the release of your recording.

You should acquire a working knowledge of the media that can benefit you, assemble mailing lists, design and print promotional materials, and develop a promotional campaign.

MARKET RESEARCH

Market research helps you plan your promotional budget and shows where to target your efforts. It will also help you answer the question, "Who is going to buy my recording?"

Market research should be done well in

advance of making your recording. It will help you define your financing needs, sales, and promotional goals. The main tasks are (1) identify your genre; (2) characterize your potential audience; and (3) analyze your competition.

Identify Your Genre

The first question most people ask once they know you are a musician is, "What kind of music do you do?"

Agents, club owners, and concert promoters want to know if your music is the type they are looking for; record distributors and store owners want to know where to put your recording in their catalogs or stores; DJs need to know whether your music fits their programming needs; fans want to describe your music to their friends.

Most genres have many subcategories, which makes it easier for bands to identify where they fit and for people to find them on the Internet. For example, rock includes alternative rock, metal, Euro-rock, angel rock, surf rock, punk, progressive rock, and thrash. Folk includes bluegrass, Celtic, contemporary, traditional, and cowboy. Christian includes praise and worship, traditional church music, black gospel, Southern gospel, and music with Christian messages in rock, rap, and country genres. Dance includes techno, rave, electronica, ambient, and creative psychedelic. New age has tonal healing, angelic, meditation, and so forth.

The answers to these questions will help you narrow your description:

- ◆ How would a fan of your music describe it to a person who has never heard you

PHOTO BY JAY BLAKESBERG

David Grisman, one of the world's great mandolinists, is the inventor of the term "dawg" music—which encompasses a hybrid of bluegrass, jazz, and just about anything else he feels like playing.

play or knows nothing of your background?

◆ What style of music is it most like?

The success of many independent labels is due to the development and growth of specialized promotional and sales networks in niche-genre markets. There are distributors such as Sandbox (hip-hop) and City Hall Records (jazz, blues, world) that handle independent labels. There are nonprofit associations, such as the Folk Alliance and the Gospel Music Association, where members trade information about performing opportunities, festival promoters, specialty magazines, and radio programming. These niche-genre networks are being given an ever bigger boost by Internet Web sites devoted to particular genres and by the improvement of Internet audio transmission.

Some genres are attached to religious, social, political, or ethnic topics, such as new age, environmental, Western Americana, Christian, Celtic, feminist, etc. As interest in these genres increases, so do promotional opportunities and sales of recordings. For example, the popularity of Celtic music has been greatly enhanced by the Irish folk-dance musical *Riverdance* and the remarkable success of singer-songwriter Loreena McKennitt, who began her career as an independent artist, and by National Public Radio's Celtic program, "Thistle and Shamrock."

Examine the Web sites of independent recording label artists to learn how those in your genre promote and sell their music. These sites have information about performance opportunities, magazines, radio stations, and associations that support their particular genre.

Characterize Your Audience

Promotional and sales efforts are best geared towards developing and increasing a following of loyal fans.

Characterizing your fans will help you design graphics and promotional materials that appeal to them, determine which media they pay attention to, and book performances they will attend.

Begin with identifying the people that already listen to your music—your friends and fans. Describe them by age, sex, social and political interests, occupation, financial status, lifestyle, hobbies, and their tastes in music and art. Isolating their special interests may open unusual avenues for you and give you ideas about what merchandise (T-shirts, coffee mugs, decals, etc.) they might buy in addition to your records.

You also need to know what technology your fans use for listening to music. How many prefer cassette players? Turntables? CD players? Other?

If your music is similar to that of other recording artists in your community, ask them if they have analyzed their audience or found any special ways to reach them.

If you are unable to describe your fans and their interests, select some people at random at your next performance and interview them or print a simple questionnaire on a card and hand it out at gigs. Include a place for names and addresses so you can add to your mailing list.

Here are five questions that will help you identify special interests.

◆ What music magazine(s) do you read?

◆ What radio station(s) do you listen to?

◆ What other bands do you like?

◆ Do you prefer CDs, cassettes, vinyl?

◆ What hobbies/special interests do you have?

Analyze the Competition

You compete with other bands for performing venues and media attention. Go to their gigs to answer these questions.

◆ How good is your music in comparison to theirs?

◆ Where are they performing?

◆ How do they promote their music?

◆ Where are they getting reviewed?

Attend music conferences that are devoted to your genre. Talk to bands and record label personnel. Get copies of their press kits. Study their Web sites. Read the magazines and newspapers in your area. Visit record stores to find out how recordings are displayed. Gathering and sharing information (networking) is free and rewarding. You might find yourself with new allies to add to your mailing lists.

Compare yourself with the top acts in your genre because that is where the real competition lies. Why should people spend money on your recording when they can spend the same amount and get one by a famous artist in the same genre? Is it because fans love your performances and you are accessible to your audiences in ways that famous performers are not? Is it because you have created music that is different and excites them?

Knowing what makes your band different or better than others will enable you to design promotional tools for a campaign that can work effectively for you.

MAILING LISTS

Assembling mailing lists before making a recording will help you decide how many copies you will give away, what promotional materials will accompany them, and how to time your campaign.

You should spend time researching conventional media outlets (local and regional newspapers, magazines, college radio stations, and the Internet). And spend some time each month to research and add new opportunities. As your career succeeds, more promotional opportunities will open and your lists will grow.

Three lists should be assembled: fans, industry, and press. Each of these can contain several subcategories.

Fan List

Fans should be the first to know when you release a recording. They have followed you from gig to gig and brought their friends to hear you. They have talked up your band and played your recordings. Their loyalty and support should be repaid with care and regard.

A great deal of the new business that businesses get is created by people that recommend them. Savvy bands court their fans and build mailing lists.

Fans are a major source of support. The "Dead Heads," fans of the now defunct Grateful Dead, number well into the hundreds of thousands. They were primarily responsible for the band's ability to fill concert halls in the '60s, '70s and '80s, although they had no radio hits until the '90s. Even after the death of Jerry Garcia, these fans still buy merchandise from the band's in-house merchandising company. Their quarterly publication, *The Grateful Dead Almanac,* sells posters, T-shirts, and records released by remaining band members and lets fans know about "The Further Festival"—concerts by remaining band members and friends.

Fan mailing lists are useful for getting people to gigs, raising money, selling records, and creat-

I first became a Dead Head in 1969. The Dead experience was powerful and cathartic. It triggered deep releases of emotional energy in me and in the audience around me. The whole community attended and left feeling purged and more attuned to their commonality.

—Alan Mande, from Paul Grushkin's introduction to Grateful Dead: The Official Book of the Dead Heads

ing word-of-mouth excitement. A good fan list provides solid evidence of a following to club owners and promoters and improves your chances of getting better gigs. Good music has a way of creating a kind of excitement ("buzz") and you need to take advantage of that. Fan lists help you do so. They enable you to send out information about gigs and new recordings and provide your fans with personal information such as causes you are interested in, other musicians you admire, etc. Some bands have reported that telling fans about their plans to make a recording resulted in offers of financial help, discounts at studios owned by fans, and so on.

To start your list, write down the names and addresses of your family and friends. They are your most dedicated supporters and are most likely to spread the word of your accomplishments.

Next, gather the names and addresses of people that come to your performances, either by having a guest book or by passing out cards they can fill out. The cards can contain questions about their interests and double as the market research needed for characterizing your audience. During every performance, mention that you are assembling a fan mailing list to let people know when and where you are playing and keep them up-to-date about your recording efforts.

If you have a Web site, ask your fans to visit. Provide a method for visitors to join your Web mailing list by providing an e-mail link or a form to fill out on-line, which can include some marketing questions.

Offer to exchange your fan list with other bands in your genre.

Industry List

Making and selling recordings adds credibility about your professionalism and your following. It creates incentive for club owners and concert promoters to hire you, and for bigger recording labels to sign you. Your recording's increasing sales figures show that you have a growing network of fans that come to your performances and buy your recordings.

Research and make a list of club owners, concert and festival promoters, booking agents, artist managers, and musical groups that might be interested in using you as a warm-up act. List the people at seminars and conferences that book showcases—opportunities to perform for industry people.

It is useful to subdivide your industry list into first priority and second priority categories. The first consists of people that seem accessible and sympathetic, such as a club owner who thinks your band shows promise or a record label that has evinced interest.

The second is for those that seem less accessible, yet, may in the future be able to give you the break you need, such as promoters of large concerts and festivals, producers, publishers, distributors, store owners, and artist managers.

Research names in major music industry guides such as *The Billboard International Buyer's Guide Directory* and *Recording Industry Sourcebook* and in guides put out by musician and songwriter associations for their members, such as the *AFIM Directory* published by the Association For Independent Music.

Many music organizations, record labels, artists, and others in the industry have Web sites that provide links to the media and industry businesses that are important to them. Artists often post listings of where they are performing and which radio stations are playing their music. There are also sites that list tour dates for hundreds of artists. Use the Internet to add to your industry and press lists and, more importantly, learn about the resources available for your genre of music.

IF YOU WOULD LIKE TO BE ON OUR MAILING LIST AND RECEIVE NEW RELEASE INFO, TOURING INFO AND GIVEAWAYS, PLEASE FILL OUT THIS CARD AND MAIL IT BACK TO US.

Ubiquity

Name
Address
City   State   Zip
E-mail address
What CD was this card in?
Purchased at?
Best store that should but doesn't carry our stuff
Would your friend like a catalog?
Name
Address
City   State   Zip
Comments

Many labels include mail-back postcards with all CDs. This one is from Ubiquity Records.

Press Lists

Press lists contain names, mail and e-mail addresses, fax and phone numbers of the people responsible for listings, reviews, interviews, stories, airplay, talk shows, etc.

Research the media that influences your target audience. Include writers, DJs, and radio and television people that might appreciate your music and give it their attention.

Subdivide your press list into the following

categories: print, radio, Web-only radio, television. Divide each of those categories into priority and secondary lists.

Research sources in your local library. Read national annual media directories—such as the *Gale Directory of Publications and Broadcast Media.* Listen to radio stations to learn if they play your type of music, and gather information from book, record, and musical instrument stores.

You must check the accuracy of all listings as names and addresses frequently change. The best method is to phone each source directly. This should be done before your first mailing is sent; and thereafter at least once every three months.

Bring your laptop computer to the gig and use it to sign fans to your mailing list with Digital Napkins, a database included in StarMaker's software program for musicians (www.stringfellow.com).

Print Media List

Identify writers at publications, and Internet sites that publish news about artists at your recording and performing level. This will be your primary print media list.

Once you start attracting notice, you can send reviews and other promotional materials to people on your secondary press and industry lists.

Read your community's newspapers and magazines and any specialty journals that are interested in the type of music you write and perform. Do not neglect the Sunday supplements of daily newspapers, which often have sections that deal with art and music.

Most large newspapers and magazines have more than one person writing about music: one may review only major concerts; another concentrates on local performances; another does record reviews; still another may write special news columns. Your list can have many names from one newspaper or magazine. If only one recording or press release is sent to a publication it will not be shared. Each person on your list must receive the information.

Spend time reading. It will help you to personalize your approach. Just as you like to know that writers hear and like your music, they enjoy knowing that you read and pay attention to their words. Take special notice of writers that do material about other-than-famous performers. It is more useful to approach writers and critics that have a history of reviewing independents than those that never review anyone who is not famous.

One person's name can crop up on several different magazines and newspapers, identifying him or her as a freelance writer. Like musicians competing for club gigs, freelancers compete for space (and pay) in newspapers and magazines by coming up with salable ideas. These are important people to have on your lists since they are always on the lookout for scoops, interesting events, side issues, and special news.

Pay particular attention to regional and national publications that serve specialized musical interests. In the last ten years, niche music magazines and fanzines have proliferated; and those that are published only on the Internet are increasing. A good place to research publications is to look at the links provided on Web sites by recording labels, music organizations, and other artists in your genre.

Some local, regional, and nonmusic publications may be interested in stories about independent labels and musicians of interest to their audience. Some examples are *MS* (women's issues); *Sierra* and *Wild Earth* (environmental issues); and *Yoga Journal* (health).

Many newspapers, magazines, newsletters, and Internet sites feature calendar listings of special events as a community service. These listings are usually free. The only rule is to get your information to the right people on time (lead time). You can generally assume that a daily publication and Internet Web site must have information three to five days in advance; ten to 14 days for a local weekly; two weeks (or more) for a national weekly; three to four weeks for local monthly publications; and three to four months for national monthly publications. Call or e-mail and ask for the name of the person responsible for calendar listings and what their lead time is.

Note whether the people on your mailing list will accept news sent to them via e-mail and in what form. Many magazine editors prefer that press releases and news articles be sent in the body of the e-mail, not attached as a word processing document.

Research the names and addresses of local organizations that send newsletters to their members. Many nonprofit music organizations have newsletters that feature reviews and stories about music projects and groups. If you fit their target audience they will want to hear from you. Religious organizations, political groups, historical societies, environmental nonprofits, and so forth, always welcome news that will interest their audience.

Radio List

Radio sells records, which is why airplay is so important. It will also boost ticket sales for live performances. With few exceptions, however, airplay on major AM and FM stations is reserved for major label artists.

Your best chance for airplay is to research and contact the radio stations that offer specialized programming or play specific genres of music. Information is available from organizations that serve the genre, from radio lists located on many musician's and independent record label Web sites, and from musicians and other music business people.

Research network programmers that deliver syndicated programming. Some of the major ones are Westwood One; ABC; Jones Satellite; National Public Radio; and Public Radio International. Find out who actually does the programming and try to develop relationships with them.

The *Gale Directory of Publications and Broadcast Media* indexes U.S. and Canadian commercial and public radio stations by 48 major musical genres. Information about radio stations and the types of music they play can be found in *Billboard Magazine, Radio and Records,* the *Recording Industry Sourcebook* and *The Album Network's Yellow Pages of Rock.* You can also research radio stations on the Internet. Many post their playlists and you can see if they play music from your genre.

When you discover DJs and radio stations that play music from independents with styles of music similar to yours, put their names on your priority radio list. Be sure to get the names of the program directors that are responsible for playlists. Include the names of DJs that have the authority to slip in cuts of music not normally on their playlists.

Inquire about the recording format each station requires, as many do not accept cassettes or vinyl.

Television List

If you are considering making video clips, investigate which television stations or programs devote some programming to independents and what quality of video they require.

Programs that air locally on public television, local cable stations, and community television are good bets. Some nightclub owners and festival promoters now produce and syndicate live shows for video programming. Appearing on one of those will increase your exposure. It is great free publicity and a good place to direct promotional efforts.

If your research shows that there are specialized shows devoted to issues that appeal to your target audience, add the names of the producers to your lists. If your project is newsworthy, contact "assignment" editors: their job is to weed through the news and prioritize it for news programming. You can find out their names by phoning the stations.

List Keeping Systems

Design a system for your lists that is easy to use, update, and break into categories. You can have an effective system on note cards or in notebooks with categories separated by tabs. A computerized database system is an extremely useful tool for organizing and managing lists. You can easily code entries by type and readily update them. You can designate special "fields" that allow you to enter relevant notes. Most database programs have mail merge capabilities that allow you to do personalized mailings and print labels.

Be sure to check names and addresses before you send out your materials.

As you research artist sites, fanzines, and radio stations on the Web, list and "bookmark" the URLs for sites you would like your Web site to be linked to and from. (A bookmark is a special software command that enables you to save the URL of a Web site and return to it without having to type in the URL.) This makes it easy for you to return to them when you have your own Web site and get permission to make the links.

PROMOTIONAL MATERIALS

Promotional materials introduce your recording, provide information about you and your music, and can induce people to play your recording or hire you for gigs. Your recording and other publicity materials are your ambassadors: they imprint the name and image of your band in people's minds. They help to create a draw for your performances and sell your recordings.

The essential promotional materials include your recording, letterhead, biography (bio), photographs, and press releases. Extras are posters, fliers, printed press kit covers, and other printed materials used to announce performances and advertise your record. Bands often use many of these materials to help promote performances in advance of their recordings and build their fan base.

They are designed to answer the questions most-asked by fans and business people.

- What kind of music do you do?
- What instruments does your band play?
- Where do you perform?
- Do you have a following outside of your home town?
- How many fans generally come and see you at your concerts?
- Do you have any recordings?
- What makes you different?

The more straightforwardly you can answer these questions, the more you set yourself apart as a professional.

Some musicians have difficulty describing their music. Those that can have a huge advantage over those who categorize their style as "unique" or "it's a blend of many styles." Vague responses give people the feeling that you do not know, or care, so why should they take the trouble to find out? Vagueness arouses resistance, not

curiosity. Moreover, if you do not define your style, others may do it for you in a totally unacceptable way. To avoid this, find words that do justice to you and your music. The more innovative your music is, the more important it becomes to give people a handle on it.

Promotional materials are placed inside a folder and the whole package is referred to as a "press kit." As your success builds, you will continually update your materials and add new ones, such as reviews and the names of radio stations that have played your recording.

Many bands make promotional materials, gig information, and other news available through their Internet Web sites. People can listen to samples from recordings and interviews with band members. This is faster, easier, and cheaper than mailing materials and provides fans and the business community with the opportunity to learn about you when it is convenient for them. Your Web site should at least contain the contents of your printed press kit.

Promotional materials are most cost-effectively designed and printed when you work with a graphic designer. Many of the basic designs you select can be used for multiple purposes to provide a consistent graphic element, which helps solidify your band's image.

Well-executed and informative materials can persuade people to attend your performances and listen to your music. If your publicity materials seem amateurish, you create the impression that your music is amateurish—even if it is not. Mediocre design and execution creates negative impressions that are hard to erase.

Other than your recording, your biggest

expense will be the initial outlay for quality promotional materials. To economize, while at the same time publicizing your recording, you should use elements from your recording's cover throughout your promotional materials.

Your Recording's Cover

The best promotional material you can have is a well-produced recording. So do not hide your music inside a poor cover. The first impression your recording makes is visual; people see it before they hear it. The cover design is the single most important graphic for your recording.

Logo design is an art. A logo can be a symbol or a special form of lettering. Logos can be trademarked.

Letterhead/Logo

A letterhead helps to establish your band as a business. It is effective in professionalizing communication with the media and other businesses. The lettering style, the colors you use, and your logo have a great deal to say about your image. You will use them repeatedly on all your publicity materials to highlight and dramatize your band and recording label's name and image.

A logo is a symbol or special lettering for your group's name or the name of your label. It helps create instant identification for your band or business.

Biography

A biography (bio) contains information about your band: what kind of music you do; instrumentation; and the performing and recording experience of the band and its members. It should describe what differentiates your band from others and discuss the musical influences that led to the development of the band's music. It should also contain one or two complimentary quotes (if you have them) from reviews and articles. Information about the birthplaces of musicians or what high school they attended is irrelevant. Try to keep bios to one page. Other information, such as a list of key performances or discography, can be provided elsewhere in your promotional materials.

Media people often use material directly from your bio when writing reviews or feature stories.

Some biographical information should also be supplied within your CD, record, or cassette package.

If you are at a loss for words, hire a professional writer to help you. Music critics and reviewers are good people to approach.

Photographs

Photographs are important promotional tools. They should help answer the questions, what kind of music do you play or what kind of image/personality do you want to create? They create interest and help cement an image with your band's name. Photographs may show the people in the band with their instruments; or they can be designed to produce an emotional or dramatic feeling. Many recording labels provide two types of photographs: one shows the musicians; the other a reproduction of the graphics on their recordings.

Photographs can be used on your recording's cover and be included in your press kit and on your Internet Web site. They can be used to create fliers, posters, postcards, and other promotional materials.

Magazines and newspapers use graphics to enliven their pages. Although most of the music photographs you see reproduced have been provided by bands (or their management), photographers are sometimes sent to "shoot" a performance. If a magazine or newspaper photographer does shoot at one of your gigs, you can call the publication's photo librarian and request a proof sheet—even if the photographs were not selected to be reproduced. The fees for buying reproduction rights of these photos range from as little as $30 to hundreds of dollars.

Newspapers and magazines prefer black and white, glossy photographs. They should be no larger than 8 by 10 inches and no smaller than 5 by 7 inches. Since photographs are often reduced ("cropped") to fit narrow columns, tight groups of people and instruments are best. For good reproduction, photographs must be in sharp focus with an uncluttered background that does not compete with the musicians (plain white or very light gray is best). Sharp black and white tones are mandatory. Grainy photographs do not reproduce well. Action shots against a white or

very light background are preferable to standard portrait shots as long as the image is sharp and clear. A common error is having a microphone or instrument cover half a face.

Color photographs are the preferred medium on Internet Web sites.

A photographer is usually hired by a graphic designer who provides art direction for the various photographs needed in your promotional materials. If you are trying to save money by bypassing a graphic designer, make sure that you hire a professional photographer who has experience in shooting musicians and can meet the varied technical and aesthetic requirements necessary to ensure your promotional goals are met.

The positioning of musicians and their instruments; lighting and camera angle are very important. A good photographer will be able to relax band members so they do not feel and look self-conscious. As a general rule, he or she will know to keep alcohol, tobacco, and drugs out of your photographs.

Photographers can be found by reading the credits on recordings and in music magazines. You can look in the yellow pages, but make sure that photographers are experienced in working with musicians by looking at their portfolios. Many photographers are posting their portfolios on the Web.

Professional photographers are expensive to hire, but will be worth it if you get results: your photo in newspapers and magazines; better gigs; or a recording cover that "begs to be opened." The publicity generated when your photos are used by the media will more than make up for the expense of acquiring them.

Dean Shostak's revival of the glass armonica, a musical instrument invented by Benjamin Franklin in 1761, provides a promotional "hook" that creates immediate curiosity and interest and easily differentiates his Celtic and Christmas music recordings from others. This unusual instrument consists of tuned quartz bowls mounted on a spindle, which is spun by using a foot treadle. Applying moistened fingers to the rims of the bowls produces an ethereal and unusual sound.

In many cases, the photos taken for your recording's cover can be used to update your image and promotional materials.

You can have prints reproduced inexpensively at a production photo facility. Firms that specialize in quantity photo duplication are listed in the yellow pages of major metropolitan areas under the heading, "Photo Finishing—Wholesale." Reproductions of black and white glossy 8 by 10-inch photographs cost from $40 to $65 per hundred. Production photo facilities can also make black and white copy negatives from your recording's cover and reproduce it on glossy paper for the same price range.

Provide the photo reproducer with copy that lists the name of the artist, recording's title, contact person, their e-mail address and phone number, and photographer's credit. This

caption should be stripped in at the bottom of the negative before it is reproduced. This costs less than $20.

Color photos of recording covers can be reproduced by color copiers in quantities of 100 or more for under a dollar per copy.

Photographers own the copyrights to their photographs and therefore the right to license their use. Some photographers charge you one fee for the "shooting session" and separate fees for the use of the photographs in various promotional materials. They will ask you to sign a "use license" for reproduction of the photograph. The license will specify the use(s) that will be made of the photograph, for what period of time, at what price, and how it should be credited. If you use the same photograph for a different purpose than is specified in the license, the photographer has the right to charge another fee and have you sign another use license.

Others sell their copyright outright, giving up all rights forever. This is called a copyright assignment or "buyout."

When negotiating with a photographer, confirm the terms and conditions of use in advance.

Additional Printed Promotional Materials

Other than notices in print, radio, and television, how does news about musical events in your community get around? By fliers and posters on utility poles and storefront windows? Chalked messages on sidewalks? Notices on community bulletin boards? Postcard mailings to fans? This information will help you figure out what additional promotional materials you need.

Many bands design fliers and posters so that space is left for filling in gig dates. Postcards and mail-order forms are commonly sent to fans to remind them of gigs and to draw attention to a band's recordings. Newsletters, either mailed or posted on a band's Web site, can provide fans and business people with more news.

Press Releases

Press releases are a very effective method of getting information to the media. They are factual ministories that capsulize information and tell who, what, where, when, and how, directly and simply. Good press releases anticipate questions and answer them. They are organized so the most important information comes first and the least important last.

Media people are swamped with more news than they can handle. They learn about your recordings and your performances from press releases. The choice of what to write about, publicize, or review is based on information that arrives in the office and what the publication's editorial priorities are. Tips, fed by long-time business contacts (managers, promoters, secretaries, and friends), also influence the choices.

Information provided in press releases is used to create articles, announcements, reviews, and interviews. You may be surprised at how many articles and reviews use the exact language supplied by your press release.

Press releases help writers supply accurate information to their readers. Hype should be omitted—with this exception: if you have some particularly favorable reviews from previous performances or recordings, include one or two quotes in your press release. Be factual and informative. Plainly written press releases work best.

Press releases should be sent monthly to the media and business people on your mailing lists to keep them informed on the progress of your career. Do not stop after your first mailing, even if you get a lukewarm response. The more press releases you send out, the better your chances of familiarizing media and business people with your name and eventually capturing their interest. Repetition works. Subsequent press releases can highlight a notice about changes in band personnel, news of success in signing with a major booking agent, additions to your Web site, reviews, gig calendars, new posters, etc. Each new booking is a valid reason for a fresh press release, letter, and phone call.

Press releases should be typed double-spaced on your letterhead. The top of the page should contain the words "Press Release" or "For Immediate Release," a date, and the name, phone number, and e-mail address of the person who can be contacted for further information.

The release should have a headline. The first paragraph should highlight the purpose of the release and most relevant facts. The next paragraphs should contain supplementary information.

Press releases that announce the release of your record should be accompanied by your recording, press kit, and cover letter.

A cover letter gives you the opportunity to add a personal tone and plead your case. You can ask for special attention because you are a non-major label artist or refer to articles or reviews by the person to whom you are writing that you

PHOTO BY FRANK RICHARDS

Guitarist Scott Huckabay.

MEDIA CONTACT: PAT HAYES   For Immediate Release
360-734-3643 or promo@soundings.com   JUNE 15, 1998

Guitar Master Scott Huckabay
To Be Featured On NPR Music Program "Echoes"

Soundings of the Planet recording artist and acoustic guitar master Scott Huckabay will be featured on John Diliberto's top rated National Public Radio (NPR) music program "Echoes." The show will air on July 1st, 5th, and 12th on over 150 syndicated stations throughout the United States. Check your local NPR station listings for specific times and days of the show. A complete list of radio stations that broadcast the program can be found at www.echoes.org.

The Echoes segment will include an in-depth interview with Scott along with a variety of musical selections from his *Peace Dance* album. *Peace Dance* climbed onto the NAV top 25 radio chart and continues to get rave reviews. Huckabay plays the acoustic guitar with precision, power, and passion. His innovative six-string attack features explosive dynamics, cascading rhythms, and soaring solos.

Scott is currently putting the finishing touches on his eagerly anticipated *Alchemy* album. In addition to his trademark solo instrumental sound, *Alchemy* will feature five energetic instrumentals with the addition of driving bass and percussion. Huckabay will be touring the Western region of the United States this summer performing a variety of old and new material.

Tour dates will be listed on the Soundings of the Planet Web site, located at www.Soundings.com.

"Scott is the most exciting guitarist since Michael Hedges in his passion and unique artistry. He is an absolute celebration of sound."
                                        —Carla Van Dyk, WDVR

"Stevie Ray Vaughn, Michael Hedges, and Jimi Hendrix all rolled into one. Scott is a dream come true for guitar enthusiasts everywhere."
                                        —Robert Walmsley, *Omega Directory*

"*Peace Dance*—Top 10 album of 1997"
                                        —Lyn Mcnut, KUAC

"When I featured the entire *Peace Dance* album one morning, my phones kept lighting up. Evidence enough of a winning album."
                                        —James Dlugosinski, WWSP

Pat Hayes
Promotions
Soundings of the Planet
promo@soundings.com

have read and liked; and you can include an invitation to an upcoming performance.

A special note: the more personal you make your mailing, the more chance it has of being opened and read. Attractive stamps and colorful mailing labels help people distinguish your mailings from junk mail.

Public Service Announcements (PSAs)

If you are a nonprofit business or community organization, or you are a band that will be performing a benefit for a nonprofit business or community organization, you can supply radio stations with public service announcements (PSAs)—brief messages that describe your activities. Commercial stations air these messages at no charge. They receive numerous PSAs daily, so submit your copy early to help in scheduling. Selection is based on interest, immediacy, balance, and variety.

The messages can be 10, 20, 30, or 60 seconds in length. Check with each station to learn their preference.

Use a stop watch and read your PSA out loud to check its time.

PSAs should be printed on the letterhead of the sponsoring organization. Sentences should be kept short, simple, and factual. Remember to include a phone number people can call for further information.

Videos

Videos are excellent, albeit expensive, promotional materials. Airing them on public, cable, or network television stations increases a band's exposure and helps catalyze sales. Videos of a band's live performance are sent to club owners and concert promoters to convince them to book the band. Video bios (visual representations of the information in the artist's bio and clips of performances) are increasingly being sent to major label recording executives as a means of persuading them to listen to a band's recordings and sign them. They are sent to stores to interest them in carrying the music or in sponsoring an in-store performance.

Videos can be transferred (uploaded) to computers to be viewed on Internet Web sites by using QuickTime software.

Labels that release specialized genres of music often provide compilation videos, which feature a variety of bands, to public, cable, and network television stations. Labels for popular music formats submit clips of individual songs to programs such as MTV.

Your videos must be well-produced to get the results you want. Videos that can compete in quality with those commonly aired on MTV can cost as little as $15,000, but the average is closer to $50,000.

Enhanced CDs

Enhanced CDs contain an extra file of multimedia content that can be viewed on a computer screen while the audio tracks are played through the computer's CD drive. Viewing the file is optional because the audio tracks can be played on any CD player.

Shock tactics got Liberties Bed, a surfer grunge alternative rock band from South Florida, a lot of media attention for the provocative (but not sexually explicit) graphics on the enhanced CD portion of the title cut "Wicked Ways."

Putting multimedia material on your CD is another way to make your band and recording more memorable. It provides an opportunity to differentiate your release from those of competing bands. It can enhance a listener's appreciation of the music; show the band in live performance; and provide musical scores and lyrics.

The minimum playback requirements for enhanced CDs are PCs with Windows 95 (though some will run on Windows 3.l) or Apple Macintoshes with 7.5 or later operating systems, quad-speed CD drives and color monitors. Computers should have at least 16 megabytes of RAM, although with the huge memory requirements of newer software, more is better.

While the music is playing on your CD drive, the computer monitor can display photographs, videos, press kit materials, bios, posters, stickers, lyric sheets, and Web site graphics. Anything that can be placed in digital files can be mastered onto the multisession file of the CD.

If you decide to make use of this promotional opportunity, the enhanced CD material should be planned in advance of your recording, even though you will not be able to finalize exactly what viewers will see until you know the final sequence of songs. Planning content in advance will let your graphic designer and photographer know that some of their materials will be used for this purpose and may help them suggest additional materials.

Here are basic questions to help budgeting and planning.

◆ How much can you spend to create content?

◆ What do you want the enhanced CD to accomplish?

◆ Do you want to provide graphic content for one song, two songs, or the entire audio?

◆ What do you want the content to convey about style, image, or music?

◆ What content do you already have?

Graphic materials are digitized by scanning, then placed into appropriate software, such as Adobe Photoshop, where they can be manipulated. Videos can be transferred to QuickTime movies.

Next, the digitized materials are transferred to an authoring program so they can be sequenced and needed enhancements, such as title page, subtitles, etc., can be created. Some suitable authoring programs are Microsoft PowerPoint, Macromedia Director, and Adobe Premier.

Authoring should be done by an experienced multimedia producer who understands the manufacturing medium, computer programs, and mastering. Multimedia producers are the equivalent of audio producers: they know how to create and make the best use of audio/visual materials; they are adept at using graphic tools to enhance and change images; and they can create imaginative segues.

The completed program is then compressed and saved as a stand-alone freely distributable file, such as a QuickTime video or Macromedia Director movie.

Finally, the file is "burned" onto the CD master that will be used for manufacturing your music. The cost of manufacturing an enhanced CD is the same as a regular CD.

Bands are not charging more for enhanced CDs and only some buyers have equipment to access them. The music portion can be played on any CD player.

Compilations

Many independent record labels provide compilations of selections from their artists' recordings (samplers) and make them available as promotional tools. Some send them to radio stations and report that DJs program music directly from them. Others send them to people on their mailing lists as inducements to buy CDs.

Some manufacturers send samplers to prospective clients to demonstrate their work and to radio stations as a value-added service for clients.

THE INTERNET

The Internet is a communication network, an encyclopedia of the modern age and collection of cyberspace storefronts. It connects computer users so they can converse, exchange mail, and share and research on-line data archives (printed information, pictures, videos, sound clips).

Compilation albums are good promotional tools for music service businesses as well as individual artists and bands.

Information, goods, and services are shared over the World Wide Web ("WWW" or the Web) via a collection of electronic pages called Web sites, which are established by individuals and companies. Web sites are accessed through a World Wide Web address, referred to as a Uniform Resource Locator (URL), prefixed by the letters and symbols http://(Hypertext Transport Protocol), followed by www and a specific Web site address. Example: http://www.folkmusic.com.

Letters, documents, photographs, audio files, and other information can be sent via e-mail. Many Web sites have e-mail links to make it easy to contact them.

People with like interests regularly communicate with each other via Usenet (users network) that provides access to a large collection of bulletin board style newsgroups on the Internet. Usenet originally required specialized programs called newsreaders for access, but today it is available through the Web at sites such as DejaNews (www.dejanews.com).

Discussions also occur on Web site chatrooms, which offer participants instantaneous communication and sharing of ideas. They are commonly used for live interviews.

The basic tools needed to access the Internet are a computer with at least 32 megabytes of RAM and a 15-inch or larger monitor. Common extras are computer CD-based (CD-ROM, CD-R) drives, external speakers, helper programs, and plug-ins for listening to Internet sound clips and playing videos. To connect to the Internet, you need a modem with a minimum baud rate of 28,800 bits per second (BPS). (Baud rate refers to

the speed at which a modem operates. The higher the baud rate, the faster the file transmission.)

To get an Internet account, you request service from an Internet Service Provider (ISP). Examples of ISPs include EarthLink Networks (www.earthlink.net), MindSpring (www.mindspring.com), and America Online (www.aol.com). Note that these companies are not the Internet itself; they simply provide access to it through their computers. Some ISPs, such as America Online, provide additional non-Internet features through a members-only on-line service. Most ISPs provide Web access to their customers through software Web browsers such as Netscape Communicator (www.netscape.com) and Microsoft Internet Explorer (www.microsoft.com/ie). Communicator and Explorer have built-in e-mail capabilities, but many Internet users install an additional custom e-mail program such as Eudora (www.qualcomm.com) or Microsoft Exchange (www.microsoft.com/exchange).

Music can be listened to on the Web through a variety of methods. You can download an audio file and play it back from your browser. This is an older method and can take many minutes (five to seven minutes for 30 seconds of sound with a 28.8 kb modem). MPEG-compressed audio (abbreviated as MP3) is a "download and play" format that is frequently used to provide CD-quality music. Another class of audio programs play music as it is downloaded (audio streaming) in quality comparable to FM radio. Common streaming audio software includes RealNetworks RealPlayer (www.real.com), Liquid Audio (www.liquidaudio.com), Apple

QuickTime 3.0 (www.apple.com/quicktime), and Microsoft NetShow (www.microsoft.com/netshow). RealPlayer and NetShow also support low-quality streaming video, which allows sites such as Streamland (www.streamland) to provide music videos online. You can listen to MIDI files (which download most quickly) through sound modules, which are sometimes built into computer operating systems or supplied by a soundcard. Some sites such as Res Rocket (www.resrocket.com) have created MIDI systems that allow artists to jam over the Internet.

Currently, the Internet and television exist as separate mediums, but technologies exist that combine them and provide Internet access using a television set or allow television broadcasts to be viewed on a computer.

A good example of this is WebTV Network (www.webtv.net), which provides a low-cost ($100 to $300) Internet "set-top box" that can be connected to a standard TV and allows Web surfing and e-mail. WebTV is a good choice for musicians that want to access the Internet but are unfamiliar with computers or have a limited budget. Many owners of indie labels have expressed hope that increased public access to the Internet will lead to increased sales of recordings and of music that is downloaded to computer hard disks and other storage mediums.

Web Sites

Web sites are major promotional tools. Many bands, record labels, music business professionals, music organizations and associations, radio stations, newspapers, and equipment manufacturers have Web sites. Many provide links to other Web sites and Usenet discussion groups as a service to their visitors.

A Web site makes it easy for fans to find you, learn where you are playing, listen to samples from your recordings and interviews, watch videos, and order recordings, related merchandise and concert tickets, and communicate with band members or their management via e-mail. A Web site is the easiest and cheapest method of providing a continuous stream of in-depth information. Advance Web site notices of concerts can sell them out without any other media attention.

Some fans get so enthused they set up unofficial Web sites that may include more information than the official ones. This information can consist of reviews, fan commentary, photos, etc. In some cases it may be incorrect or unauthorized. Permission must be obtained for the use of any copyrighted material—articles, photographs, illustrations, or music. Placement of copyrighted material on a Web site without authorization constitutes infringement. Recording or placing live music on a Web site without the authorization of the artist or artist's manager constitutes copyright infringement. If you want to correct misinformation or request that copyrighted material be withdrawn, e-mail the site's owner.

Web sites provide business people with an easy way to learn what your band is up to. But make sure they also receive your recordings and printed promotional materials.

You can obtain a Web site by renting space from an Internet Service Provider (ISP) that offers this service (domain hosting). Some ISPs charge by the amount of megabytes used; others by how much information is downloaded each day, week, or month. There may be additional charges for such extras as analyzing a mailing list from your account, or analyzing visitor logs; audio and video downloads, message boards, or secure commerce capability. Once the space for the site and a domain name is secured, you can hire a Web designer to produce the site. Typical costs for independent site development range from several hundred to thousands of dollars. However, increasing numbers of musicians are designing their own sites. (Information on registering your Web site name [domain name] is found in the chapter, Business. Information on Web site design is found in the chapter, Graphic Design and Printing.)

You can also create a site on the larger Web sites of Web hosting companies, such as the Internet Underground Music Archive (www.iuma.com) and Kaleidospace (www.kspace.com)—communities of bands and businesses with related information (magazines, record labels, business resources). These large sites rent space from a domain host. Many offer marketing, sales, and other services to artists. (The Web hosting company only hosts Web sites but does not offer dial-up access as does an ISP.)

Some Web hosting companies, such as Xoom, GeoCities, Hypermart, and Angelfire, provide Web page space for free. Generally they provide up to 11 megabytes of space and give you some easy page builders so you can create your own pages. These are good for musicians that have a limited budget and are taking a do-it-yourself approach.

If you decide to change your Web hosting company or ISP, you will have to make a major promotional effort to let people know your new Internet Web site location.

Some artists have their own sites and provide links to the larger music sites that sell and help promote their recordings. This is done by reciprocal agreements between Web site owners, and no fees are charged. You can also hire a Web designer to include links from other sites to yours. Fees can range from hundreds to thousands of dollars, depending on the number of links that are provided.

Many independent label distributors have Web sites for the bands whose music and merchandise they sell and often link their sites to the bands'. Shared space is sometimes offered free, but more often these distributors charge an annual base fee that may include two or more text pages; two or more images; sales of your work; and one or two song samples. They charge additional fees for including video clips, additional images, songs, and text. They also take a percentage of sales. However, these are usually lower than the rates charged by standard record label distributors.

Print information and a few high-resolution photos on a Web site can take less than 10 megabytes of memory, but dozens of high-quality images with song and video clips take much more. Make sure that your domain or Web host can rent you enough space to accommodate your current and future needs, and the provider is not clogged with more traffic than it can handle. Ten full-screen pictures with 40 seconds of MP3 audio and 20 seconds of QuickTime

In November 1998, the community links on John McCutcheon's Web site (www.folkmusic.com) included: The Virginia Organizing Project; Paul Robeson Centennial Celebration; Artists for a Hate Free America; *The Onion*: A Madison, Wisconsin-based satirical news weekly; Veterans for Peace; Cherish the Ladies; The Progressive Directory; Rounder Records; Handgun Control; Bias Recording Studios; AFM Local 1000: The Musician's Union "UnLocal" created by and for acoustic, traveling musicians; Baltimore Orioles; Community Organizing Home Page; Sing Out! Magazine; community FM radio station WMNF; Steve Riley & the Mamou Playboys (a Cajun band); and the Literacy Volunteers of America.

Community listings are a way of enriching your own community. I've included a number of sites for your fun and edification. Some are people doing important work, some are friends of mine, some are real-life diversions, some are all of the above. Some will remain on this community page forever, most will change monthly. Adds come in at any time. Each of these spots is a starting point, linking you to their own web of communities. Information, inspiration, input: that's what the Web can be about. Have fun and thanks for including us in your travels.

—John McCutcheon

video require at least two to three megabytes. Streaming audio and video are much more efficient; a single megabyte can store 10 minutes of RealPlayer-encoded audio and over a minute of streaming video. Once you have a site of your own, make reciprocal agreements so that your site can be linked directly to other sites of interest and vice versa.

The first page visitors commonly see is called the home page and it can be as long as you like. Many bands, however, use their home page as a directory to lead visitors to other information, such as bios, photographs, audio samples, tour information, order forms, etc. Make your site's purpose very clear and make changes to the home page as often as feasible by providing new information and special offers.

The best sites are updated regularly to give visitors a reason to return. The updates can be performance dates, tour itineraries, new samples of your CD, interviews, newsletters and business information, and interesting links to other sites. A sophisticated tool that can increase interaction between visitors and the Web site is a database of information provided by the Web site that is accessed through key-word searches.

Downloading complex and colorful graphics can be very slow. Give people the option of selecting only text and provide thumbnail photos that can be enlarged at their choice.

Put your Web site and e-mail address on all your printed materials. During your performances, be sure to invite fans to visit your site. Visitors seldom discover a band's Web site through random surfing of the World Wide Web.

Post your Web site in all the search engine

directories (Yahoo!, HotBot, AltaVista, etc.) and supply them with key words and phrases that identify you with your genre and make it easy for people to find you. Include the title of your recording and your band's name. Do not describe yourself only as a rock musician, a key-phrase search on rock musician will bring up thousands of names. But a search for "industrial rock" on the Yahoo! search engine brings up less than 20 references.

List your site on specialty Web site music lists, such as the Ultimate Band List (www.ubl.com).

Your ISP can give you access logs that tell how many visitors (hits) came to your site and whether they found your site from a search engine or a link from another Web site. A popular addition to many Web sites is a "counter" program that records access to the page along with the current date and time. A wide variety of these programs are available. Check out Digit Mania (http://www.digitmania.holowww.com/) and Text Counter (http://www.worldwidemart.com/scripts/textcounter.shtml).

Web Radio

Improvement of Internet audio transmission has led to the rapid growth of Web sites that transmit music programming on the Internet (Web radio). AM and FM radio stations can convert their content to a RealAudio format and be heard over the Internet virtually any place in the world. The broadcast quality varies, due to a variety of factors, including your modem and computer's processor speeds, type of phone lines, cable access, etc.

Web radio is increasing because the Internet is not limited by channels, time slots or geographical location. These stations emulate AM/FM radio stations: programmers select the content and the stations get revenue from banner advertising and a percentage of the sales of recordings ordered by fans.

There is also growth of Internet-only Web radio sites owned by large independent music labels and distributors, such as Navarre's NetRadio, which play music from the labels they sell. This sophisticated promotional tool enables listeners to immediately link to the distributor's Internet sales site to make purchases.

Most Internet stations provide users with the ability to program their own music and download selections, for a fee, onto a CD-Recordable (CD-R). In order to provide content that is different from what is available on AM/FM radio, many Internet-only stations program music from many more genres than those currently offered by major AM/FM stations. They actively solicit music from independent labels. For example, www.spinner.com provides selections from more than 60 genres of music.

Web radio stations that operate in the United States are required to file use licenses with performance rights associations so performance royalties can be paid to composers. (This subject is dealt with in the chapter, Copyrights.)

Use e-mail links to make inquiries about how programming is selected on Internet stations. If they are interested in your music, ask how they would prefer it be sent to them—via Internet or mail.

WWW.SPINNER.COM DELIVERS MORE THAN 120,000 DIGITIZED SONGS IN MORE THAN 100 HIGHLY SPECIALIZED MUSIC CATEGORIES. ◀- - - -

It reaches more than two million listeners worldwide, broadcasting more than one million songs per day. Song information is displayed as music is played. Internet radio now offers many more choices to listeners than what are available on commercial radio and provides an easy way to purchase music. The following list of categories offers independent recording artists ideas about how to classify their music. Spinner.com channels are arranged within ten music genres. Where does your music fit?

Rock	Oldies	Themes	Top Hits	Mood Food	Classical
Jazz & Blues	Urban & Dance	Country & Folk	World & New Age		

CHANNELS

20th Century	A Taste of Avant Garde Classical	Bop	Get Dizzy with the Bud, Bird, Miles & Monk
8trax	Songs from the '70s	Brit Invasion	Paul Revere Beware: The Beatles are Coming!
'90s Rock	AlternaPop from the Early-to-Mid-'90s	Bull Market	Songs about Rolling in the Dough
Acid Jazz	Hybrid Incorporating Elements of Jazz, Funk, Hip-Hop & Soul	Celtic	Do a Little Jig to these Irish Folk Faves
African	African Rhythms	Chicago Blues	Blues Blowin' in from the Windy City
All Blues	Blues You Can Use		
All Jazz	Jazz in All Its Colors	Christian	Inspirational Rock, Pop & More
Alt. '80s	The Roots of Alternative Music: '80s Classics Heard Here!	Classic Country	Hank, Kitty, Johnny & Patsy
		Classic Rock	We Built This Channel on Rock 'n' Roll!
Alternative '90s	Truly Alternative Stuff from the Early-to-Mid-'90s	Classical 101	Classical Standards & More
Alternative Country	Rock Tunes with a Twang!	Country	10-Gallon Tunes!
Alternative Now	Beyond the Boundaries of "Alternative" Music	Country Blues	Roots Grown North of the Delta
Ambient	Refined Electronic Expression	Crooners	Take A Sentimental Journey
		Delta Blues	Home Grown in the Mississippi Delta
Avant Garde	Step Outside … If You Dare		
Awesome '80s	Back to the Days of Parachute Pants & Valley Girls	Dinner Jazz	Mellow and Romantic Sounds
		Disco	Bell-Bottomed Dancers: Shake Your Groove Thang
Ballads	The Love Channel		
Baroque	Get a Handel On Your Bach: Classics from the 17th and 18th Century	El Nino	To Help You Weather the Storm(s)
		Electric Blues	Plugged-in Blues
Bear Market	Drowning Your Cash Flow Woes	Female Blues	Ladies Sing the Blues
		Female Focus	All Women, All the Time
Big Band	Big Bands for Big Jazz Sounds	Folk	Tales of The Common Man
		Funk	I Wants to Get Funked Up!
Bluegrass	A Fiddle Playin', Banjo Pickin', Partner Swingin' Good Time	Fusion	Jazz + Rock = Fusion
		Gospel	Can I Get an "Amen"?

CONTINUED ON FOLLOWING PAGE

CONTINUED FROM PREVIOUS PAGE

Gothic	For the Dark @ Heart	New Age	Audio Therapy
Great Guitar	Music Made for the Guitar	New Wave	Synth-Pop of the '80s
Heavy Rock	Contemporary Rock 'n' Roll with an Edge	Old Skool	Breakdance to Hip-Hop's Roots
HiNRG Dance	Pop, Miami Bass, and Euro Dance Music	Oldies	Rock 'n' Roll Hall of Fame
Hip-Hop	I Got Two Turntables and a Microphone	Opera	Experience the Drama
		Progressive	Experimental Rock for Experimental Types
House	House Music All Night Long!!!	Psychedelic	Lava Lamp Listening
Indie Rock	Tunes from Independent Labels: No Sell-outs Here!	Punk	I'm More Punk than You Are!
Industrial	Music by Machines	R&B-Fresh	Today's Freshest Urban Grooves
Jungle/D&B	Future Urban Breakbeats … Step to It!	Reggae	Riddims of Dancehall, Rock Steady, Roots and Ragga. Go Deh!
Just-4-Kids	For Kids' Ears Only!		
Latin	Que Pasa? Tune in. Find out!	Relax Trax	Quality Mellow Tunes for Stress Relief!
Latin Jazz	Jazz Picante Style		
Laugh Trax	Songs & Stand-up to Tickle Your Funny Bone	Rock 101	Four Decades of Rock 'n' Roll
		Show Tunes	Your Ticket to Broadway's Best
Lilith Fair	Female Artists Coming Soon to a Venue Near You!	Sinatra Style	A Tribute to Old Blue-Eyes
		SKA	Skank to the First, Second & Third Wave!
Lite Rock	Ms. Dion, Mr. Bolton, and Ms. Carey Found Here!	Slow Jams	Laid Back Smooth Grooves for an Unobtrusive Mood
Live Channel	Is it Live or Is it Spinner?		
Lounge	Cocktails, Anyone?	Smooth Jazz	Take the Edge Off
Love Gone Bad	For You Lonely Hearts: Check into the Heartbreak Hotel	Soul	Food for the Soul from the Godfather, Queen, and King
Lust	For Those with "Healthy" Appetites	Swing	It Don't Mean a Thing if It Ain't Got That…
Mega BPMs	Electronica's Best Found Here	Techno	Breakbeat, Electro & Detroit Techno Beats for Your Feets
Melancholia	Sounds of Sadness: Pop's Version of Gothic	The Piano	Ivory Ticklers of Jazz, New Age & Rock Persuasions
Metal	Headbanger Heaven!		
Modern Blues	The Contemporary Collection	Top Country	Current Country Hits
Modern Love	Ballads Crooned by Today's Alternative Bands	Top Jammies	The Beatz from the Chartz
		Top Pop	Top 40 Tunes Compiled from Weekly Charts
Modern Mix	A Mix of Current AlternaPop Hits	Trance	Electronica for an Altered State of Mind
Mod Rock Grrls	Today's Fem Rockers & Alterna Queens	Trip-Hop	Hip-Hop for Spaceheadz
Motown	R&B Oldies That Got SOUL!	Urban Divas	Sisters, Homegirls, and Assorted Soulful Singers
Movie Scores	Silver Screen Composers		
Movie Tunes	Tinseltown Treats!	World Music	Music From Around the Globe
Nature Sounds	Mother Nature Originals	World Class Rock	This Is Not Your Father's Rock 'n' Roll
New Acoustic	Light Sounds sans Electrons		

PROMOTIONAL CAMPAIGNS

A promotional campaign is the month-by-month use of your mailing lists and press kits to familiarize people with your name of your band and your music and attract the attention of media and industry people. The more specific you are about your goals, the easier it will be to design a campaign to meet them. If this is your first recording and most of your performances are confined to the city where you live, your goals will be different from those of an artist who has released three independent albums and performs in a five-state area. As you gain success, promotional opportunities will increase.

Make your plan well in advance of making your recording because you need to know how much money to budget for your promotional tools and mailings. Once your recording is out, your plan will remind you when to send out mailings. If your success is more rapid than you anticipated, you can adapt your plan to meet the new circumstances.

Prepare your sales and promotion campaign so it can go into high gear once your recordings arrive. Ready your mailings, update your lists, and visit the stores that have offered to take your recordings and let them know when you will have inventory.

Even if you get your recordings early, do not begin your campaigns until you have all your promotional materials, mailing lists, and sales arrangements ready. That will be frustrating, but make up your mind you are going to do it right to make the most of the sales and promotional potential of your recording.

The keys to success are a constant flow of news to the people on your priority list and phone follow up. Unlike major labels that concentrate their efforts on promoting new recordings for only a month or two after their release, you can take a year or more to get your record off the ground. Each booking gives you a new reason to barrage the people on your mailing lists with press releases, photographs, fliers, and pleas for attention. Eventually your persistence will bring reviewers or DJs to hear you or will persuade them to listen to your recording. If they like your music, they will review it or play it on the air. This will lead to better gigs, more important reviews, more airplay, more excitement, more fans, and more sales.

Make samples of your recording available on your Web site; and on music sites that sell your record to provide people with a convenient way to sample your music.

Always follow mailings to people on your priority mailing list with phone calls to make sure the material has been received. This establishes personal contact and enables you to provide any additional information needed. Spend no more than a minute or two on the phone. Be brief and friendly. Say something like, "I'm George from the band 'KiX.' Last week I sent you our newest recording and invited you to come to our performance. Did you receive it? Have you had a chance to listen to it?"

Phone calls are also the way to correct misinformation or make changes (such as a different starting time for the performance). This information can be given to a media assistant or secretary.

Industry people are used to these phone calls; and they are often very polite about putting you off the first few times. If you get a secretary who tells you that the person you are trying to reach is out of the office or "in a conference," say something like, "I'm just calling to make sure that he or she got my mailing announcing my recording. Will you pass my message along?"

Be patient and polite. Perseverance always furthers. Never get angry with a media person for not using your press release or not showing up at a performance as promised, even if it is the tenth time it has happened. You will often be preempted by famous groups and more skilled promotional efforts. Remember, media and industry professionals are just overworked people in demand. A friendly attitude and cooperative manner are more likely to achieve the results you want.

Free Recordings

Giving your recording away is part of any promotional plan. The difficulty with giveaways is drawing the line. Use them where they are likely to accomplish tangible results: performances, airplay, reviews, in-store play, a store or distributor to carry the record.

One of the purposes of assembling a priority list and making a promotional plan is to figure out how many recordings you will give away.

Record Release Performance Party

The release of your new recording is news for your fans, industry people, and the media. Most bands celebrate with a performance (record release party) at the best venue they can book.

Club owners and concert promoters know bands will work extra hard to promote the concert and bring in media people.

Bands that have regional followings should hold a series of release parties in key cities. Telling a club owner or promoter that you want to use the gig for a record release party may give them just the extra incentive needed to book you.

The best time for the party is six weeks after you send out your first press release announcing the release of your recording. This gives time to book the best venue and provides another opportunity to create excitement and barrage fans and the media with mailings and invitations.

A sample promotional plan for a record release party is found on page 35.

Send invitations to your fans and ask them for special support, particularly if you know key media or industry people will be attending. A record release party is a good time to thank fans and friends for the support and help they have given. Some bands sell their recordings at a special discount for that night and give some small item away with each sale or have a drawing for free records or other items.

Promoting Performances

Artists on independent labels must perform live if they expect to promote and sell their recordings and gain media attention. Getting and promoting gigs are as equally important as promoting your recordings.

You may, however, be surprised at (and perhaps offended by) the low wages offered for playing concerts and showcases or for touring with other groups. But, it is important to remember that a platform from which you can create excitement, or a showcase gig for festival promoters, can be worth a great deal more than a decent wage for that particular performance. This is a common trade-off in the music business. Many new bands (including those signed to major labels) lose money while touring to support their first recording. In the balance, they gain media attention, increase their draw, add new fans, and sell recordings. Keeping your long-term goals in focus will help you make clear decisions about which performances are worth your while.

Once you have a performance contract, it is your responsibility to find out what you can do to supplement the promotion efforts of the club owners, record companies, or concert promoters. Find out how far in advance they need publicity materials. Let them know you will send supplementary notices to your fan list and post the performance on relevant Web sites. Tell them that although you are willing to expend extra efforts to get media attention, you do not want to duplicate their efforts and need to find out what they will be doing. Some club owners only send notices to free calendar listings, and do not include writers, reviewers, or radio DJs. Some expect bands to put out fliers and posters. You will find it helpful to prepare a list of poster and flier destinations and a map that lists postering opportunities to help volunteers do their job as quickly as possible.

Let your fans know where you are playing and ask them to bring their friends. Mail postcards with a month's worth of dates and post the information on your Web site and on other Internet calendar listings.

Phone trees are an excellent technique for getting the word out for special occasions and packing a venue with enthusiastic fans. A phone tree is similar to a chain letter. You call five special fans and say, "I particularly need lots of people to come to this performance because some very important industry people are showing up. Would you mind calling (or e-mailing) five others and letting them know and ask them to do the same?"

Send press releases and personal invitations to media and industry people on your priority list. Although they may ignore these mailings, the repetition provides evidence of frequent performances and increasing success. At some point, they will pay attention.

Follow up your invitations with phone calls. Always ask if they have had a chance to listen to your recording. If they say they have misplaced it, be gracious about sending another.

Make arrangements for the free tickets you will need. Club owners and promoters will usually grant you a number of free passes for the media because that generates publicity for them as well. Even if you have to spend some of your own money to buy tickets, a favorable review or high paying gig should more than compensate.

When you invite guests to your performance, make absolutely sure their names are on the guest list so the person at the box office or the door will not hassle them. Failure to remember this can lead to adverse publicity. Have press kits and extra recordings to hand out.

If invited guests do show up, call them the next day for feedback. Immediate contact can make the difference between getting a gig or review or not. It is also good form and helps solidify your contacts.

When you do get reviews, make copies of them to use in subsequent mailings and post them on your Web site. People are impressed when you receive attention from others and it often prods them into action. DJs and program directors often need a little extra input to decide to listen to your record and give it airplay. Do not forget to add copies of these reviews to the promotional materials you use to book gigs.

Getting Feature Stories

Every newspaper and magazine uses a regular staff and freelance writers to find and write feature stories. The writers are easy to spot because their stories have bylines. It is your job to interest them with ideas.

Feature stories include more information about a performer or group than do reviews or press releases. They can be interviews, biographies, or articles about particular aspects of a performer or group. They can capture an event through a series of photographs. Although feature stories are usually reserved for name performers, exciting controversial subject matter from less well-known groups can draw the attention of certain feature writers.

Dream up unusual angles about your endeavors and frame your ideas in a brief letter or phone call to editors. One or two enticing sentences should be enough to arouse curiosity. The more specific you can be about your idea for a story, the better. Here is an example of a short pitch to interest a writer in a good story.

"Singer continues fight to drain Glen Canyon Dam."

Follow your letter with a call to check responses and provide additional information. Do not get discouraged if your ideas are rejected. Think up new approaches and try again.

Photo stories can sometimes be placed in magazines or newspapers more easily than interviews or articles because they have visual appeal and few people take advantage of this form of promotion. A photo story showing how you recorded your CD might make an excellent feature for a Sunday supplement or local music magazine.

When a writer responds to your ideas and does print a feature story about you or your group write a note of thanks. It is always appreciated and helps cement your relationship.

Reprint reviews and stories on your letterhead, include them in your mailings. Hype breeds hype. When people in the media see favorable reviews and articles about you it stimulates them to jump on the bandwagon.

Getting Airplay

Before you ask radio stations to play your recording, make sure it is available in stores or through large Web sites. Radio stations will take a recording off the air if listeners call in to say they cannot find it. Include a list of the stores and Web sites that carry your recording in your personal letters to the stations.

Let programmers and DJs know which cuts are best for their stations. One way is to place a sticker on the front cover that lists them; another is to mention them in your letters.

| SAMPLE PROMOTIONAL CAMPAIGN FOR A RECORD RELEASE PERFORMANCE PARTY | ◀ - - - |

The following plan outlines a schedule for mailings to promote a record release party. This is best scheduled for six weeks after the date you are scheduled to receive your recordings, which should allow time for any manufacturing delays and for you to get the recordings into stores and book a performance in a venue you can publicize.

Note that each mailing contains a new press release and different promotional materials.

SIX WEEKS PRIOR TO PARTY

Announce the release of your recording and record release party by sending a press release, press kit, and recording to everyone on your priority media list. Include personal letters of invitation and make a personal plea for attention. Make sure the invitation includes an extra guest.

Send the same material to club owners and concert promoters that are most likely to offer bookings. Deliver some of these personally.

Send a press release announcing the recording to fans. Include an order form. Tell them to watch for a special invitation to your record release party.

Post the information on your Web site and others that have calendar listings.

FIVE AND FOUR WEEKS PRIOR TO PARTY

Follow mailing of recordings with phone calls. If you get a secretary or voice mail, leave a short message stating that you are following through on your mailing of the previous week and are calling to make sure they got the package.

Send a press release that announces the concert to all media and Web sites that have calendar listings.

THREE WEEKS PRIOR TO PARTY

Send a press release that announces the concert, along with a black and white photograph and another personal letter of invitation to all the media and industry people to whom you sent your initial recording and press kit.

Phone them three days after they should have received the release. Ask if they have had a chance to listen to your recording and review the contents of your press kit. Do not be put off if they tell you they have not. Be gracious and tell them you hope they will attend the party.

Send your fans a special invitation to the record release performance party. Include another order form.

TWO AND ONE-HALF WEEKS PRIOR TO PARTY

Send a press release that lists stores and Web sites where your recording can be purchased to everyone on your mailing list. If any reviews have appeared, make copies of them and include them in this mailing. Include a short personal letter to people on your priority lists urging them to come to the performance.

TWO WEEKS PRIOR TO PARTY UP TO PARTY DAY

Call media and industry people that have accepted your invitation to reassure them that tickets or guest passes will be there. Thank them for accepting.

Get ready for the party. Double-check all arrangements with the promoter and technical people. Make sure your guest list is in order. Keep talking the party up to fans and friends. Make sure you have extra press kits and recordings on hand.

Give the guest list to the owner of the venue; and double-check that the person who takes tickets has that list at the door.

DURING THE PARTY

Put on a great show and be sure to thank everyone that attended.

AFTER THE PARTY

Call the media and industry people that showed up to thank them again and ask for feedback. Kick your sales and promotion campaigns into high gear.

Your pleas for airplay have the best chance of being heeded when you combine them with performances in the listening area. As soon as you know you will be performing, send personal letters, press releases, and recordings to people at those stations that are likely to play them. Follow with calls and visits to remind them you need their help. Invite them to your gigs. Make absolutely sure their names are on the guest lists.

Public performances, favorable reviews, fans that request your recording, and your own persistent mailings of press releases and attractive promotional materials are very persuasive in getting radio attention. And once you have received airplay on any station, include that information in your personal letters. As soon as one radio station "goes" on your recording, you can persuade others to follow.

If you anticipate getting airplay on commercial stations, you can hire Broadcast Data

Systems (BDS) to track it. They track airplay by radio station, time of day, frequency, and size of the listening audience. The formats they currently track are adult contemporary, mainstream rock, modern rock, country, Spanish, adult album alternative, rap, rhythm and blues, and top forty. More information about their services can be found at http://www.bdsonline.com.

Getting Videos Played on Television

Sales generated by having your video shown on television can exceed those generated by radio airplay. Television producers are inundated with expensive and very well-produced clips from major and independent labels. Be especially persistent and patient when you identify stations that may be receptive to your videos.

Using Professional Services

Public relations (PR) firms work to persuade

print media people to write about their clients and help stir up excitement. They also arrange radio and television interviews. Independent record promoters are paid to get airplay for their clients, their services can be expensive.

They need to know what your goals and expectations are; what past success you have had; where you plan to perform; and what promotional materials you can provide.

Before hiring a PR firm or independent record promoter, find out what success they have had in getting print and airplay for independent label artists at your level. Ask how they can help you.

The best time to talk with PR people and record promoters is about six months prior to the release of your recording. Show them your promotional materials and ask them for help in getting as much media attention and airplay as possible for your record, record release party, and performances or tours. Determine how far in advance of your recording they want to start and how many press kits and recordings they need. Have them write out what they think they can accomplish so you will have a means to measure and evaluate the results.

The best way to find a good PR firm or independent record promoter is to ask people that have used their services. Do not hire firms that promise to do large mailings of your recording, but not the painstaking personal follow-through that brings results. Ask for references and check them. Talk to bands that used their services.

Average monthly fees for PR firms that work on a national basis are $1000 to $2000, plus expenses, and they can be higher depending on the scope of work. Fees should be lower when a firm is hired to publicize only one performance. The fee for an independent record promoter usually starts at $1000 a month.

PR firms and independent record promoters will charge you for every phone call they make on your behalf and every stamp used. Before you hire one, find out what expenses you will be paying for and ask for a written estimate.

Promotional Services Offered by CD and Cassette Manufacturers

Some free or very low-cost, value-added services are now offered by a number of manufacturers. These include booklets of marketing and promotion tips; CD samplers (compilations) that include one of your songs sent free to radio stations; mailing your CD to radio stations; stocking your recording in Internet music superstores; free labels on promotional copies, which tell that your recording is available at an Internet superstore; and free bar code graphics. Some of these services are very valuable and should be investigated at the same time you request manufacturing and printing estimates.

Advertising

Paid advertising works best when you carefully target your audience, have already achieved results from other promotional efforts, and are combining advertising with other promotional efforts.

Initially, the best places to advertise your recording are in publications that reach your target audience—either in the classified sections, which are inexpensive and often effective (especially for genre music), or in display ads that

Twelve CD samplers from Oasis CD and Cassette Duplication—including *OasisAcoustic*™, *OasisBlues*™, *OasisAlternative*™, *OasisWorld*™, and others—are sent to radio programmers and music business people that enjoy the mix of famous to completely unknown artists from major and indie labels. They are manufactured and promoted completely at Oasis' expense. Contact information for each featured musician is included with the discs.

include a mail-order coupon. Display ads are generally placed in the body of a publication.

Another good place is a banner ad on a Web site that targets your audience and is linked directly to a site where people can hear and buy your recording. Fees for banner ads range from hundreds to thousands of dollars. They are called banner ads because they usually appear as an approximate 2 by 9-inch ad at the top of a Web site page.

Every media source that carries advertising has a media kit, which contains its advertising rates, circulation, and information about its audience. This information is invaluable in targeting your promotional efforts. You can receive media kits by writing or calling advertising managers and requesting them. Web sites that carry banner ads have links on their home pages that carry rates or links that allow you to ask them to e-mail further information.

When you advertise, you must conform to federal regulations regarding mail-order sales (see the segment, Federal Mail-Order Regulations, in the chapter, Sales). Offer your brochures or catalogs for free.

If you place ads in more than one publication, code the return addresses so you will recognize the source of orders.

Some magazines are willing to trade space in return for a percentage of sales. This is referred to as a "per inquiry" (PI) deal. The record company provides a camera-ready ad that contains an order coupon. The magazine provides the ad space. Orders are sent to the magazine. The magazine sends the record company the coupon and its share of the money plus the shipping and handling fee. The record company ships the recording. Magazines want to build their mailing lists and prove that advertising in them is worthwhile. They are most likely to make PI deals when advertising is slow, commonly January and August.

Radio advertising is most effective when it is combined with an advertisement for an upcoming performance—and airplay. Sometimes buying a radio ad provides leverage towards getting airplay, especially when the ad contains some of your music.

promotion - ➤ 39

Ubiquity Recordings

UBIQUITY RECORDINGS, FOUNDED IN 1993, CAME ABOUT BECAUSE OF JODY and Michael McFadin's love for collecting rare "groove" vinyl records, and their deejaying at San Francisco Bay Area clubs and running a store, Groove Merchant Records. The increasing demand for the records they had stockpiled provided the catalyst for them to license the rights of some of their rare records and manufacture them under the name Luv N' Haight Records. Ubiquity has since branched out into dance electronica, jazz, and hip-hop (Ubiquity); and Afro-Cuban jazz and Latin jazz/soul (CuBop). The different imprints (label names) make it easy to distinguish the genres.

We started as historical preservationists, to keep alive a genre of music that would have been permanently buried. Today we deal with music we love. What continues to drive us and excite us is discovering something new, seeing it through to a final recording, and turning people on to the music.

In the beginning, we had no knowledge of the business. Our naiveté was a benefit because we didn't believe certain things were not possible. We called any independent store we could think of; went to the New Music Seminar in New York with a travel cart of our recordings and networked, and sent mailings to our customer list.

Michael and Jody McFadin
Founders

We have two goals. The first is to please our customers. One reason we have a Web site is to be convenient. Our catalog got so large so quickly that when stores are out of records our customers lose out. The other goal is to please the musicians we sign. We give them creative freedom and they almost always produce their own recordings. We settle on a budget, write the check and allow them to deal with the session. This has given our recordings an authenticity that has become identified with our labels.

—Michael McFadin, cofounder, Ubiquity Recordings
www.ubiquityrecords.com

sales
sales

Independent artists and labels use a variety of methods to reach buyers. Direct sales at performances, fairs, craft shows and educational workshops; mail-order promotions to fan lists; museums; artists' Web sites; record stores and nonrecord store chains; specialty music mail-order catalogs (*Ladyslipper*—women's music, *Sounds True Catalog*—new age products, *Frontiers CDs & Tapes*—Western, cowboy, alternative country, blues); wholesale gift shows; and wholesale distributors are all used in the quest for consumer dollars.

At first, expenses will probably exceed income from sales of your recordings, because you will be spending money on promotion and sales efforts. Selling at performances nets immediate income. If you consign your recordings or sell them to a wholesale distributor, income will be deferred up to six months or more. You will have to do most of the sales work yourself and try to set many different elements into motion at the same time. Most stores and distributors want to be assured that performances and promotional support are forthcoming before they agree to handle your recording; and people will not buy your recording until they see you perform, hear it played by a friend, read about it, or hear your music on the radio or a Web site.

Coordinating this can take months of hard work, so try to set reasonable and specific sales goals and work hard to accomplish them.

Many artists begin by selling direct and consigning recordings to stores in those communities where they perform. As their sales and performances increase, they may find distributors or make deals with independent record companies that specialize in their genre of music. (The deals and clauses common in record contracts with independent labels are discussed in the chapter, Recording Contracts.)

FORMAT AND PRICING

Recordings are manufactured in many formats: analog cassettes; compact discs (CDs); MiniDiscs (MDs); and vinyl (7-inch 45s, 12-inch extended play records (EPs) manufactured to play at 45 revolutions per minute (rpm), and long playing records (LPs) manufactured to play at 33 1/3 rpm.

Information on Digital Video Discs (DVDs) is not included because its future as an audio format is unpredictable. The future of MDs is equally unpredictable. Few MiniDisc consumer players have been sold and it is not expected to be a popular consumer format.

The record company decides on the retail list price of each format, but store discounts are common and many performers offer discounts for direct sales at performances or by mail order. Remember that you, not the retail store, decide on the retail list price.

The retail list price helps to determine the discount price at which stores frequently sell to customers (determined by the store) and the discount price at which performers sell to fans (determined by the artist).

The price at which distributors buy from recording companies, the distributor wholesale price, is set by the record company. This is commonly 50% to 55% of the retail list price depending on the volume of inventory ordered. The discount can go as high as 60%.

The price at which stores buy from record distributors, the store wholesale price, is determined by the distributors. This is commonly 35% to 45% off of the retail list price. Most artist-owned labels consign their recordings to individual stores at a store wholesale price.

┌ ─ ► FOLLOWING IS A CHART OF PRICES COMMON IN THE INDUSTRY:

RETAIL LIST PRICE	DISTRIBUTOR (JOBBER) WHOLESALE PRICE	STORE WHOLESALE PRICE
CASSETTES		
$8.98	$4.04-4.49	$4.94-5.83
$9.98	$4.49-4.98	$5.48-6.48
7-INCH VINYL 45s		
$2.98	$.89-1.00	$1.18-1.28
12-INCH VINYL EPs		
$4.98	$2.24-2.49	$2.46-3.23
$5.98	$2.69-2.98	$3.28-3.88
COMPACT DISCS AND LPs		
$15.98	$7.19-7.49	$8.78-10.38
$16.98	$7.64-7.99	$9.33-11.03

SELLING AT PERFORMANCES

Performances are the most effective method for giving people a taste of your music and letting them know your recording is available. Performing regularly exposes your music to people, helps you win new fans and can create excitement among media people that may lead to reviews and airplay.

Selling at performances is good business. It generates fan enthusiasm, they will play your recordings for friends and encourage them to get copies of their own and attend performances. They will call radio stations with requests, and look for copies in recording stores. The demand created by fans can persuade stores and distributors to handle your recording and reviewers and DJs to give it attention. Buying your recordings at gigs gives your fans a chance to thank you directly. It is also a quick way to make back some of the money you invested in producing your recording. You do not have to give stores or distributors a cut or wait to be paid. Hopefully, direct sales will at least cover your monthly promotional and sales expenses.

A live concert is so powerful an introduction to a recording that many

labels will not sign artists that are not willing to perform on a regular basis and sell their recordings at performances. If your band records for a record company, you have to buy your records from them at the price established in your recording contract.

Major labels have shown a new willingness to allow artists to sell recordings at performances. In the past, they were opposed to this practice because they said it took away sales from retail stores. Now they know retail sales are catalyzed by fans that introduce the music to others.

PHOTO BY HENRY DILTZ

Sonic Joyride kicked off their 1999 tour with the release of their new CD, *Breathe,* by giving performances and selling recordings from their custom tour bus, "Cosmic Sled," in support of a national radio and retail campaign. On top of the bus is a stage set, video screens, and a 10,000-watt sound system. Inside is a 16-track digital recording studio. Videos of each performance will be uploaded to the band's laptop computer and placed on their Web site in QuickTime so that fans can plug into their road adventures. The band's innovative 1998 tour received generous media coverage from MTV, CNN, *Billboard,* and *Musician* and sponsorship from many local radio stations.

A great resource for musicians that want to learn how to successfully book gigs.

Club and Concert Performances

Club owners generally agree to have recordings sold at performances. Sometimes they will go out of their way to be helpful, particularly if the artist has involved them in their overall plans. If you want to sell at a club, make arrangements in advance of your performance.

Most concert promoters provide some means for the sale of recordings and promotional items at concerts, especially at concerts in genres that are not popularized by major recording labels. They understand that the recordings of unusual or unknown artists may be difficult to find in stores.

Arrangements are made at the time you negotiate your performance contract. Try to set up convenient space for a display or sales booth. Find out about special fees, insurance requirements and other red tape. Make sure you let the promoters know you are willing to do most of the work involved and you do not intend to add to their burdens.

Sales arrangements vary. Sometimes there is no charge or there can be a flat fee or a percentage of the sales. Do not depend on volunteers to staff your booth. That is a job that requires responsibility, time, and energy, and you should pay whomever helps you.

You can ask other performers on the bill to share the space and the tasks.

The sales of recordings and promotional items at large concerts and festivals has become big business, often generating more gross income than the box office. Sometimes the promoter sells booth and display space to recording labels or merchandise distributors. Sometimes sales are exclusively handled by a separate merchandising company or record distributor that has made arrangements with the promoter. The promoter charges a rental fee, a percentage of sales, or both. The merchandising company buys products from the record company or record distributor.

Artists that make recording deals with major labels will find that negotiating merchandising rights has become a standard part of any contract.

Increasing Sales at Performances

Here are some suggestions for increasing sales at performances.

Perform songs from your recording: it is a good way to interest the audience in buying it. This might seem obvious, but many performers become carried away with new material and get tired of performing old songs. When you do perform those songs, be sure to tell the audience they are on your recording.

Announce at least once during each set, preferably right before your last song, that your recording is available for sale and where it can be purchased. The announcement should be simple and short. "Many of you know that we recently released a CD (or cassette) called (_____).

For those of you who would like to buy a copy we have some on sale here in the main lobby for ($_____). It is also on sale at these locations (_____)."

Reinforce your announcements with a sign on your display table that shows your recording graphics and the words "ON SALE HERE." Make sure someone is on hand at all times during the performance to make sales and answer questions.

Consider offering a special performance discount. Display that fact prominently on your poster: "SPECIAL PERFORMANCE PRICE." Round off your price so that you can make

PHOTO © 1998 BY ROBERT CORWIN

"Hot stuff," said folk music legend Tom Paxton about *Hot Soup!*, a recording from Sue Trainor, Christina Muir, and Sue Ribaudo. The trio, based in the Washington, D.C./Baltimore, Maryland area, is well known for performances and workshops at local schools. The title of their recording provided plenty of fodder for promotional merchandise and their imaginative tabletop sales display. It also gave reviewers clever headlines for their stories: "Only the Finest Ingredients," "A Blue-Ribbon Recipe," and "SOUPer Harmonies."

change easily—like $10 or $15. Most states require that sales tax be collected for recording sales so build the correct sum into your rounded-off price. Keep accurate sales records; you will need them for tax purposes.

Consider giving away small promotional items to help people remember the name of the recording and where to buy it when they leave the concert. These can be postcards, newsletters, matchbooks, posters, bumper stickers—whatever you dream up and can afford.

Add each buyer's name and address to your fan list. Someone who buys your recording will appreciate being notified of future performances, new recordings and other relevant news.

Have press kits and business cards on hand for invited guests and any unexpected media and business people that show up.

SELLING IN RECORD STORES

Long before you start recording or designing cover graphics, you should visit stores to see what they stock and how they price. Pay particular attention to the small mom-and-pop stores, they often specialize in regional music or specialized genres. Notice which recordings from independent labels they carry and how they are displayed. See if there is a selection of your type of music. Explain your project to the owners and ask if they would consider carrying your recording. When you find a store that is receptive, add the owner and buyer to your industry list. Keep them informed about your performances, let them know that promotion is a regular part of your business and assure them that you will be promoting your recording.

Getting your recordings in a store does not, however, guarantee sales. Customers generally know what they are looking for when they go to a store, and are not likely to find and buy your recording by some happy accident. Even the smallest stores carry as many as 500 titles; the largest up to 100,000. No matter how good your recording is, it will not sell until you create a demand for it. Tell the store owner where to file your record. If there is no designation, create one. In the '80s the file name "Dance/electronica" did not exist in record stores. Today it does. Some record companies are placing the words "file under (name of music genre)" just below the bar code on their recordings.

Initially, sales will be slow. It can take up to six months of promotion and performances to convince people to buy your recording. Recognizing this will spare you the frustration caused by unrealistic sales expectations.

You will find that the most receptive stores are small and specialize in particular kinds of music. The owners of these stores are often sympathetic to individual business efforts. Like independent labels, they provide customers with recordings not always found in the larger stores.

The large discount record stores depend on huge volumes of business for their success. They make their money on the biggest-selling recordings from major labels. But the rising popularity of music from independent artists and labels means that most of these stores now carry a range of genres.

The large stores and chains prefer dealing with record distributors, not artist-owned recording labels. This avoids complicating their bookkeeping, and past experience has led them to believe that individual artists will not service accounts regularly or keep recordings in stock. They will carry your recording only if there is a demand for it or to complement other recordings they offer in your particular genre.

Once your recording is out, bring it to the stores that were receptive. Return to the more reluctant ones when you have proven sales at performances and other stores. Keep all stores up-to-date with news of reviews, airplay and reports of sales in other places. Send them all your press releases.

If you perform in their area, invite store personnel to attend so they will be aware of your efforts to promote your recordings.

Make your greatest promotional push after you have set up distribution in enough stores so that people can find your recordings easily. This may sound like a catch-22, but, hopefully, you will find some nonchain stores to sell your recording, particularly if you make them aware of your promotional and performance plans. Once your recordings begin to sell and your promotional efforts begin to pay off, you have leverage to get your recording into more stores.

Increasing Sales in Record Stores

The best way to support record store sales is to tell your fans where your recording can be purchased. This also provides free promotion for the stores.

Independently owned record stores may be willing to feature a poster of your band or your recording when you first release it or are doing a concert. Store clerks may play it on their sound systems or set it in a counter display without

---

Consignment Agreement

Date _____

Consigned to _____
              name of store

address _____ phone _____

_____ copies of the recording titled _____

_____
name of label   catalog number

Suggested retail price: $ _____

Price to consignee: $ _____

Payment is due when additional recordings are consigned or _____ days after the receipt of an invoice for records sold. Full returns accepted.

Recordings are the property of _____
                                 name of label
and may be removed at their discretion.

Thank you.

_____
signature of consignor

_____
signature of consignee

---

charge. Be sure to give them any written materials or press releases that name their store(s). You can also make a "bin" card to describe your recording's musical genre to prevent it from being filed in the "miscellaneous" section.

Many stores provide listening posts, private listening booths or headphones near displays, where potential buyers can hear selections from featured titles. These selections are usually not chosen by the retailer, but by the record company or distributor that pays the store for the privilege. The fees can range from $500 for three months display to many thousands of dollars. Exceptions to these fees are occasionally made for artists that are not affiliated with large independent or major labels, especially if they are popular where the stores are located. It never hurts to ask.

Some retail record stores have sound systems that play music continuously throughout the day. With few exceptions, the selections are paid for by recording labels.

Retailers often charge for space to stack recordings on the floor or in some prominent location near the entrance and for wall space to display posters.

Talk to store managers about their policies and fees.

Discounts and Consignments

Most stores buy recordings from labels and distributors on consignment: they pay only for goods they actually sell, commonly on a quarterly basis.

If a recording has not sold within a reasonable length of time, usually 90 days, the store will return it. Record companies always take back defective recordings without charge.

When you work with individual stores, a simple consignment agreement can act as order form and receipt. When the store needs more recordings, you collect for the ones sold and make out a new consignment agreement.

As long as you service stores personally, they will usually pay for the last order each time you consign more recordings. This method eliminates delays in payment, something you will appreciate once you start working with distributors and pricing and billing policies become more complicated.

Servicing Accounts

Once you have put recordings in a store, it is your job to keep track of them. Only in the case of incredible demand will store managers call you when they run out of your recording. You must make it as easy as possible for the stores to carry your recordings. Regular servicing of accounts, and courtesy on your part, are essential to a good working relationship. Visit the store at least once a month to check on sales and stock. Do not phone; clerks do not like taking time from in-store service to check inventory.

Store owners want one person to assume responsibility for your account and at some point you may have to hire someone to handle all your store accounts.

SELLING TO NONRECORD RETAIL STORES

Do not limit your sales efforts to music stores. Try to place your recording in health food stores, art galleries, coffee shops, bookstores, toy stores, truck stops, craft outlets, museum stores, religious goods outlets, and other specialty shops. Any store that is frequented by your target audience can be a good outlet for your recordings. Some may even play your recording on their music systems to help create interest.

There are three ways to reach these stores. One is to contact them personally and consign your recordings; another is to sell to the retail distributors that service them. The third is to rent booths at gift shows, which are regularly attended by store owners for the express purpose of buying inventory. There are gift shows that specialize in jewelry and crafts, clothing, toys, etc. The easiest way to find out about the ones that interest you is to ask stores in your community that carry records, the Chamber of Commerce, and associations that deal with particular classes of merchandise.

SELLING AT FAIRS AND ARTS AND CRAFT SHOWS

Many artists rent booths at fairs, arts and craft shows, etc., to sell recordings and related merchandise. If you do this, provide a method for playing your music through a sound system or headphones. The more attractively the recordings are displayed, the more you will sell. You might also make arrangements to share the booth rental with other recording artists or with someone who sells items that appeal to your target audience.

DISTRIBUTORS

Consigning recordings to stores and servicing accounts is hard work. From the beginning, you will wish that someone would do it for you. That is the business of a distributor.

Distributors make money by buying recordings from many different labels and selling them to as many stores as they can. They will not take on your recording until they believe it will sell.

When you prove sales through your own distribution system and show some success with promotion and touring, distributors will want to talk with you.

With few exceptions, recordings from independent labels are handled by entirely different distributors than the ones that service major labels. Most independent recording distributors cover specific geographical territories or specific genres of recordings. A rack jobber is the name of a special type of distributor that supplies department stores and chain outlets, such as Target and Wal-Mart. Most independent record labels deal with a number of record and non-record distributors, seeking them out region by region to be assured of total coverage.

In general, you should start with distributors in your area that specialize in recordings similar to yours. They will be interested when you can show good sales in many stores and you will have leverage for convincing them to carry your records, particularly if you can show them that you have booked gigs in the area and have plans to promote them.

If you think there might be a demand for your recording outside of your region, find a distributor in that area. Seek out the smaller distributors first, because they will be more willing to take you on and can give your account service and attention.

Finding a Distributor

The best way to learn about distributors and their reputations is to join the Association For Independent Music (AFIM), formerly the National Association of Independent Record

Distributors and Manufacturers (NAIRD). Members are owners of independent labels, distributors and manufacturers. The AFIM publishes an annual directory of member distributors and labels.

Attend the AFIM's annual convention to meet the distributors. Play your recording for them, acquaint them with your promotional and performance plans, and ask questions. At the same time, you can speak with the owners of labels that use independent distributors. It is in your interest to find out about different distributors' reputations for service and payment. (More information on the AFIM is provided in the chapter, Business.)

Ask the owners of the stores that carry your recording. They can provide information as to what other labels their distributors carry and what their business reputation is.

Ask artists that record in your genre of music, visit their Web sites and the Web sites of their recording labels. They often name their distributors or provide links to distributor Web sites. Researching artists by name on the Internet can also lead to the names of distributors.

Information about record distributors is available from associations devoted to particular genres of music and in many magazines that specialize in particular genres.

You can find a list of recording distributors in *The Billboard International Buyer's Guide Directory.*

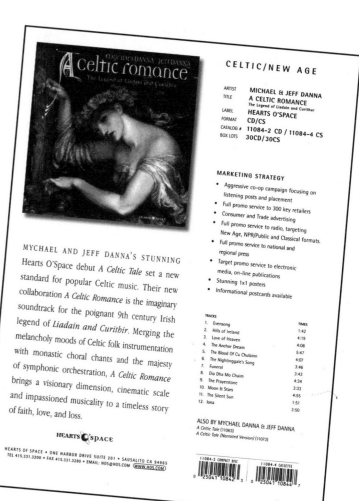

A one-page sell sheet provides distributors with concise information to convey to their store accounts.

Distributors and Promotion

Once you find a distributor you have to work to keep that distributor interested in your recordings and working on your behalf, especially if you do not have a proven volume of sales. Think of the distributor as a business partner who is working with you to achieve a mutual goal: selling your recordings.

News about your successes and performances is important because distributors will use it as leverage to persuade stores to carry your product. Send them all press releases. Offer to supply copy for their one-sheets, which are universally used by distributors as quick reference sheets. They contain the artist's name, name of the record, label's name, date of release, UPC bar code number and catalog number. They also provide a brief description of the recording, its genre, unique qualities, highlight well-known musicians, quotes from reviewers, and important tour dates.

In the last few years, several independent recording distributors have increased their services to supplement the promotional efforts of their labels. These include sending out regular newsletters that feature tour dates, news of airplay, and clips from favorable reviews; paying for listening posts at retail record stores; booking concerts at retail outlets; taking out ads; sponsoring Internet radio stations that feature music from the labels they carry; and linking their Web site to Internet music stores.

When you are going to tour in an area that is serviced by your distributor, tell them in advance so they can persuade stores to take extra stock and put up special displays. Offer to meet store owners and salespeople. Let the distributor know about your plans for getting reviews and airplay and ask them for suggestions. Even if you are not touring, send your distributors all your press releases and favorable reviews to inform them of your progress.

Find out about your distributors' salespeople and deal with them personally. Add them to your mailing list, phone them occasionally and visit them when you are in their vicinity. If you deal with distributors that handle many different labels, you will find that the salespeople are not always acquainted with all the recordings they sell. Any input from you will give your recording an extra push.

Doing Business with a Distributor

The price at which distributors buy from recording labels is commonly 50% to 55% of the retail list price. Variations are based on your discounting policies, leverage in the marketplace, and number of recordings sold.

Written agreements with your distributors should specify the discounts, when and how often you will be paid, and the amount of promotional recordings you will provide.

Discounts as high as 60% are given to distributors for large volume buys.

Distributors order inventory and, being wary about paying for product that might be returned, specify that payment will not be made until the stores have paid them. Stores pay distributors on a monthly or quarterly basis; they return unsold merchandise, generally after 90 days. The label and distributor agree to take back unsold and defective recordings. This means the record label consigns recordings to distributors and the distributors consign them to the stores.

Distributors make accountings to labels on a quarterly, semi-annual, or annual basis.

They will want some free promotional records and want to make at least one copy available to each store they service, as a way of introducing your music. Your written agreement with them should specify how many recordings they can make available as promotional giveaways or samples. Ensure that these copies are

We are now requesting secured inventory agreements from our distributors. This means the product is technically ours until we're paid for it. In case of a bankruptcy, or sale of the business, the agreement allows us to come in and claim the inventory so that it doesn't get tied up in legal limbo and we have a way to recoup.

—Pat Hayes, Promotion,
Soundings of the Planet

not just extras that will be returned for credit by using stickers that say "Promotional Copy, Not for Sale" or by otherwise distinguishing "promo" copies from sales copies.

Once you have received an order from a distributor, you must ship or deliver the recordings at your expense. Include an invoice that states the terms of sale with each delivery.

Collection

The biggest headache in dealing with distributors is the long wait for payment. Their primary reason will be that store payments are delayed. To speed payment, distributors may offer incentives such as, an additional 10% to 15% discount for cash on delivery with returns accepted only for damaged merchandise, a sliding scale discount,

and a one-for-ten policy. The label gives the distributor a free recording for every 10 bought and paid for within a specified period, usually 30 days. Distributors assess stores for late payment, usually 2% to 5% of the amount owing. You can use some of these same tactics with a distributor.

Many labels report that a lapse of six months is common before they see the first payment for new inventory. And there are distributors (and stores) that delay payments for a year or more or never pay, a practice that has occurred often enough to warn you about it here. The practice is often discriminatory: the distributors first pay labels whose products sell faster than others and those that have done business with them for a long time; they delay payments to new labels and labels with sloppy business practices.

Collecting money is one of the least appealing aspects of selling. If you are not persistent, distributors will think that you do not care when you are paid. The labels that are the most persistent are usually paid first.

Therefore, it is important to find out something about distributors' payment reputations before you deal with them. Ask owners of other recording labels. People are usually willing to share their experiences, particularly the negative ones.

You have real leverage to collect only when your recordings are selling quickly and your distributor must reorder, or when you put out a second recording to follow a record that has been selling. Many labels report cutting off distributors from receiving more product the very first time payments lapse beyond 90 days. This may sound hard-nosed, but it is accepted as good business practice and lets companies know you are not willing to be taken advantage of.

You can speed up the collection process only through constant diligence. Develop a personal working relationship. Visit and talk to your distributors as often as you can. Tell them about your performance and promotional successes. Regular and personable communication is the best method for assuring they will not neglect you.

Always put an audit clause in your agreements that specifies you have the right to visit their accounting offices once during a calendar year and audit their books for your account.

Sell or consign only small numbers of recordings to distributors at first, so if sales increase rapidly and the distributor will need more recordings to keep up with demand, you can refuse to provide them until the last consignment is paid for. Your chances of getting paid are better anyway, since the amounts involved are small. Distributors know their retail accounts and can make fairly accurate estimates about the rate of sale for your recording. Their initial order will be based on that knowledge.

Be extremely diligent about collections. If distributors miss an accounting period, send the distributor a certified letter stating that they missed the payment date. Start phoning and ask to talk to the bookkeeper. If you are told repeatedly that the bookkeeper is "out of the office," complain to the person on the phone. Keep bothering them. Recognize that you are financing the distributor. Not getting paid on time means that they are using your money for maintaining their own cash flow.

An alternative to trying to speed up the collection process is to simply accept the fact that you have to wait to be paid. Even so, you must set limits on what you will accept.

The foregoing is not meant to discourage you from using a distributor, but to inform you that it often takes awhile for money to get back to you, so plan accordingly. When you do find distributors that sell recordings for you and pay on time, acknowledge them graciously. Consider any move to a new distributor very carefully, weigh possible profits against the loyalty and hard work of your current distributor.

SELLING MUSIC ON THE INTERNET

The Internet is an ideal medium through which to make your music available. Recordings are sold at artists' Web sites; independent artists' collective Web sites, such as Kaleidospace (www.Kspace.com) and Internet Underground Music Archive (IUMA) (www.IUMA.com); major and independent labels' Web sites; and Internet superstores, like CDnow (www.cdnow.com) and Amazon.com. Sales of individual artists' products can reach $10,000 a month and more, depending on their success in promoting their music.

Some independent labels and large music Web sites have begun to make music available through electronic delivery. Customers can preview cuts and either (1) download them, for a price, to their hard drives or other digital storage mediums, such as CD-R or MiniDisc; or (2) purchase selected cuts that will be placed on a CD-R and sent to them. These cuts will be encrypted (watermarked) to prevent direct copying. Liquid Audio is the first company to offer encryption services. Its partners include Intel Corporation and RSA Data Systems, a leading supplier of encryption tools. While direct downloads are potentially very exciting for the music industry, a recent study by Forrester Research, a market research company that specializes in Internet commerce, indicated that its contribution to overall sales will be less than 10% for several years to come.

You can ask people to print out your mail-order form and send it with a check or money order. And many artists have reported that sales immediately escalated by as much as 50% when they began taking credit card orders.

Most Web sites allow listeners to sample music, see QuickTime videos, look at artists' bios, tour dates, and so on.

One method for an artist owned label to sell recordings on the Internet is to make arrangements with a large independent collective, such as Kaleidospace or IUMA that already has sales and fulfillment mechanisms in place. Even if you have your own Web site, you may find that providing basic information on these large sites and linking your site to theirs is by far the easiest and cheapest method to sell recordings on the Internet. You will have to pay a nominal fee for placing web pages on these sites (typically under $400) and either a sales commission, typically 20% to 30%, or a monthly fee.

Another method is to find a distributor that provides Internet sales or is linked with a large Web site that does. Internet CD superstores such as CDnow buy their products from independent and major label distributors. Their on-line databases make it easy for people to search by genre, artist, and title. Many of these superstores are linked to Internet radio stations, so if someone hears music they like, they can order the recording.

Amazon.com, Inc. has a program to help independents list their CDs on its Web site. Visitors can see a display of cover art, read liner copy and reviews, listen to 30-second sound clips from two tracks on a CD, and order with the Amazon.com guarantee "usually ships in 24 hours." Amazon stocks the title(s) and e-mails the label when stock is low. For full information contact: www.amazon.com/advantage.

A partnership between Muze Inc., a provider of in-store information systems for music, books, and videos (*Muze/Phonolog*), Baker & Taylor Entertainment, a leading distributor of videos, CDs, and cassettes, and Liquid Audio, a supplier of on-line music delivery systems, gives artists that are not currently represented by a label the opportunity for their recordings to be promoted over the Internet, sold to retail accounts, and listed in the *Muze/Phonolog* catalogs. Fans that visit the Liquid Audio Web site can listen to artists' cuts in Dolby Digital sound, purchase the music for download on their PCs, and store it permanently on a CD-R or MiniDisc. Artists' tracks are included in the Liquid Music Network, a large database of commercially available downloadable tracks. Your recordings are entered into the Muze database, which is used by 90% of traditional retail stores and 75% of on-line retail stores. If your recordings do not have distribution or additional distribution is needed, Baker and Taylor

Entertainment will take five on consignment and fill orders for your recordings from Internet or traditional retail music stores.

If you want to sell only a few recordings through your Web site, the easiest method is to find an Internet service provider (ISP) that offers this service (sometimes called a virtual "shopping cart program") as an enhancement to their basic service. You provide the mail-order form on your site. Make sure the ISP provides secure credit card transactions. According to author Jeannie Novak, in her book *Creating Internet Entertainment,* "The Internet is a relatively safe place to conduct transactions—certainly safer than giving credit cards to strangers over the phone or at restaurants…. Current fraud rates on credit card numbers collected by traditional means (e.g., phone orders) run to several percentage points—vastly higher than any statistics thus far reported for the Internet."

You can link your Web site to a service provider that has electronic commerce services (e-commerce), which include credit card processing and sales fulfillment. A good one is Cartalog from Virtual Spin, an Internet company that provides a variety of e-commerce software and services. The fees are established according to the number of items and disk space used.

The search engine Yahoo! (www.yahoo.com) also provides e-commerce services through its Yahoo! Store system. This site is particularly notable for providing access to sales statistics that store creators can access through their Web browsers.

You can buy software that enables you to create your on-line store. Relatively simple ones

PHOTO BY JOHN KLICKER

Any type of music you can find nationally you can find on a local level—and sometimes it's better. There's more honest feeling. We got tired of big interests telling our friends what they want them to hear; and we got tired of seeing local product hidden in bins where even diehard consumers had a hard time finding it. That's why we opened our store. Now we're expanding our horizons and starting a Web site called Locals Online—a Global Collection of Local Music (www.localsonline.com)—where independents from anywhere in the world can contact us, fill out a description of their music, and consign us records at their wholesale price to sell on our site.

—Dan Sause, co-owner, Locals Only, Portland, Oregon

like ShopSite Express from ICentral, Inc. provide customizable options for payment, shipping, and secure credit card handling. More expensive software applications can enable you to develop a fully coordinated and integrated on-line catalog that links to a database system, which provides

Digital delivery of music over the Internet will most likely be the primary way of purchasing music within the next three to five years. This is great news for independent musicians. They will not have to rely on the uncertainties of traditional distribution methods. The money saved by eliminating manufacturing costs can be put to use as part of the all-important marketing budget. Artists' customers will be able to pay for music and have it delivered immediately to their computers. This will give artists access to marketing information about their customers that is not available through traditional retail.

Currently, the vast majority of download-and-play music offered for sale is provided through MPEG (MP3) compressed audio at sites such as www.mp3.com. The site carries lots of news and commentary, downloads of free MP3 software, and thousands of full-length songs in MP3 format created by independents, which can be legally downloaded and saved.

–Jeannie Novak, author and cofounder of the Kaleidospace Web site (www.kspace.com)

real-time inventory, pricing, ordering, and bookkeeping functions.

RETAIL RECORDING CATALOGS AND DATABASES

When you offer your recording for sale, you qualify for listing in recording catalogs and databases that list information about recordings. These resources are used by retailers to locate and order recordings for their customers. It is important to be listed so people that hear of your recording can order it directly from you, or through music stores or distributors.

The *Phonolog* published by Muze Inc., is a comprehensive loose-leaf catalog that lists currently available recordings cross-referenced by label, title, artist, and category. Subscribers receive weekly updates. *Phonolog* print listings are also accessible by using Muze's software Phonolog for Windows.

Muze also publishes *Muze for Music*, a comprehensive music database that is available as an in-store interactive information system for tradiional retailers, and as a licensable database for on-line retailers. This database contains over 200,000 music titles and associated album information, including title, artist, label, catalog number, length of recording, track list, liner notes, reviews, and etc. Both album and song titles are searchable by key words.

Listings in *Phonolog* and *Muze for Music* are free and open to all recordings, which are on sale and generally available in record stores. To be listed, send a copy of your recording, including associated packaging, along with production notes and promotional materials.

The *Schwann Artist*, an annual guide to classical performers, and *Schwann Opus*, a quarterly classical guide organized by composer and piece, list CDs and cassettes currently available in the United States. The *Schwann Spectrum*, a quarterly guide to nonclassical listings, is being redesigned and is expected to resume publication sometime in 1999.

Listings in Schwann publications are free, but recordings must be available through a U.S. telephone number and address or be distributed nationally to stores. In order to be listed, labels must send a copy of their recording(s) and information about the record company (name, address, phone number, contact person).

The addresses for these catalogs are listed in the Directory of Resources. When you send the catalogs your materials and information, include the names and addresses of distributors that carry your recording. List information as it is shown on your recording's label, "A"-side first.

MAIL-ORDER SALES

Sales can be generated through mailings to people on your fan list and rented mailing lists, and through mail-order catalogs that specialize in your musical genre, recordings in general, or sell a variety of merchandise. Success depends on accurately assessing your audience, researching and obtaining the right mailing lists, and sending out advertising packages that effectively communicate your message. Mail-order information should also be included in the printed materials for your recording.

Mail-Order Package

If your goal is to sell just to fans that are already interested in your music, an attractively designed mail-order form may be all that you need.

Add a shipping and handling fee to the price of the recording; and provide your customers with shipping choices. That fee should cover the cost of shipping, the mailer, and the time spent preparing the package and logging the sale for tax and business purposes.

If you want to interest others, have your graphic designer prepare a special mailing package that uses the graphic elements from your recording's cover and promotional materials. This package should include a business reply card or return postage paid envelope. The easier you make it for people to respond to you, the higher your sales.

Independent label owners have found that the number of responses to mail-order offerings are higher when more than one recording or complementary items like T-shirts, decals, and posters, are available.

If you want Christmas orders, advertisements should be mailed no later than October 15.

You can save money and increase sales by doing a cooperative mailing with other independent labels.

Renting Mailing Lists

Specialized mailing lists can be rented, often in the form of self-adhesive labels. The company renting them to you will specify they are for one time use only and will seed the list with decoy names to protect against unauthorized use.

The varieties of mailing lists will astonish

you. To research mailing list companies, look in the yellow pages under "Mailing Lists." Many of these companies can research specialized lists, for instance, all the banjo teachers in America. Many music magazines, associations, and nonprofit

Ladyslipper Catalog

Music by Women & More

Autumn 1998

The most complete catalog of women's recordings from major and independent labels worldwide. Their entire catalog is now on-line at their Web site www.ladyslipper.org.

groups will rent their lists for as little as $40 per 1,000 names. Fees are seldom higher than $100 per 1,000 names.

Expect no more than a 2% return from any mailing. If you want to test the value of renting a list, do a trial run by buying no more than 2000 names. You can judge by the response whether a larger mailing will be worth the effort.

Some mailing list companies can computerize and update mailing lists for your use at regular intervals. They can prepare your advertising and graphics, handle the mailing, and do order fulfillment.

Mail-Order Catalogs

The number of mail-order catalogs that specialize in particular genres of music or particular subjects is growing. You can find recordings being promoted in museum, clothing, environmental, toy, and new age catalogs. Inquire about how you can get them to carry your recording. Tell them why you think people that receive their catalog would want to buy it. If they are interested, ask what their initial order is likely to be, what the range of annual sales for recordings similar to yours is, and what their payment policies are. Research their reputations by getting in touch with some of the other recording artists featured in their catalogs. Many of them will have Web sites and e-mail addresses.

Federal Mail-Order Regulations

In 1976, the Federal Trade Commission issued the Trade Regulation Rule on Mail-Order Merchandise that imposes certain obligations on sellers that market products by mail order. The FTC had received numerous complaints from customers that paid for products but never received them or experienced long delays in receiving them. The purpose of the rule is to protect mail-order customers from abuses by mail-order merchants.

In any advertisement for mail-order sales, the seller must state when the seller expects to ship the product. If no time is mentioned, it is assumed the product will be shipped within 30 days of the buyer's order. If the seller is not able to meet the delivery date, the buyer must be advised of a new shipping date or told why a revised date cannot be set and be given a chance to consent to the delayed date or cancel the order. In case of cancellation, the buyer's payment must be refunded in no more than seven days.

If the new shipping date is no more than 30 days after the original shipping date, the buyer is automatically deemed to have accepted that date unless the buyer notifies the seller otherwise. If the new date is greater than 30 days or a new date cannot be set the seller must notify the buyer that the order will be canceled unless the seller receives notice from the buyer within 30 days consenting to the delay or the seller actually ships the product within 30 days.

All notices to the buyer must be by first-class mail and must provide the buyer with an opportunity to respond by enclosing a business reply card or a postage paid envelope. If the seller decides the order cannot be filled, the buyer must be notified and refunded their money in no more than seven days.

Finally, the seller is required to maintain a record of compliance with the rule. If the seller does not, there is a rebuttable presumption that the seller has failed to comply with the rule. Sellers should keep records of their notices to buyers and any evidence of shipment of the product or refund. If there is a dispute, the better sellers can document transactions the stronger their defenses will be against buyers' claims.

SALES PLANS

A sales plan outlines how many recordings you project you will sell in a year. Until you estimate how many recordings you are likely to sell, you will not know how many to manufacture at first or how much you can reasonably spend on recording, manufacturing, business, and promotion. Your long-term goal is to eventually show a net profit. Your short-term goals are better gigs, more exposure, and maybe interest from larger independent or major labels. Gross profit is the total income you receive from all sales; net profit is what you have left after all annual business expenses that relate to your recording have been met.

Add the number of recordings you plan to give away to the number of recordings you project you will sell. This figure determines the total number of recordings you will manufacture.

To arrive at a reasonable estimate, do the research outlined in the Promotion and Sales chapters and use the worksheet, Sales, found on page 221.

According to hundreds of interviews conducted with independent label artists, you can reasonably expect that 10% of an audience will buy a recording. If you know how many performances you are likely to do in a month that will reach substantially different people, you can make a pretty good guess about how people will hear you during a year's worth of performances.

Count the number of people on your fan mailing list and guess how many new people will sign up after you release your recording, based on the rate of sign-up at gigs and concerts. Expect that 2% of the entire fan list will buy your recordings by mail. (Presumably, some will have bought the record at gigs, stores, etc.)

Your research about stores that are likely to carry your record should provide you with some idea about the rate of sales. Store managers should be able to estimate that number based on their experience with recordings similar to yours.

If a distributor, independent label, or record catalog sells your record, they should be able to provide you with estimates based on sales of other recordings they carry.

SAMPLE SALES PLAN FOR A FIRST RECORDING

The following is an example of a modest three-month sales plan for an artist who has been playing regularly at clubs in a large metropolitan area and doing an occasional concert. The recording is the first one to be released and the plan assumes the release will be accompanied by a promotional campaign that will use the recording to increase the number and improve the quality of the venues where the artist performs. The goal is to sell at least 400 recordings within three months in stores, at performances, and by mail order. If this goal is met, an artist can reasonably expect to sell a minimum of 1600 recordings the first year. Meeting these goals will also provide the leverage to persuade a distributor or record catalog to carry the recording.

FIRST MONTH

Set up distribution in 15 small specialty record stores. Sales expectations are two recordings a month in each store (30 recordings).

Sell 50 recordings at performances.

Sell 20 recordings through the mail or to family, friends, and others.

Total month's sales: 100 recordings.

SECOND MONTH

Add five new stores. Sales expectations are two recordings a month in each store (10 recordings) plus another 30 recordings sold from the first month's stores. Total 40 recordings.

Sell 50 recordings at performances.

Sell 30 recordings through the mail.

Total month's sales: 120 recordings.

THIRD MONTH

Add five stores in adjacent areas. Sales expectations are two recordings a month in each new store (10 recordings).

Use promotion to increase sales in the first 25 stores and estimate that approximately half of them (12) will sell three recordings a month in each store (36) and the rest will continue to sell two (26). Total 62 recordings.

Increase the amount of your gigs so that you are selling 75 recordings at performances.

Sell 50 recordings through the mail.

Total month's sales: 197 recordings.

Total sales for three months: 417 recordings.

Quinlan Road

Loreena McKennitt
Founder

LOREENA MCKENNITT DEVELOPED A LARGE, PASSIONATE FOLLOWING FOR HER unusual, and not apparently commercial, genre of music by learning and doing the business herself. Today she is an internationally renowned performing and recording artist who has sold over eight million records in 40 countries worldwide. She manages herself and her business, Quinlan Road.

Between 1985 and 1989, she released three independent recordings. *Elemental,* her first cassette, was sold at her street performances in Toronto's St. Lawrence market. *To Drive The Cold Winter Away,* released two years later, featured obscure, traditional Christmas tunes she recorded in a monastery in Ireland and in a historic church in Ontario. When Loreena released *Parallel Dreams* in 1989, she was filling concert halls throughout Canada.

The Warner Music Group and Loreena reached agreement in 1991. Since then, she produced four recordings distributed by Warner worldwide: *The Visit* (1991); *The Mask And Mirror* (1994); the EP, *A Winter Garden: Five Songs For The Season* (1995) and *The Book Of Secrets* (1997). She has won two Juno awards (the Canadian equivalent of a Grammy). A live double album is in the works.

By the time major record companies began to be serious, I was running a very good business for myself. I didn't need an alliance with one in order to do what I loved. I was making over $100,000 a year in record sales. I knew what my manufacturing units cost; what the wholesale discounts and return percentages were. But more than that, I knew what it had taken for me to build a successful career. I knew very well that I didn't have to settle for a conventional artist's record deal. The only way I was going to do a deal was as a symbiotic partnership. The record company that seemed most in tune with that approach was Warner Canada. They were willing to throw out the rulebook, deal directly with me, and figure out a contract that was mutually beneficial. During negotiations, I was treated as an individual who was bringing her own repertoire, a strong knowledge of her strengths and weaknesses, and a very healthy business.

—Loreena McKennitt
www.quinlanroad.com

recording contracts

by Edward R. Hearn, Esq.

the purpose of this chapter is to make you aware of options, suggest ways of investigating those options, and help you understand the primary considerations involved in any contract proposed by a recording or production company. It is always advisable, when faced with a financial or contractual situation, to solicit the advice of an attorney or accountant who is familiar with the music business and the way recording and publishing contracts are structured.

An alternative to raising funds to produce your recording is to approach other recording labels. These may be major labels, labels with distribution deals with major labels, or wholly independent labels.

While investigating sales outlets for your recordings, research the labels that promote and distribute recordings that are similar to yours. Write to ask for their catalogs. If you think you will fit in, supply them with information about you, your performances, and your plans for recording. If they are interested, ask about their distribution network, and how many of your recordings do they project could be sold in the first year or two.

Within the last decade, independent recording labels that specialize in particular styles of music have become very successful in reaching and developing niche markets. You might find one that successfully markets music of your style and is interested in producing, manufacturing, and distributing your recording.

Some of these labels have made recording deals with major labels or distribution networks. How do you know whether independent labels are subsidiaries? Look for the logo, name, or trademark of a major label or distribution network on the spine or back of the recording.

Before examining the issues involved in negotiating with a recording label, it would be useful to summarize the major advantages and disadvantages between producing, manufacturing, and distributing your recording through your own effort, compared to turning some or all of that responsibility over to a recording label.

The advantages are you retain quality and aesthetic control over all elements involved and realize a larger amount of the income that results from recording sales, thus providing a quicker return on your investment.

The disadvantages include—limitations of the geographical area of distribution you can handle; the difficulty of collecting money from retail stores and intermediate distributors; financing the costs of production, manufacturing, and inventory as well as marketing, promotion, and distribution. These activities take substantial amounts of time and money and must be weighed against using that time and money to further develop your talents.

PROS AND CONS OF MAKING ARRANGEMENTS WITH A RECORDING LABEL

The chief advantage of releasing your recording with an independent recording label is it generally has a distribution mechanism in place. It is organized to handle the time and expense of financing and administering the production, manufacture, marketing, and distribution of recordings. It can better bear the financial risk, including the risk of not collecting money from the buyers of recordings. In addition, the company may have developed a reputation in the music community for a certain style of music and can move a greater volume of recordings in a wider geographical territory.

Bear in mind that if a small label invests time and money in your career and is successful

in generating a reasonable level of income for you, you should carefully weigh the benefits of signing with a major label if asked (where you will be one of many)—against staying with the smaller one (where you may be the star!). Far too often, the benefits of a smaller label are discovered only after an unhappy relationship with a major recording label occurs. Much depends on the style of music involved, for example, pop and rock may get more attention from a major label than jazz, new age, children's music, or Yiddish folk songs. Both small and large labels have demonstrated effectiveness at heavy metal, dance, and rap music.

The negative aspects of distributing through a recording label include—less income per unit sold; a longer period of time to receive that income; loss of control over elements of your career or music; and a possible long-term commitment for future recordings as a partial exchange for the company assuming the expense of financing, production, manufacture, marketing, and distribution of your recordings.

One of the realities of the music business is that the distribution artery is the most congested when it comes to the flow of money to the seller of the recordings. Frequently, there is a substantial delay between placing the recordings in the market and the return of income to the artist. Consequently, any distributor or recording label should be investigated carefully to determine its success and reputation for honesty and financial responsibility.

Here are some options with smaller labels not usually available to musicians that sign with major labels.

Distribution Deals

In this type of deal, you deliver an agreed amount of fully manufactured and packaged records, cassettes, or compact discs to a record company. Some labels may only distribute product, while you do the marketing and promotion; others may do everything.

In a distribution only deal, the record label will either contract directly with stores or deal with networks of independent distributors or both, selling to them at wholesale prices.

If the company only distributes your record, you will receive a sum equivalent to the wholesale price, minus a fee of 20% to 30% and other direct expenses that you authorize the company to spend, but you pay for all the manufacturing and all associated marketing and promotion costs. A standard contractual agreement is that you receive money only on records actually sold.

These types of deals often result after bands release recordings for a regional audience, find themselves with growing popularity, and use that as leverage to make a deal to broaden their sale base.

Pressing and Distribution (P & D) Deals

In P & D deals, you deliver a fully mixed recording master and artwork to the record label, which assumes the responsibility of manufacturing and distributing your recordings. If the label advances the manufacturing costs, it will reimburse itself out of the sales of your recordings and take both a fee for the use of its money and a distribution fee.

If the record label also picks up promotion, publicity, and marketing, then the deal is usually structured as a royalty deal that will leave the record label with a sufficient margin to cover all of its costs and make a reasonable profit. The royalty is sometimes higher than in standard recording contracts because you have already invested the costs of recording and producing. That is not always the case, however. When negotiating this type of deal, ask that any royalty percentages be specified as "net cents per unit" for each configuration.

As an alternative, if marketing and promotion duties are involved, these expenses could be deducted as direct costs also, along with the distribution fee and manufacturing costs, with the balance paid to you, but more likely the deal will be structured on a royalty basis of anywhere from 14% to 18% of retail, plus mechanical royalties.

Production Deals

In this type of deal, you sign as an artist with a production company. The company is responsible for recording your music and for obtaining distribution through independent distributors or a record company. In many cases, contracts for these deals are similar to recording contracts because the production company will make a P & D deal with a record label that also includes marketing and promotion and then contract with you for a percentage of the royalty paid to it by the record company.

For example, a production company may have a deal with a record company that pays 14% to 20% of the retail selling price on recordings sold, depending in part on whether the recording costs are paid by the production company or advanced by the record company. The production company then contracts with the artist to pay a royalty from between 6% and 10% of the retail selling price or 50% to 60% of the royalty paid to the production company by the record company.

Francisco Aquabella is arguably the greatest conga player in the world. He has played with all the greats, including Dizzy Gillespie, Frank Sinatra, and Tito Puente; and he was a founding member of the Latin group Malo. Being so in demand made it hard for him to record his own solo projects. Fantasy Records recorded a debut LP in the early '60s and original copies of this vinyl LP have traded hands on the collectors' circuit for over $500 per copy.

I first saw him perform at a club called Steamers in Fullerton, California when he sat in with a band called the Banda Brothers that usually plays with Pancho Sanchez as his rhythm section. Then I saw him again in Burbank at The Baked Potato nightclub, playing with his band. I was hooked. We sat down with him and his associate, Frank Marrone, and talked and did a deal. We will be releasing a new album of his music in 1999; and we will be re-releasing any other music of his we can get ahold of.

—Michael McFadin, Ubiquity Recordings

If you are contracting with a production company, ask whether they have an existing subsidiary deal with an independent label or whether they hope to obtain one on the strength of the recording they make with you. If it is the latter, you should clarify what will happen in the event that no such deal is made.

RECORDING CONTRACTS

If you succeed in finding a recording label for your project, you will have to negotiate and sign a contract. Careful consideration must be given to the terms of the contract, since it will govern the rights and responsibilities of the label and you.

Although contracts with independent labels can be very similar to those negotiated with major labels, smaller independent companies sometimes work out arrangements that do not mirror those standards. With increasing frequency, however, the smaller labels are reflecting the contractual style and approach of the major labels, perhaps because of the investment costs and financial risks incurred in developing an artist and the desire to have a secure contract with the artist that is sufficiently strong so a larger label will not be able to tempt the artist to switch labels without the smaller label participating in the benefits of that switch.

It is always wise to ask the recording label for a projection of how many recordings they expect to sell. Many independent labels will provide information about average sales of first recording releases. That way you can compare what the contract offers against what you can realize on your own. You may find that even though a recording label may double your sales, the actual income will be less than what you can do yourself.

Be aware that the money financed for recording and touring, as well as cash advances are considered advances or loans against income and will be deducted from your royalty earnings before any royalty payments are made to you.

The following outlines the major negotiating areas included in almost all recording contracts. Major and independent labels tend to have obtusely written contracts that have been developed over a long period of time. Although most major labels no longer insist the label participate in some or all of the music publishing, many independents do. This is an issue that must be examined carefully and be the subject of a separate publishing deal.

Duration of the Contract

Recording contracts often obligate the artist to a one- or two-year period for the initial term and subsequent option periods for one album each, usually for four to six options. The recording label generally retains the authority to decide whether to exercise any options. The actual duration of the recording agreement can be from five to seven years and sometimes longer, with the artist being obligated to produce from five to eight albums.

Long-duration contracts increase the label's chances to profit from the time and money spent developing your career and a market for your recordings. Contrary to media hype, fame and fortune are seldom achieved overnight. In fact, a small label may insist on a long-term commitment since its investment in you will have a greater financial impact on it than a major label's investment will have on the major.

From the artist's perspective, the best approach is to limit the term of the agreement to one album plus two or three options, with one album to be produced during each period of the contract. Limiting the term of the contract

provides the opportunity to negotiate a more substantial agreement with the company or go with another label if that seems to be the best course to follow in advancing your career.

If a major label deal is your goal, a limited duration contract with an independent will increase your opportunity to sign with a major without it having to buy out the small label's agreement with you.

Royalties

Every record company uses a different formula to identify the royalty percentage paid to an artist. The percentage can be based on the retail selling price for recordings sold or paid for or on the wholesale cost to distributors or record stores.

Industry standards for first recordings vary, but an artist royalty range, not including fees or percentages paid to a producer, typically varies from 6% to 10% of retail. The royalty rates for singles are generally lower because the expense of promoting singles can be very high, particularly if the recording labels are paying promotional fees to independent promoters to gain airplay (costs that may be charged back to your royalties). The wholesale standard varies from 12% to 20%. Some companies base the royalty on 100% of sales, while others base it on 90% of sales.

Some labels agree to increase royalty percentages based on success. For example, an artist might earn a royalty of 8% up to the sale of 250,000 records; 10% on the sale of up to 500,000 records; and 12% for sales after 500,000 records.

Some record companies deduct a sum for packaging, which can range anywhere from 10%

to 25% of the retail or wholesale selling price. This percentage is deducted from the price used by the record company to compute your royalty.

The most important thing you and your lawyer can do when negotiating royalties is to ask for a net cents per unit. Being told that you will get a certain percentage per recording without determining how it translates into actual net cents per unit will not provide the information you need. Since royalties are paid only after advances, production, and recording costs are recouped (sums that should be specified in your contract), you should figure out how many records the company will have to sell to recover those costs before you see your first dime. The company will also want to recoup tour support and radio promotion costs from your royalties.

For example, one label may offer you 10% of a $15.98 retail price, with a 25% packaging deduction, based on 100% of sales. The net cents per unit would be $1.1985.

Another may offer 85% of the same 10% on a $15.98 retail price, with a 20% packaging deduction, based on 90% of sales. In this case, the net cents per unit would be $.98.

Recording labels often provide a certain number of "free goods" to retailers and wholesalers based on the number of units they purchase (effectively a discount on quantity purchases). Generally, royalties are not paid on free goods.

For example, on the purchase of 100 units perhaps 15% are free and 85% are billed. In the examples given above, your net cents per unit would be further discounted by another 15% when measured against the actual number of units shipped.

CD Royalties

The royalty rates payable on compact discs are a controversial negotiating item between artists and recording companies. At the time CDs were first manufactured, labels argued that royalties should be less than those paid for albums or cassettes (generally 15% less), because of increased manufacturing costs. With few exceptions, major labels have not increased these rates, even though manufacturing costs have decreased and retail prices have stabilized at the figures established when CDs were first released.

Performance Sales

Independent labels sometimes encourage the sale of recordings at performances or through mailing lists. In this case, a clause should be added to your contract that states you can buy recordings at a specified price. Typically this is equivalent to the lowest wholesale price available. If you do not pay for this inventory when you get it from the company its value will be treated as an advance against royalties or other fees that will be owing to you.

Foreign Sales

Most contracts address the distribution of recordings in foreign countries. For these sales, the amount of royalty paid to the artist is 50% to 75% of the domestic royalty. The rationale for this deduction is the recording label must license a company in another country to manufacture and distribute the recordings there. If the arrangement for foreign distribution is made with a company that has no relationship with the recording label itself there is justification for the reduction in royalty. If, however, the foreign company and the recording label are related, the justification is weakened though not completely eliminated, since the foreign affiliate has its costs of doing business and generally has to be a free-standing profit center. The arrangement with the recording label should provide for an alternate scale of foreign royalties depending on the relationship, if any, the recording label has with the foreign distributor and what that distributor is paying the recording label.

Recoupment of Expenses and Advances

Typically, a recording label advances the costs of producing, manufacturing, promoting, and distributing the record and charges the production and recording costs against the artist's future royalties. This is called an advance against royalties.

It is extremely important to determine a ceiling for these expenses in your contract; and to make a reasonable projection as to how many retail sales must be generated before the advance is repaid.

Sometimes record companies advance a bonus sum to the artist for signing, as well as money for touring and videos. These sums are also charged against the artist's future royalties.

Financial Statements

Your contract should specify that you will receive financial statements from the recording label within 60 to 90 days of the end of a calendar quarter or semiannual period. These statements should itemize the amounts spent on production that will be recouped from royalties. In addition,

the first and all subsequent statements should show the amount of recordings that have been distributed and whether those recordings were given away as promotional copies or actually sold. The total amount of money earned will show either as a debit or a credit.

Authority to Use Your Name

The recording label will want the authority to use your name, likeness, and biographical material in its promotional activity for the recording. You will have to give the recording label the authority to do that. You should strive to have the label grant you the right to have a say in how it promotes you, so you feel comfortable with the image projected.

Merchandising

Many record companies will try to acquire ownership rights for merchandising. These include the right to use your name, image, and the artwork on your recording for T-shirts, posters, concert booklets, etc. Since this activity can mean additional income for you, particularly when touring, you should try to retain these rights.

Promotion

The promotional commitment of the recording label is critical in any arrangement you make. It will do no good to have a recording contract and an inventory of recordings with no commitment from the company to actively promote the recording. While it may seem strange that a recording label would spend money to produce and manufacture recordings and not promote them, it does occur.

We first heard Alison Krauss on a demo tape from a group called Classified Grass. She didn't sing lead until the fourth song on the tape. Her voice so piqued our interest that we got her home phone number and asked for more material. Today, she is a bluegrass superstar, earning three Grammy awards in 1997: Best Bluegrass Album; Best Country Performance by a Duo or Group with Vocal; and Best Country Instrumental Performance. Many major labels have asked her to sign with them and, so far, she has turned them down.

Our advice for bands seeking to record for Rounder is this:

First, get our catalog and make sure your music fits with the kind of recordings we are issuing.

Second, go to a good-sized record store and look in the bins to see what other labels are putting out music you feel is similar to yours. When you write us, tell us why you think your music will compete with what you have found in the bins.

Third, put together a good press kit that contains a bio, reviews, and letters of support and recommendation from people in the field, such as artists, and radio disk jockeys.

Fourth, include a demo or CD with your strongest songs first.

Fifth, keep us informed about where you will be performing and any changes in your career.

—Ken Irwin, cofounder,
Rounder Records

You should try to get your recording label to commit to at least a minimum promotional level and perhaps work out a promotional plan of attack with it. This may include the label advancing costs for touring. Most recording companies resist making such contractual commitments, arguing they want to wait until after the music is recorded. In this situation, your ability to retain good communication with key people at the label will provide the best chance for your recording to be promoted.

Publishing

Many labels, both small and large, ask that publishing rights be assigned to them. You should remember that publishing in the music business often involves large sums and whoever owns the publishing rights winds up with most of those dollars.

In the last decade, artists and their lawyers have been successful in not assigning publishing rights to recording labels, arguing that a recording label's primary job is to sell recordings. A publisher's job is to sell songs, and since most recording companies do not actively provide that service, artists should be free to assign that right to a publishing company of their choice.

Recording companies will argue that participation in publishing income helps offset their investment risk in producing and marketing recordings.

The Residents

In 1972, THE RESIDENTS RELEASED THEIR FIRST EP, *SANTA DOG*, OUTRAGING Bay Area rock and punk music iconoclasts with a lyric that started "Santa Dog's a Jesus fetus" and was accompanied by music that was equally weird. This started a cult following that grew right along with the creativity and bizarreness of the Residents. By 1980, the band had released six LPs and two more EPs, each continuing to ruin just about everyone's notions about outrageous and bizarre music. The Residents also acquired a very savvy group of managers called The Cryptic Corporation.

To this day, the Residents appear masked, providing a graphic hook that has led to some of the most memorable and inventive cover art, posters, mail-order catalogs and Web site in the music industry. And what a grand mystery! No matter how sincere and diabolical the attempt, no one has come close to unmasking their identities or successfully describing their music.

Since 1980, the Residents have expanded their creativity into performance art shows, which included *The Mole Show, The 13th Anniversary Show* and *CUBE E: The History of American Music in 3 E-Z Pieces*. They also created ideas and music for multimedia videos, laser discs, and CD-ROMs. In 1991, they released an album, *The Freak Show*, which became the basis of their first CD-ROM. *Freak Show* received positive press from *Rolling Stone, Computer Life, The Wall Street Journal* and *Time Magazine*. A live version played for 21 days in Prague in 1995. *Bad Day on the Midway*, released in 1995, won two multimedia awards from The Macromedia International User Conference People's Choice Awards, "Best Entertainment Title" and "Most Innovative Use of Multimedia."

A compilation of the music of the Residents, *Our Tired, Our Poor, Our Huddled Masses*, was released in 1997 by Rykodisc. Their newest work, *WORMWOOD*, released in Fall 1998 by NOsides (distributed in the U.S. by East Side Digital) explores some very curious biblical tales.

The Residents are planning a 1999 world tour.

www.residents.com

THE RESIDENTS
FREAK SHOW
ORIGINAL SOUNDTRACK

THE RESIDENTS
HAVE A BAD DAY

Identities Unknown!
Founders

graphic design and printing

attractive and well-designed covers and promotional materials will help you attract the attention of business and media people and help make your name and your image memorable.

The cover is the single most important graphic for your recording. Its value as a vital sales and promotional tool cannot be overemphasized. The cover often determines if the recording will have a chance to be sold. It has to compete for a buyer's attention along with the best and most well-known artists in your genre of music. Cover graphics can make the difference between a promoter, DJ, or reviewer being curious enough to listen to the recording or placing it in a reject pile.

THE GRAPHIC DESIGNER

The elements of design—copy, typography, paper, photographs, drawings, colors, shapes, lines—must be skillfully related so they visually present the music, image, ideas, and emotions the artist wants to convey. Design themes must provide a clear, consistent, and memorable identity throughout all your promotional materials. The skillful execution of ingenious visual ideas is as demanding an art form as creating memorable music.

Unless you are skilled in design or have limited sales expectations and budget, you will do best to seek the assistance of a professional graphic designer. Most graphic designers have completed four years plus of education to acquire the knowledge required to produce good design. Those whose work has originality, wit, attention to detail, proportion, and distinguishable style are highly sought after and very well paid.

The more experienced and talented your designer is, the more likely you are to wind up with a package that will please you and attract others.

A good designer, like a good producer, knows how to cut corners and save money when necessary. Having the artwork for all your materials designed at the same time as your cover will help ensure that your ideas are translated into designs that reflect your music and personality. Many of your graphic elements, such as logo, photographs, and type style, should be repeated in all your materials to provide design continuity and save time and money during production and printing. A piecemeal approach often leads to promotional pieces looking as though they are entirely unrelated.

The graphic designer may work with photographers, illustrators, typographers, printers, and others to coordinate the complex process of producing finished artwork that is ready for printing.

Graphic designers perform many tasks on computers. These include type selection, design, layout, line art, borders, illustrations, and so on. Computers allow designers to economically prepare design comps (presentations of graphic ideas in sketch form) and final artwork, make changes to copy easily, scan photographs and illustrations and readily manipulate them. They understand printing techniques and will correctly prepare artwork according to printers' specifications.

Choosing a Graphic Designer

Start your search for a designer by looking at the credits on covers you like. Call the recording label and get the designer's phone number. Do not hesitate to approach designers that have worked for major labels; they may be willing to work with you too. Call for referrals from the American Institute of Graphic Arts (AIGA), a highly respected graphic design organization; professors at universities and colleges that offer graphic design courses; and local graphics cooperatives and companies that are listed in the yellow pages under "Advertising Agencies," "Art–Commercial," and "Graphic Designers." Your graphic designer may be able to suggest a Web site designer; if not, e-mail bands whose Web site designs you like and ask for suggestions.

Do not assume that because a designer is famous, he or she will be too expensive or inaccessible. And do not be misled into thinking that just because a designer is famous, he or she is right for you. You will want to see samples of their work and judge for yourself.

Once you have names and phone numbers of several graphic designers, call and make appointments with them. Spend at least an hour with each to review their portfolios and discuss the steps and costs of your project. Discuss what materials are needed and for what purposes (covers, letterhead, logo, photographs, posters, etc.).

Tell them your design budget. This helps determine whether one-, two-, three-, or full-color will be used and how lavish your materials will be.

Your initial discussions should end with requests for preliminary proposals that outline the cost for the services you need. If you have already chosen your recording manufacturer, provide the designer with their estimates for printing your covers. Ask the designer to prepare separate printing estimates for the other promotional materials you have described. It should

take a week to ten days to prepare these estimates. Do not expect a figure on the spot. The
interviews should help narrow your choices and
provide insight about the working relationship
you will have.

Proposals will be based on the complexity of
design, number of materials to be designed and
the designer's experience and reputation. They will
provide the basis for further discussion and final
decision about who you choose as your designer,
and what you can realistically afford to accomplish. Proposals and estimates are usually free.

Designs produced for your cover and other
promotional materials are original creations that
will be copyrighted in the name of your graphic
designer. If the designs are produced on a computer, the designer will not provide copies of the
files to prevent you from changing them.

Manufacturer Design Services

Many cassette and CD manufacturers now offer
professional design services and can produce
recording covers at very economical rates. Some
even include these services as part of the total
manufacturing costs.

Their graphic designers can turn out excellent work, if you are clear about your goals. You
will be responsible for educating them about
your project, providing copy, photographs and
illustrations, and proofreading and approving
final artwork. Send them your other promotional materials to help ensure that your cover
will be visually compatible. Hiring your own
photographer and using a manufacturer's
design services can be an effective method for
saving money.

If you supply photographs and illustrations,
copy them and provide the instructions about
size and cropping on the photocopies. Package
original photographs and illustrations carefully
so they do not get damaged during shipment,
and insure them against loss.

If the photographs need to be altered in any
way, the manufacturer will charge an hourly fee
for doing it. Be sure to get an estimate on this
work beforehand.

If you do not have photographs or illustrations, you have to educate the designers about
your music and your target audience so they
can choose appropriate stock photographs or
illustrations.

The manufacturer will present you with
design concepts to approve before proceeding to
final production. If you do not like what you see,
they will prepare another set of concepts. Once
you have approved a concept, changes in design
and words will cost extra.

Being Your Own Designer

Many independents take a do-it-yourself
approach and try to design promotional materials themselves, using desktop publishing,
scanners, and illustration software. They ask a
friend who likes to draw or an amateur photographer to provide visual images. While this
approach may save money in the short term, it
rarely provides satisfactory and professional
results. There is a steep learning curve to understanding how to use the hardware and software
and produce final artwork that meets printers'
specifications. Improperly prepared artwork
leads to expensive changes and delays.

The art of graphic design is immediately apparent in the way four design elements of a business card are handled—logo, business name, person name, address/phone. The logo's design, arrangements of words, size and selection of typeface, leading (spacing between lines), color, and paper determine whether or not a card is attractive and suits the style and image of the business.

If you choose to do it yourself, you can increase your chances for producing a good design by making your type legible and spending money on either a professional photographer or illustrator. The former is preferable because he or she will provide multiple shots that can be used for a variety of promotional needs.

Most manufacturers can furnish design templates showing the exact dimensions required for your CD and cassette packaging and inserts.

THE DESIGN PROCESS: PRINTED MATERIALS

The design process is typically broken up into (1) design input; (2) copy; (3) design concepts (rough drawings and sketches); (4) purchase and direct outside services, e.g. photography and illustration; (5) final artwork production and (6) prepress.

It can take up to two months from rough design to final art that is ready for printing. About four to six weeks of that time will be spent on design and production. Designers often juggle many jobs at once, so budgeting adequate time is a must. Another two weeks or more will be spent preparing the final artwork. It can take another four to six weeks after the artwork is delivered to the printer before it is printed.

Scheduling enough time with your graphic designer in the preparatory stages is important. Arrange to be available when you are needed for approvals and proofing.

Working with Designers

A good working relationship with your designer is essential for the production of successful promotional materials. You enter a partnership, much like that between musician and arranger and each of you has specific areas of responsibility.

Your chief responsibilities—

- ◆ Agree on a budget for design and printing
- ◆ Decide what materials are needed and in what quantities
- ◆ Provide deadlines
- ◆ Provide information that helps your designer create a design concept
- ◆ Supply the words (copy) for the front, back, spine, and insides of your cover; and bios and other written materials
- ◆ Approve drawings, photographs, and preliminary sketches
- ◆ Carefully proofread all artwork and copy
- ◆ Approve all final artwork proofs

Design Input

The graphic designer has to know about your music and those that composed and recorded it; your potential audience and how you expect to reach them; and the image you want to project. Tell them your feelings about design. Do you prefer illustration or photography (or neither) as the main graphic? Which colors do you like? You can communicate your feelings about design by bringing examples of covers or posters that appeal to you (or do not). Try to describe your taste with visual aids as well as verbally.

If there are graphics you already use, like a logo, performance photographs, banners, or posters, bring them along. Sometimes they can suggest a design concept. Your designer will tell you if they are of adequate quality for the goals you have outlined. If you like a particular pho-

tographer or illustrator, let your designer know from the start.

The more explicit you can be in this early stage, the more smoothly the production of your materials will progress. Do not rush these discussions; it may take a few hours of communication for the designer to feel he or she has enough information to provide preliminary sketches and concepts. The failure of a designer to please a client can often be attributed to the failure of that client to communicate what is important.

Designers will want assurance you understand their job well enough to communicate your needs and then allow them the freedom to work creatively. You must be able to relinquish control and trust the job will be done well.

Logo design is a specialty skill. A logo's role is to create instant identification for your band or business and it will be repeated in all your promotional materials. Memorable logos are not quickly and inexpensively designed. Their cost can equal or exceed the cost of your cover. Although using clip art for logos is cheap, their use will brand you as an amateur.

Universal Product Code

Final artwork for CDs, records, and cassettes that are going to be sold in stores must contain a bar code termed a Universal Product Code (UPC). Distributors require that your product carry a UPC.

The UPC, which is controlled by the Uniform Code Council (UCC), Inc., is used extensively on all types of products. UPCs allow the use of automated checkstands. The checker passes each item over an optical scanner that reads the UPC symbol, decodes the UPC number and transmits the number to a computer that stores price and other information on all products carried in the store. The item's price and description is transmitted from the computer back to the checkstand to be printed on the customer's receipt. Simultaneously, the computer records information that aids inventory control.

In the record industry, UPC codes are also downloaded to a service called Soundscan, a company that tracks over-the-counter sales of recorded music and makes information available to paid subscribers. Soundscan can give you and your distributor a report on how many CDs you sold and in which cities they were purchased.

The UPC is a 12-digit number accompanied by a corresponding bar code symbol. This number, when properly assigned, uniquely identifies a product. The first six digits (company prefix) identify your company. The UCC selects the first five digits of the company prefix and requires that you select the sixth digit when you apply for your UPC. The selection number, which identifies a specific recording, is assigned by you and consists of the last digit of the company prefix plus any four additional digits. Next is the configuration digit, a one-digit number that identifies the medium of the item (CD, vinyl records, cassette, VHS tape, etc.). When you receive your company prefix from the UCC they will furnish you with a list of current configuration digits. The last digit in the UPC number is a "check" digit and is provided by the company that produces your bar code label. The Uniform Code Council can furnish a list of firms that

produce film masters for bar codes, or your recording's manufacturer may be able to produce your bar codes. Some manufacturers offer free bar code graphics as a value-added service. You supply the first 11 digits of the number; they generate the bar code and place it on your recordings.

Specifications for size, location, and printing standards for the UPC symbol are contained in the manual *UPC Symbol Location Guidelines* and the *Symbol Specification Manual* provided by the UCC when you receive your UPC company prefix.

You can also request that your UPC be printed on adhesive and be placed on the top edge of your CD's jewel box.

In 1998, the price for obtaining a UPC code for a company was $350. Once your company is registered you do not have to reregister every time you put out a new recording. You only have to change the four digits that identify the specific recording, the 11th digit for each recording format, and the 12th digit, which depends on who produces the bar code label.

It usually takes 10 to 15 business days for your application to be processed. Your graphic designer or manufacturer will place the UPC on the final artwork for your CDs, vinyl records, and cassettes. (If your manufacturer places the UPC code, you should instruct your graphic designer to leave room for it so it does not cover essential information.)

For information on how to obtain a UPC company prefix, call the Uniform Code Council, Inc. at (937) 435-3870 or write to them at 7887 Washington Village Drive, Suite 300, Dayton, Ohio 45459.

Graphic continuity was established on Katie Lee's CD and cassette projects by hiring the same illustrator as was used for her book, *All My Rivers Are Gone*.

Copy

Writing the words (copy) for your promotional pieces first will make design concepts easier to achieve and help you synthesize your ideas. It will help your designer make sketches of how to size the words in relation to other graphic elements such as photographs and illustrations.

Write down all the words that you want to appear on each promotional piece you will be producing. The only way to insure that each piece contains what you want is to prepare the copy for each separately. Later, you can use your originals to check final artwork. Although many elements will be common to each piece, placement and typographical treatments will differ.

Use a word processor to prepare the copy. This makes it very easy to make changes—and there are always last-minute changes. Double-

space the copy and leave wide margins. The neater the copy, the easier it will be to design the typography.

Have your copy edited and proofread. This is best done by someone skilled in doing so. Check carefully for errors in spelling, numbers, addresses, punctuation, grammar, and consistency of style. There are always errors and they are not always obvious. Double-check everything with a suspicious eye and a clear head.

When you are finished, provide your designer with a printout of the copy along with a computer disk containing it.

Copy for Recording Covers

CD booklets and cassette J-cards can be manufactured with from two to 24 panels of information, but the most economical formats

It's a hell of a long journey but music's been traveling for years.... So take this journey—a musical trip that begins with the blues in New Orleans, stops in Lake Charles for some cajun gumbo, runs through San Antonio, Austin and Fort Worth for some Texas cooking and some Mexican peppers, then winding its way...towards a chance gig at the Edmonton Folk Festival that turned into something that's still a little ad hoc...but dozens of dates together since have Krazy-glued this band as tightly as any musicians can get....

—From the cover copy, *Return of the Formerly Brothers,* Stony Plain Records Edmonton, Alberta, Canada

for CD covers are two to four panels and for J-cards, four or six panels.

You need to balance economic considerations with your sales and promotional goals. You must decide what information is important and what is not. A common mistake is cramming too much copy into too few panels and compromising by making the type so small that is it virtually unreadable, which defeats the purpose of including it.

Unless you have some very good reason for doing otherwise, the name of the artist(s) should take first billing on the cover, not the title of the recording. It is your name that will be important for people to remember in the long run, especially as you release more recordings.

Because many people will only have your recording, it is especially important to include biographical, mail-order, and booking information. This may mean that you cut the long list of friends you want to thank. You can thank them with copies of your recording.

If you can afford extra panels, include lyrics. Fans love them. And they will be helpful if you are going to make a strong attempt to sell your songs to other performers or publishers.

One error that occurs often is incorrect matching of the songs on the label with songs on the recording. Double-check!

A checklist of recommended copy items for each recording format is included on pages 91–95.

Design Concepts

This is the idea stage of the design process. Your designer will use your copy to prepare concept sketches (roughs) based on your preliminary discussions, which show the placement of photographs and illustrations, and you will be shown the portfolios of the illustrator or photographer the designer wants to use.

These sketches usually contain some typographical choices—lettering style (fonts), size, case (upper and lower), format (bold, italic, plain), and their positioning—and color usage.

You will be asked for additional input, and you need to indicate what you like and do not like. You may like the concepts well enough to choose one and go right into the next stage—tight design comps—or you can ask for further roughs.

The designer will next provide tight design comps based on your input. These will show how your project will look when completed, and you will be given accurate quotes on the costs for illustrations, photography, and the production necessary to provide final artwork ready for printing.

After you have discussed and approved the comps and the budget, your designer will order photographs and illustrations.

Some designers quote separately for roughs and tight design comps. If you do not like the roughs, no more money is owed. Others will provide proposals that include roughs, design comps, and production, but quote separately for photography and illustration.

Purchase of Outside Services

Your designer will hire a photographer and arrange and direct a session, after which you will help select photographs. The photographer will be asked to shoot black and white as well as color.

Color transparencies and slides are the preferred format because they provide the most direct transfer to color separations. Transparencies cannot be duplicated without loss of color, so photographers often take three or four shots of the same pose, at the same settings, to have duplicates in case one gets lost or mishandled. Color negatives must be transferred to color transparencies, with some color loss. Contrast and detail will be diminished when

color is converted to black and white. In the latter two examples, corrections can be made on a computer by a person skilled in that technology. If this is to be done, request an estimate.

If your budget is tight, the designer can use stock photographs for your recording covers. These are available from many vendors and are cheaper than hiring a photographer. Some stock houses offer 100 high-resolution photographic images, arranged by themes, on a computer disk for as little as $250. There are no further royalty or licensing fees for the use of these photographs. Fees for stock photographs from individual photographers are based on use and start as low as $100. (More information on photography is included in the chapter, Promotion.)

If original drawings or paintings are needed, your designer will ask an illustrator to prepare preliminary sketches for you to review before ordering completed artwork.

Production

Assembling all the graphic elements for each promotional piece and preparing final artwork for the printer is the next stage. This is usually the longest part of the process because it is so exacting and detail oriented.

Separate artwork is prepared for each piece, according to the printer's specifications. These specs are critical because an error can result in the need for a re-print. Your designer must also make sure the label artwork contains a matrix number that matches the one assigned to your master tape, so your labels go on the right record and on the right side. (A convenient marking system is to end the matrix number for side one with "-1" or "A" and side two with "-2" or "B." This helps avoid error and the mismatching of labels and sides.)

Photographs and illustrations will be scanned, cropped, color corrected, and properly sized. Final colors will be selected for typography and other graphic elements such as borders. Paper will be selected.

You will be asked to proof the final artwork and give your final approval. Check carefully for omissions by comparing the final copy with your originals.

Often, bands make the most copy and design changes after they see the final artwork, adding expense and time to the project. Up to this time they have not seen the final assembly of all the graphic elements in correctly sized formats and recognize only then some important element they have forgotten or want to change. Copy changes are relatively inexpensive to make; changes to design, illustrations, and photography are not. Keep this in mind throughout the process as you give approvals to various segments of your design work.

Paper

The choice of paper (stock) is another critical design and budget consideration. There are thousands of different textures, weights, and brands of paper ranging from industrial packaging to coarse newsprint to the glossy stock used for high-end commercial printing.

Most graphic designers know how artwork will look when it is printed on different paper. They can help you choose the appropriate stock for your project.

Design and Production Fees

Fees for design roughs are based on the amount of time spent, plus materials. Fees for providing roughs for covers and promotional materials start as low as $500, but the average is $1000 to $1500.

Material costs may include scans (between $5 and $15 per scan, depending on size), color laser copies, special art materials, etc.

Although graphic designers will include an estimate for production work, they generally charge by the actual number of hours spent. Hourly rates vary from $15 to more than $100 per hour.

Fees for logos can be as low as $300, but $1000 to $2000 is average for experienced designers working with new bands. Graphic designers that are especially good at logos have commanded fees in five-digit figures.

Photographers' fees range from $200 for a half-day shooting session and go as high as $2000 per day. Separate fees are charged for use licenses. (A more complete description of licensing fees is found in the chapter, Promotion.)

Commissioned illustrations range from $25 to $1500 and up per drawing. Illustrators charge separate use license fees, copyright their work, and want to be credited on your recording's cover, as do photographers.

Color

Generally, the more colors you use, the higher the cost for printing and the more difficult it is to control quality throughout the design and printing process.

Printers use two methods to reproduce color: spot color (match and custom color) commonly

---

RECYCLED PAPER ⬅----

Recycled paper is made from the scrap produced by paper mills and from unsold books and magazines (preconsumer); from discarded (postconsumer) paper; or a combination of pre- and postconsumer papers.

The cost of recycled paper depends on the type of paper from which it is produced and the chemical processes used to remove dyes, inks, and coatings. Recycled paper can be de-inked without using chlorine, acids, or bleaches, but the final result has some ink specks and is not bright white.

Although costs continue to drop, recycled paper is usually more expensive than comparable nonrecycled paper.

---

referred to as the Pantone Matching System (PMS) for one- or multicolor printing and the four-color process. The system provides a full range of hues and assigns each a reference number. The Pantone Matching System is incorporated into most publishing and illustration software to provide a standardized method for choosing colors and specifying them to printers.

For spot color, different inks are blended to produce a single color.

Printing with a black ink is the cheapest method of printing. A substitution of other colors rarely costs more than $40 (unless it is a very long print run). Metallic inks are specialty items and may cost more.

Multicolor printing is achieved by using two or more ink colors. Each color is printed in sequence.

Duotones, made from black and white photographs, are printed in tints of two colors of ink to add extra luster and depth. Often, black is one of the colors.

We print our newsletter on 100% postconsumer recycled paper that has been de-inked without using harmful chlorines, acids, or other bleaches. Many of our environmentally conscious clients ask that we use the same paper for their CD and cassette covers, even though it adds expense.

—Jim Bosken, QCA Inc., Cincinnati, Ohio

The four-color process method blends dot patterns of the four process colors—magenta (red), yellow, blue (cyan) and black—to reproduce your color artwork and photography. This is achieved by separating the photograph or artwork into four negatives. Additional runs can be made to add spot colors such as a metallic color for the name of your recording.

Prepress

Prepress is the conversion of final artwork (copy, photographs, and illustrations) from electronic files into film negatives. It is usually done by a printer or prepress service bureau (imaging service, color house) that owns the complex equipment needed. Few graphic design houses or advertising agencies have this equipment.

One negative is made for each color you specify for multicolor printing.

For four-color process printing, color illustrations, prints, slides, transparencies and artwork are converted into four halftones (separations), one each of the four process colors, blue (cyan), red (magenta), yellow, and black or "key" (CMYK).

Color separations can be produced photographically and with digital scanners and image setters.

Your graphic designer may want color separations done by a reputable service bureau whose work he or she knows and trusts. Their cost will be comparable to those at most printers, unless you have been quoted a special economy package price that includes them. When you request printing prices, ask that color separations be quoted separately.

The cost of color separations varies, depending on the size of the artwork, the reputation of the lab, and the nature of the artwork.

Proofs

The next step is to order and check proofs. You and your graphic designer must be satisfied that the proofs are correct before giving your printer the go-ahead. You are responsible for errors, no matter how much at fault the service bureau or printer may be.

Proofs can take a number of forms.

For a one-color or simple two- or three-color job, a blueline or brownline composite photographic print is made. It is furnished on paper of the same dimensions as the press sheets for your job. The blueline is used to check page sequence (as for a CD or cassette booklet), trims, folds, and the density of borders and other line art. An experienced eye can determine if the halftones will reproduce the original photographs or screen tints with fidelity. Bluelines are usually included with every job at no extra charge, but you should confirm this. A whiteprint (Velox) is a contact print of the negative. The contact print will show how the photographs and screen tints will print. Velox prints cost from $10 to $15.

A color proof (Integral color proof, Agfaproof, Cromalin, Matchprint, etc.) is a composite print that is made from the four-color separations. It is used to check the quality of the color separations, registration of the process colors, and to match color during printing. Usually color proofs are included with the cost of color separations, but you should confirm by asking. If the colors do not match your specifications, the work should be redone for no charge.

Storing Artwork

Store all the photographs, illustrations, proofs, color separations, and electronic files on which your artwork was created together in a safe place. Although your graphic designer can do this for you, the best thing is to take on that responsibility yourself. Most graphic designers, however, specify that electronic files belong to them. If this is the case, make sure they have at least two electronic backups of your artwork and one copy is stored off-site.

PRINTING

Your project might require you to work with more than one printer: an offset lithographer for your stationery package and press releases; another lithographer for press kit covers, posters, postcards, and fliers; silkscreen printer for T-shirts; and a specialty printer for recording covers.

Lithographers

Fine-quality color printing is most economically done by offset printers (lithographers). As quantity increases, price per piece decreases, with breaks commonly beginning after 500 pieces.

Printers use special screens to break up the images on the negatives into a grid of crossing lines, which gives the printed piece a dot pattern that is visible only with a magnifying glass. The screens are available in sizes of from 50 to 300 lines per inch, but 85 to 175 are most commonly used. Generally, the finer (higher number) the

line screen, the sharper the printing. Coarser line screens are generally used for silkscreen printing.

For economy and efficiency, four-color recording covers, postcards and one-page sales sheets are often gang run on large sheets of paper that can accommodate many projects from different recording labels. Since color separations vary slightly from one to the next, the inks on the press are adjusted to match the colors on your color proof as best as possible. However, the colors for gang-run projects will be close but not necessarily identical to those indicated on the color proof and you can expect a 5% to 10% variation. If the colors are not acceptable, you can use your match print to negotiate a re-run at the manufacturer's expense. If you want a very close match, request a special print run. The cost may be 50% to 100% higher, depending on quantity.

Silkscreen Printing

In silkscreen printing, commonly used for one- two- and three-color CD and cassette labels (imprinting), T-shirts, banners, and other merchandise, ink is forced through a stenciled wire screen or polyester mesh. Small quantities can be done by hand; large quantities are run on commercial screen presses.

Print Estimates

Detailed bids for all your recording formats and promotional materials should be sought from several prepress service bureaus and printers, as well as the CD manufacturer. Request them to send samples of comparable materials.

Since quality, price, and service vary, it is best to get recommendations from your graphic

These soft CD packages were manufactured through Oasis CD and Cassette Duplication as "eco-friendly" alternatives to the plastic jewel box. They are less vulnerable to breakage and cheaper to mail. James Durst's CD, *My Country is the World,* consists of three panels made from recycled paper printed with vegetable-based inks. Each of the two end panels is a sleeve—one holds the CD, the other an informative booklet. Trapezoid's "jewel-free" box is sturdier: it has a thick spine and a protective plastic tray with a locking mechanism to hold the CD firmly in place.

designer or other people you trust. Touring a large offset print shop that uses sheetfed and web presses will help familiarize you with the machinery and processes and provide the opportunity to ask questions.

Printers are listed in the yellow pages of your phone directory.

Estimates allow you and your graphic designer to make comparisons, question prices that appear out of kilter, get a feeling for service and attention to detail, and provide you with some leverage for negotiating. If you are provided with a low price from one printer,

you can ask others whether they are willing to match that price.

Once primary decisions about printing have been made, the designer will prepare a request for final bids from several firms, negotiate final price, and get a print contract.

Any special requirements, even ones that seem minor to you, can result in higher costs, as will any changes required once the processes have been initiated.

Estimates for CD, Vinyl, and Cassette Covers
Prices for printing covers from recording

manufacturers are generally lower than those of other lithographers because their presses are set up to accommodate the exacting requirements for packaging and they order paper in huge quantities.

You may be very surprised at the price variations. For example, in late 1998, estimates for printing 1000 six-panel J-cards with four colors on one side and black on the other (4/1), ranged from $182 to $250 and 2500 cost from $212 to $400. Estimates for 1000 four-panel, 4/1 CD booklets and tray cards ranged from $219 to $450; and 2500 cost from $317 to $650. Prices fell dramatically for higher quantities.

Most CD and cassette manufacturers will discourage you from having another printer do your recording covers because of their experiences in receiving the wrong sizes.

Some firms print covers as part of a package that includes vinyl, CD, or cassette manufacturing. Some will, however, quote separate prices for printing and manufacturing.

When requesting estimates, specify whether or not you will be supplying film negatives and color separations or require prepress services in addition to printing. Include all the options you are considering, such as six- and eight-panel CD booklets; six- and 12-panel J-cards, mail-order catalog inserts, alternative cardboard packaging, recycled paper, stickers, top spine stickering, special coatings, full-color imprinting on CDs, metallic inks, etc.

Detailed estimates allow you to decide if you can order more printed covers than your initial run of recordings to take advantage of reduced prices for larger print runs. This is wise if you anticipate reordering your recording.

Stationery Packages and Other Promotional Materials

For quantities under 500, the most economical price for letterhead, business cards and mailing labels is obtained by printing black on white or colored bond paper and using a photocopier and laser printing service or your own laser printer. You will need to buy mailing label stock. Business cards can be printed on a card stock, ten to an 8 1/2 by 11-inch page for as low as forty cents a page; and stationery costs about four cents a page. Some laser printers can print envelopes.

Use a lithographer if you need quantities greater than 500 copies.

Return of Artwork

Request that all artwork, film, computer disks, and other materials be shipped back to you insured after your pieces are printed. Confirm this as part of your printing agreement.

THE DESIGN PROCESS: WEB SITES

Another demanding challenge is organizing, creating, and designing Web sites that are congruent with the design of your other promotional materials. It is not as simple as just translating pages from your promotional pieces into the appropriate programming language and adding audio samples. Web pages tend to have a higher density of text-based information and fewer graphics than print media. A designer who promises to faithfully duplicate your CD liner or promotional posters may not understand the unique challenges of Web site design—particularly those requirements that ensure fast downloading and easily accessible information. Different sized computer screens, modem speeds, and Internet software add technical considerations that make it difficult for nonprofessionals to design Web sites people like to visit. Some common complaints are—poorly organized information; slow loading graphics; poor audio quality; too much information; too much hype; Web pages that do not work; and getting lost on a site.

For the best translation of your promotional information, audio/video samples, and graphic materials into a pleasing Web site, hire a web designer who will put your materials into the correct programming languages and test the site to make sure that every page and link works.

Here is what you can do to help make the job go efficiently and save yourself some money.

First, figure out what materials you want to make available on your site. You can include contents from your press kit, photographs, posters, reviews, lead sheets, and lyrics. Decide what audio and video samples you want to include.

Second, provide a written outline of what you want viewers to read, see, and hear on each Web page (which can be many screens in length). Use the terms second-tier, third-tier, fourth-tier Web page, etc., to designate how many mouse clicks away a viewer is from the home page.

The home page generally contains basic information and a table of contents to other pages. Give thought to how you want people to navigate to and from the home page and other Web pages on your site. What icons or words will be included on every page so that people can return to the home page or other key pages (commonly called a navigation bar), such as tour dates, recordings, biography, news, and e-mail contact? You may want to include an outline as a separate Web page, which is accessed from the main navigation bar and is titled "Table of Contents" or "Site Map" to provide an easy way for visitors to access specific information.

Other pages are sequenced so that the most important information is included on the second-tier pages. Many Web designers advise keeping their length to less than three screens. People want to get information fast; three screen pages are the maximum most people will pay attention to before they want to view another page.

Third- and fourth-tier Web pages are used to provide more detailed information that requires pages longer than two or three screens, slow loading graphics, and audio and video samples.

Try to confine each Web page to one subject, such as a biography, a list of tour dates, current news, recordings, etc. Secondary navigation bars or icons can be included on other Web pages to help people travel to pages that have related material. For example, a second-tier page, "Recordings," may contain summaries of all the recordings you have released. A secondary navigation bar can direct people to pages that contain audio samples and detailed information on each recording.

Third, figure out which of your materials can be supplied electronically, others will have to be scanned.

Fourth, supply a list of the addresses of other Web sites you would like your viewers to be aware of. A short description of what viewers will find on these sites is helpful.

Fifth, supply key words and phrases that will be encoded into Internet browsers so your site will come up when people search on those words when using search engines. Be sure to include the last name of the artist; band's name; musical genre (be very specific); album name; and any unusual musical instruments.

Finally, visit existing Web sites and see how they are organized. Notice which graphics are appealing so you can provide some direction to the Web designer about your likes and dislikes.

Here are some technical parameters your Web designer is likely to use:

- ◆ Web pages will be sized for 15-inch computer screens, the average size, (600 x 400 pixels). This is to make sure that most users will not have to move the design vertically or horizontally on their computer screens to view the page.
- ◆ Background colors for Web pages containing predominantly copy will be neutral—white, tan, or other light pastels—so if people want to print pages, they will be readable.
- ◆ Words and graphics on first- and second-tier Web pages will be confined to 70 kilobytes (K) so pages load quickly even if users do not have high-speed modems. The designer can provide the viewer with a choice to enlarge especially dramatic graphic images to fill the screen.
- ◆ The electronic files for printed materials, such as brochures, mail-order forms,

newsletters, and posters can be converted to Portable Document Format (PDF) using Adobe Acrobat software when you want the viewer to see or download an exact version of the document. The program has a command which enables you to place security on those files so no one can change them. PDF files can be viewed by using Adobe Acrobat Reader, a plug-in program now supplied by most World Wide Web browsers including Netscape Navigator and Internet Explorer.

Finding a Web Designer

Graphic design firms often have in-house web designers. If yours does not, ask your graphic designer for a reference.

Experience in desktop publishing or graphic design does not automatically prepare a person for Web page design. Make sure the person you use is familiar with this medium.

Seek references from artists and business firms that have Web sites you like; ask at computer stores and at computer and design departments in universities.

If your Web pages will be located on someone else's site, they should be able to provide you with the name of their webmaster.

Fees are generally based on the number of pages and audio samples required; and on the organization and design work needed. Ask what the charges will be to add pages to your site and to update information. Ask the webmaster to teach you how to make common changes, such as tour dates, by yourself.

I can't stress enough the importance of a band finding four or five Web sites they like and would like a Web designer to use as models. The band and the designer should look at these sites together and the band should explain what they like best. That way the designer knows right away what the band finds appealing. If a band cannot hire a Web designer, there are numerous Web sites that will put up a page for free. Sites like Xoom, GeoCities, Hypermart, Angelfire, will give you from five to 11 megabytes of space. Some include easy page builders. These sites are good for musicians that want to do a page on the cheap or experiment with ideas before getting a designer involved.

—Dan McAvinchey, Guitar Nine Records

Being Your Own Web Designer

You can design Web sites yourself. Many programs are available to help you create your own site and offer full control of layout, graphics, audio, video, and animation. Good programs for Web design and maintenance include Microsoft FrontPage (www.microsoft.com/frontpage), Macromedia Dreamweaver (www.macromedia.com), and GoLive CyberStudio (www.golive.com). Check Killer Sites (www.killersites.com) for examples of good work and Web Sites That Suck (www.websitesthatsuck.com) for things to avoid.

CHECKLIST OF RECOMMENDED COPY FOR RECORDING COVERS, BOOKLETS, INSERTS, AND LABELS ◀---

This checklist can be used to prepare copy for each recording format you manufacture. These suggestions are recommendations. It is up to you to decide what information is needed and where it should be placed.

CD packaging

BOOKLET/INSERT
Front Cover
- Recording's title
- Your name (or your band's) if different from title
- The words "Bonus Enhanced CD" (if applicable) can be placed on the cover or on a sticker, which is applied to the shrink-wrap.

Interior Pages
- Song titles (in sequence) and length of playing time
- Name(s) of composer(s)
- Name of publishing company(ies)
- Copyright credit[1]
- Performing rights organization (ASCAP, BMI, or SESAC)[2]
- Lyrics
- Names of musicians and instruments played
- Sampling credit (if applicable)
- Total length of playing time
- Producer
- Graphic designer
- Photographer
- Illustrator
- Engineer
- Arranger
- Courtesy credits for appearances of musicians from other recording labels. Example: "Jon Smith appears courtesy of ABZ Records"
- Recording studio
- Mastering studio
- Manufacturer
- Record label's address/phone and fax numbers/Web site URL and e-mail address
- Mail-order information

- Booking information
- Publisher's address
- Biographical material
- Quotes from reviewers
- Information about enhanced CDs should include (1) complete technical information about what types of computers, operating systems, software, and CD drives are required; (2) a short description about the content; and (3) a disclaimer, written by a lawyer, in case anything unforeseen should happen to the computer while playing the CD (e.g., a hard-drive crash). These problems are rare, but they do happen occasionally, particularly when the consumer does not follow instructions or does not use the computer/software indicated on the CD.

TRAY CARD (Backliner)
Back
(Note: The back of the tray card is visible through the back of the jewel box. Include only the information that is important for your marketing needs. Other information can be included in the CD booklet.)
- Recording's title
- Your name (or your band's) if different from title
- Record label's name
- Record label's logo
- Recording's five-digit catalog number (also called selection number)[4]
- UPC and bar code symbol
- Words above the UPC that indicate how recording is to be filed in record store bins. Example: "File Under Latin/Latin Jazz"
- Song titles (in sequence) and length of playing time

CONTINUED ON FOLLOWING PAGE

CD packaging

- Total length of playing time
- Copyright notice for the compositions[1]
- Copyright notice for the recording Ⓟ
- Record label's address/phone and fax numbers/Web site URL and e-mail address
- Any information that will add to the salability of the recording, such as a quote from a reviewer, well-known musician, or producer
- Country of origin of manufacture and printing. Example: "CD manufactured in USA" or "CD booklet printed in Canada."[3]
- The words "All rights reserved. Unauthorized duplication is a violation of applicable laws."
- Enhanced CD information (if applicable). Include abbreviated information about what hardware and software is needed. More specific information should be included in the CD booklet.

TRAY CARD
Spine

(This information is printed on the left and right edge of the back of the tray card, which folds up and is visible through the sides of the jewel box.)

- Recording's title
- Your name (or your band's) if different from title
- Record label's name
- Record label's logo
- Recording's five-digit catalog number (also called selection number)[4]

Front

(Note: This is located underneath the plastic tray that holds the CD in the jewel box. If you choose jewel boxes that have clear or translucent trays, you can print the tray card with a graphic. Sometimes a quarter-inch vertical strip is visible through the left front side of the jewel box. This space can be used to repeat the recording's title or band name; or show part of the printed graphics.)

OPTIONAL STICKERS
Top Edge Sticker (Under the Shrink-Wrap)

- UPC and bar code symbol
- Recording's title
- Your name (or your band's) if different from title
- Record label's name
- Record label's logo

Front Cover Sticker (Outside the Shrink-Wrap)

- Suggested song for airplay or quote from review or name of famous musician who played on the recording.
- The words "Bonus: Enhanced CD" (if applicable)

PRINTING ON CD

- Recording's title
- Your name (or your band's) if different from title
- Record label's name
- Record label's logo
- Recording's five-digit catalog number[4]
- Universal Compact Disc Logo. (A mandatory requirement.) CD manufacturers will supply artwork in various sizes to your graphic designer.
- Copyright notice for the Recording Ⓟ
- Song titles (in sequence) and length of playing time
- Country of origin of manufacture Example: "Manufactured in USA"[3]
- The words "All rights reserved. Unauthorized duplication is a violation of applicable laws."

cassette packaging

J-CARD
Front (Cover)
- Recording's title
- Your name (or your band's) if different from title

Spine
- Recording's title
- Your name (or your band's) if different from title
- Record label's name
- Record label's logo
- Recording's five-digit catalog number (also called selection number)[4]

Back
(Note: Include only the information that is important for your marketing needs. Other information can be included in the J-card interior.)
- Recording's title
- Your name (or your band's) if different from title
- Record label's name
- Record label's logo
- Recording's five-digit catalog number[4]
- UPC and bar code symbol
- Words above the UPC indicating how recording is to be filed in record store bins. Example: "File Under Latin/Latin Jazz"
- Song titles and length of playing time (numbered sequentially for each side)
- Total length of playing time per side
- Copyright notice for the compositions[1]
- Copyright notice for the recording ℗
- Record label's address/phone and fax numbers/Web site URL and e-mail address
- Noise reduction used and logo (if applicable)
- Type of tape and EQ settings if different from those normally associated with that type of tape.
- Any information that will add to the salability of the record, such as a quote from a reviewer, well-known musician, or producer
- Country of origin of manufacture and printing. Example: "Cassette manufactured in USA" or "J-card booklet printed in Canada."[3]

Interior Panels
- Song titles (in sequence) and length of playing time
- Name(s) of composer(s)
- Name of publishing company(ies)
- Copyright credit[1]
- Performing rights organization (ASCAP, BMI, or SESAC)[2]
- Lyrics
- Names of musicians and instruments played
- Sampling credit (if applicable)
- Total length of playing time
- Producer
- Graphic designer
- Photographer
- Illustrator
- Engineer
- Arranger
- Courtesy credits for appearances of musicians from other recording labels. Example: "Jon Smith appears courtesy of ABZ Records"
- Recording studio
- Mastering studio
- Manufacturer
- Record label's address/phone and fax numbers/Web site URL and e-mail address
- Mail-order information
- Booking information
- Publisher's address
- Biographical material
- Quotes from reviewers

OPTIONAL FRONT STICKER
(Outside the Shrink-Wrap)
- Suggested song for airplay or quote from review or name of famous musician who played on the recording

CONTINUED ON FOLLOWING PAGE

cassette packaging

CASSETTE CASING PRINTING
(Direct On-Cassette Imprinting)
- Side one/side two designation
- Recording's title
- Your name (or your band's) if different from title
- Record label's name
- Record label's logo
- Recording's five-digit catalog number[4]
- Copyright notice for the recording ℗

- Song titles (in sequence) and length of playing time
- Country of origin of manufacture. Example: "Manufactured in USA"[3]
- The words "All rights reserved. Unauthorized duplication is a violation of applicable laws."
- Noise reduction used and logo (if applicable)
- Type of tape and EQ settings if different from those normally associated with that type of tape.

vinyl packaging

JACKET
Front Cover
- Recording's title
- Your name (or your band's) if different from title

Spine
- Recording's title
- Your name (or your band's) if different from title
- Record label's name
- Record label's logo
- Recording's five digit catalog number (also called selection number)[4]

Back Cover
(Note: You may want to use some of this information, particularly the lyrics, on the inner sleeve as well.)
- Recording's title
- Your name (or your band's) if different from title
- Record label's name
- Record label's logo
- Recording's five-digit catalog number[4]
- UPC and bar code symbol
- Words above the UPC indicating how recording is to be filed in record store bins. Example: "File Under Latin/Latin Jazz"
- Total length of playing time per side
- Copyright notice for the compositions[1]

- Copyright notice for the recording ℗
- Names of musicians and instruments played
- Sampling credit (if applicable)
- Producer
- Graphic designer
- Photographer
- Illustrator
- Engineer
- Arranger
- Courtesy credits for appearances of musicians from other recording labels. Example: "Jon Smith appears courtesy of ABZ Records")
- Recording studio
- Mastering studio
- Manufacturer
- Record label's address/phone and fax numbers/Web site URL and e-mail address
- Mail-order information
- Booking information
- Publisher's address
- Song titles (in sequence) and length of playing time
- Name(s) of composer(s)
- Name of publishing company(ies)
- Copyright credit[1]
- Performing rights organization (ASCAP, BMI, or SESAC)[2]

vinyl packaging

- Lyrics
- Biographical material
- Any information that will add to the salability of the record, such as a quote from a reviewer, well-known musician, or producer
- Speed (e.g. 33 1/3 or 45 rpm)
- Country of origin of manufacture and printing. Example: "Record manufactured in USA" or "Jacket printed in Canada."[3]
- The words "All rights reserved. Unauthorized duplication is a violation of applicable laws."

OPTIONAL FRONT COVER STICKER
(Outside the Shrink-Wrap)
- Suggested song for airplay or quote from review or name of famous musician who played on the recording.

LABELS
- Side one/side two designation
- Recording's title
- Your name (or your band's) if different from title
- Record label's name
- Record label's logo
- Recording's five-digit catalog number[4]
- Copyright notice for the recording ℗
- Composition titles
- Country of origin of manufacture. Example: "Manufactured in USA"[3]

For all CD, Cassette and Vinyl Packages

1. If all songs are written and published by the same entity, just list the copyright credit and performing rights organization following the list of songs. Example: "All songs Copyright 1999 J. Smith, BMI."

2. Many bands do not join ASCAP, BMI, or SESAC because they think it is a waste of time and money. They believe they will not be paid for the scant radio airplay they happen to receive and will receive no other benefits. However, the right to publicly perform music is an essential copyright that must be licensed from the copyright owner. If a radio or TV station (or other entity) plays music from a band's recording and the band is not affiliated with one of these performing rights companies, these entities are doing so without a license and are, technically, in violation of U.S. Copyright laws.

3. To avoid problems clearing customs, the country of origin information must be included if your recordings are manufactured outside of the USA for sale in the USA; or manufactured in the USA for sale in other countries.

4. The selection number is a five-digit catalog number that identifies a specific recording. The same number is used for your UPC. It consists of the last digit of the company prefix plus any four additional digits. Do not get tricky. Number 1001 is a good start. Future recordings should be numbered sequentially.

Soundings of the Planet

SINCE 1979, "PEACE THROUGH MUSIC" HAS BEEN THE MOTTO OF DEAN AND Dudley Evenson, cofounders of the recording label, Soundings of the Planet. The Evensons have sold more than 1.5 million copies of their tapes and CDs and seven recordings have made the *Billboard* adult alternative charts.

The goal of these talented musicians—Dean plays flute; Dudley plays harp—is to bring listeners in touch with nature and themselves through recordings that incorporate natural sounds gathered from all over the world—streams, bird songs, wind rhythms, ocean waves, and acoustic instruments. The music is usually improvised by their accomplished friends, many of whom have their own recordings on the label. *Ocean Dreams,* their most popular recording, has sold over 250,000 recordings and received a Parents' Choice Award.

Dean and Dudley Evenson work closely with public school teachers that use the label's melodic instrumental/nature music in the classroom to enhance creative writing skills and help students relax and lower stress levels. They give stress reduction workshop/concerts, called "Health Through Music," in several regional schools and in local chapters of the American Cancer Society, Children's Hospital, and the Ronald McDonald House Foundation. They also work with ACCHORD, an organization that works closely with at-risk youth to teach anger management skills by involving them in hands-on musical instrument workshops and concerts.

We want to create peaceful, joyous environments for people to live in by bringing nature, music and humanity together in harmony. Music is a useful tool in helping people calm their thought patterns. It helps listeners focus on harmonies that vibrate with their whole being, mentally, physically and spiritually. As we vibrate with peaceful music, so we become peaceful within ourselves. Talking about peace on a global scale is meaningless unless we apply the concepts and principles in our daily lives. We must start with our own inner harmony, then inner harmony can expand and have an effect on the world around us.

—Dudley Evenson
www.soundings.com

recording options

every aspect of making your record involves decisions, but the greatest variety of choices involve recording.

Making recordings differs radically from sharing your music live. You must perform to a far-removed audience, without the aid of lights, theatrical effects, and your stage personality. Presenting your music on a recording requires you to learn different techniques and skills. You must evaluate yourself and the other musicians involved in the project and judge whether you can make decisions that are both objective about and appropriate for your music. Assess whether you can and want to provide the leadership necessary to execute those decisions during the planning and production stages. Preparing musicians for recording and directing sessions requires a wide range of skills—most of them learned through experience. Decide how much you want to do on your own and how much to rely on the experience of others.

You must be clear about your resources and goals and determine how much money you have to spend on recording. Recognize also that no amount of money will ever seem enough.

Many independent records have been made under less than ideal recording circumstances. Stories abound of makeshift improvisations and improbable schemes that got the job done. Wonderful records have been made on small budgets. Bad recordings are often the result of the musicians' lack of adequate technical or musical information.

If you have never been in a recording studio or recorded on someone else's album, be prepared for learning a new discipline. If you buy and operate your own equipment, the learning curve will be steep.

There are a wide variety of services and tools available that can help you record some or all of your project in your own studio and tailor it to fit several manufacturing formats. The important questions are—what product is going to be manufactured? What sound quality do you desire? Do you prefer to record and manufacture in analog or digital mediums? How many of these goals can you attain with the money and skills you have?

This chapter considers the choices that will confront you: arrangements, recording methods, recording environments, and personnel. The chapter, Recording Procedures, will familiarize you with the equipment and recording and mastering procedures common to all methods of recording.

MUSICAL ARRANGEMENTS

Music is produced in several ways: performing on acoustic or electric instruments; modifying acoustic or electric instruments with a variety of electronic devices; performing on electronic instruments; sampling a variety of sounds and modifying them electronically; and any of these in combination.

Your first decision is how to arrange your music for recording. You can record your music as you perform it; add supplementary instrumental or vocal parts to your regular arrangements; or rearrange it entirely.

Many independents choose to use their performing arrangements because they count on initial sales to come from people that regularly attend their concerts and club dates. Their audiences want to hear the music they are familiar with and may be disappointed if the artist makes a recording full of arrangements that cannot be repeated on stage.

You may find, however, that some of the arrangements you use for performing do not work equally well for recording. They may sound too cluttered, or have overlong tags or instrumentals. In the critical atmosphere of a recording studio, where each instrument can be isolated and each part analyzed, you may simply hear how to arrange your music better.

You should not completely rearrange your music unless you have prior experience at both arranging for recording and recording itself. If you change your original arrangements or add new instrumental or vocal parts, the recording process will become more expensive and time consuming. Musicians will have to learn new parts and extra musicians or composers may be needed. Additional parts also complicate the execution of a mix.

It is not easy to hear how a new part or an added instrument will work in the final mix. It takes considerable skill to play a new musical line with the precision required by overdubbing procedures. All too often, bands that are recording for the first time recognize these problems only after recording sessions have begun. They test and practice new arrangements in the studio. When the recording environment becomes an arena for experimentation, nerves fray and costs skyrocket.

To avoid turning expensive recording sessions into practice sessions, many musicians improvise and perfect arrangements on electronic instruments. They create virtual tracks using sequencers (either stand-alone or computers that run sequencing software), which tell the synthesizers what to play and when to play it, using the machine language known as MIDI. They can then choose to replicate these arrangements with live musicians.

Regardless of how you plan on arranging your music, consider seeking some professional assistance well before you begin recording. If you are going to use new arrangements, test them to make sure they work musically and can be played competently.

RECORDING METHODS

There are two general philosophies regarding the sound of recorded music. According to one, the most beautiful and natural sound results when the signal is recorded with minimal equipment and as little change as possible. The most direct route from original signal to master is achieved by using high quality microphones and two-track recorders. No alteration is done, since the more processing a signal receives, the greater the possibilities for sound degradation.

The second philosophy acknowledges that multitrack recording provides unlimited possibilities for editing sound and minimizing distortion and noise. The goal is to produce a captivating sound, not necessarily duplicate the original live sound. Thus, recording is a creative endeavor in which technology plays a part in producing the art.

Both approaches can produce recordings that are technically excellent and musically brilliant. The selection of recording method is interrelated with the choices you make about arrangements, recording environments, and personnel.

Direct to Two-Track

The simplest way to record music is direct to two-track, using one recorder and no more than two microphones, even if more than two instru-

ments are being recorded at the same time. The instruments and voices are recorded and mixed simultaneously directly on a digital or stereo analog recorder.

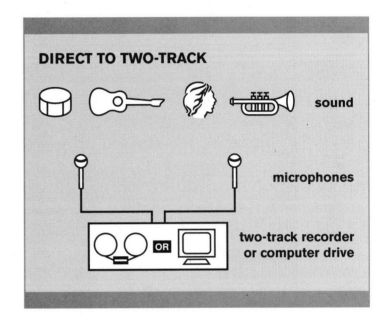

The engineer determines the best position for the microphones while the musicians try to balance their sound by controlling their performing dynamics. This method allows for some flexibility in editing; if the music is played consistently, multiple takes can be recorded and the best parts of each spliced together.

Direct to two-track has three advantages over other methods of recording. First, it allows for the greatest mobility and ease of setup. Some two-track tape recorders can be battery operated. Second, it permits great ease of performing. Musicians do not have to be set apart from each other, headphone monitoring is unnecessary, and the simplicity of the equipment and the method minimizes tension. Finally, direct to two-track is usually the least expensive method of recording. Generally speaking, this method works best for acoustic music and not as well for mixtures of acoustic and electric instruments, or instruments and voices. However, with the right engineer, good equipment, and well-performed music, excellent recordings can result.

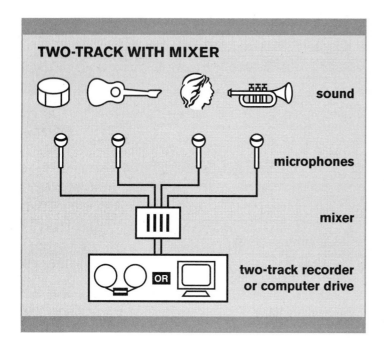

Two-Track with a Mixer

With this method of recording, each instrument and voice is given a separate microphone and the signals are routed through a mixing board. The music is simultaneously mixed and recorded as it is performed.

The musicians must be able to hear each other and the engineer has to distinguish recorded sound from room sound. This usually requires that everyone wear headphones and the engineer works in a separate room or in a truck outfitted as a recording studio (remote unit). In a concert situation, the onstage monitor system allows the musicians to hear themselves while the recording engineer monitors signals through headphones and meters or some other monitoring system, such as speakers mounted above the mixing console.

The need for a simultaneous mix means that the musicians and the engineer share the responsibility for controlling the dynamics of the music, although more control is vested with the engineer. Each microphone should be placed to minimize leakage. Sometimes this is accomplished by placing the musicians at greater distances from each other than they are accustomed to when performing or rehearsing. Baffles or other separating materials can be used. If a concert performance is being recorded, the engineer may hang additional microphones at a distance from the performers to add depth to the sound. The goal is to control the mix so solos can be turned up, important parts are emphasized, and lead voices are brought to the foreground. Special effects can be added to selected instruments or voices. As in direct to two-track, the results can be edited by recording multiple takes of each song and splicing together the best parts of each.

This method is a compromise one. It has neither the simplicity of direct to two-track nor the advantages of multitrack recording for controlling the sound and dynamics. It is best used when acoustic and electric instruments or voices cannot be recorded successfully direct to two-track or when multitrack recording is not financially feasible. It is essential the engineer be thoroughly familiar with the music and a spirit of trust and cooperation exist between the engineer and musicians.

Multitrack Ensemble

The musicians perform together, but each instrument and voice is recorded on a separate track of a multitrack recorder. The mix is postponed until all the music has been recorded.

This method permits the engineer to concentrate on capturing each instrument as clearly and accurately as possible. Different versions of the final mix can be made and tested until the right balance is achieved, and there is much more editing flexibility than with two-track recording.

By performing the music ensemble, the musicians can preserve much of the spirit and spontaneity of an actual performance, while they keep the time spent in recording sessions to a minimum. This method is a good compromise for groups that cannot afford many hours of studio time, yet want to maximize control over the dynamics of the final mix. Multiple takes can be spliced together, single tracks can be overdubbed, and some tracks can be left open for additional parts.

Multitrack/Overdubbing

Dividing the music into sections or layers and recording the parts on different tracks at different times is called overdubbing. Mixing is postponed until all the tracks are completed. This allows the most flexibility in arranging and editing.

When the music involves a complex arrangement for many different instruments and voices, the foundation is recorded first (laying down basic tracks). These tracks generally consist of drums, bass, rhythm guitar, and keyboards—whatever instruments carry the rhythmic and melodic foundation of the music. A trial

("scratch") vocal is often recorded with the basic tracks to remind musicians what they are providing tracks for. Once the basic tracks have been recorded satisfactorily, other voices and instruments are added in overdub sessions. Lead and solo instruments are usually added first followed by harmonizing and secondary instruments ("sweetening"). Lead vocals and harmonies are

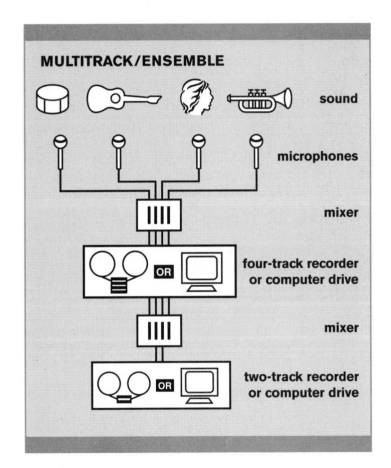

recorded last. Lead vocals and lead instruments are recorded individually, strings and brass are usually recorded in groups.

In a typical overdubbing session, the engineer plays the previously recorded music through headphones for the musicians while they add parts.

The main concern of the engineer and producer is a precision performance of exact pitch and tempo from the musicians, especially during recording of basic tracks. Sometimes musicians will be asked to repeat parts many times, until

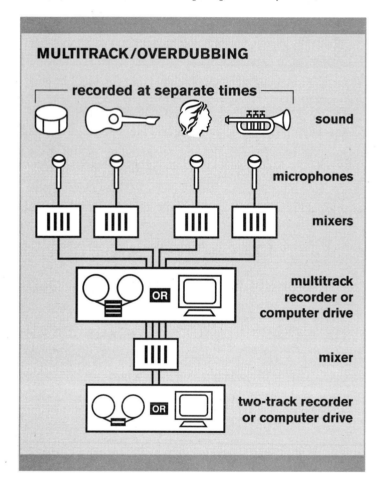

MULTITRACK/OVERDUBBING

recorded at separate times

sound

microphones

mixers

multitrack recorder or computer drive

mixer

two-track recorder or computer drive

they are satisfactory to the producer, engineer and other musicians. A "click track" can be added through the headphones to help musicians keep time.

Overdubbing is extremely demanding. Performing ease is difficult to achieve in an atmosphere where precision playing is a priority, and the start and stop procedures of sessions are often uncomfortable. Much more time is

spent listening than playing. Musicians can become so analytical that every note is played self-consciously, or so critical that nothing sounds right. Indecision and disagreements can take over the session. And overdubbing can be expensive, hundreds of hours can be spent before satisfactory results are achieved. For these reasons, you should consider carefully whether you want to take on multitrack overdubbing.

Best results are obtained when the procedures are thoroughly grasped, the music is well-rehearsed and arranged, and, in most cases, the entire project is led by a producer. Mastery of multitrack recording can be extremely rewarding for musicians. The ability to control their sound precisely opens exciting new dimensions. It is no wonder that most musicians want to try it at some point in their careers.

Premixed Tracks and Ping-Ponging

When finances do not permit the luxury of one track per instrument, fewer tracks can be used to obtain similar effects. In one method, instruments are grouped together and are recorded on one track (mono) or on two tracks to present a stereo image. Thus, additional tracks are reserved. Premixed tracks can be further processed, but the individual elements that created these premixes cannot be separated. Basic tracks, lead and harmonizing vocals, and string or brass overdubs can all be recorded successfully with this technique.

In another method, instruments are assigned individual tracks and those tracks are then premixed onto one track, freeing up the original tracks for further use. Several premixed tracks can be further premixed to one track. The

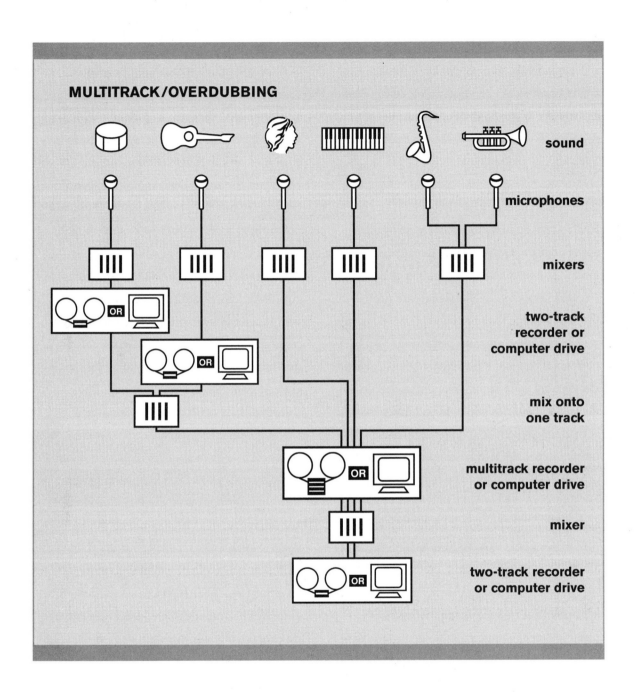

MULTITRACK/OVERDUBBING

sound

microphones

mixers

two-track
recorder or
computer drive

mix onto
one track

multitrack recorder
or computer drive

mixer

two-track recorder
or computer drive

method is called ping-ponging: going back and forth between recorded and empty tracks.

When the recording is finished, all the premixed tracks are mixed to two tracks. A disadvantage of this method is that noise levels build up quickly on the ping-ponged tracks, resulting in sound degradation (the effect is more pronounced with analog recording than with digital).

Sometimes both methods are used; for example, a live concert that has been initially recorded direct to two-track can be transferred to a multitrack medium and the other tracks are used for overdubbing.

The goal of both methods is the same: economizing on the number of tracks to cut recording costs. Although the concept sounds simple, the execution is relatively difficult. Instruments must be grouped so that they can be recorded in ways that produce properly premixed tracks.

Direct-to-Disc (Vinyl Only)

In direct-to-disc recording, a master lacquer is cut on a disc-mastering lathe directly from the music. The instruments are usually given separate microphones and the signals are routed through a mixer to the lathe.

This method requires perfection from both performer and engineer, since the music must be played from start to finish for the entire side of the lacquer without pause. Every time a mistake is made, due to either equipment failure or musical error, the lacquer must be scrapped and the process begun again. Direct-to-disc recording can unnerve even the most seasoned musicians and engineers, because there is tremendous pressure to perform correctly and brilliantly. Days can go by without one satisfactory lacquer being cut. This method is definitely not recommended for musicians that are inexperienced with recording, or unaccustomed to performing their music perfectly under pressure.

The advantage of direct-to-disc is an excellent quality recording. This method produces analog recordings with the least sound degradation because the route from sound to record is almost direct. Furthermore, a much greater dynamic range is possible than with magnetic tape recording and some people say this sound is more pleasing than that produced by digital recording.

Some direct-to-disc facilities use multiple lathes that maximize the number of lacquers (and records) that can be manufactured from one performance. Each lacquer can produce only a limited amount of stampers, which produce approximately 12,500 records each. Most direct-to-disc records are cut by independent companies and are marketed primarily through audiophile stores.

RECORDING ENVIRONMENTS

Any recording method (except direct-to-disc) can be used in the recording environment of one's choice: recording studio, club, concert auditorium, rehearsal studio, or home. In choosing an environment, the important considerations are acoustics and comfort.

Recordings are affected by the acoustics of the room in which they are made. Each environment has its own reverberation pattern. Reverberation can enhance the sound of a recording, as with classical music recorded in concert halls or it can cause muddy, distorted recordings, as with electric music recorded in an empty gymnasium. It can be entirely eliminated in the studio or be added artificially as an effect in the mix. Because all environments differ acoustically, you should listen to tapes made in the ones you are thinking of using and decide whether you like the sound quality. Personal preference is the most reliable guide.

Finding an environment where you and your musicians can perform effectively is vitally important. The pressure to perform well often escalates into anxiety. Here are some factors to consider that will help you judge how you are likely to feel in a particular environment:

- ◆ Can the room accommodate your musicians, their equipment, and all the recording gear, comfortably?
- ◆ Are the aesthetics of the space conducive to performing? Color and lighting are extremely important to temperament and mood.
- ◆ Are temperature and humidity regulated? Playing in a cold or hot room, or one that is drafty or excessively humid, can make you uncomfortable and affect the sound quality of your instruments.
- ◆ Do you need an environment free of external distractions or interruptions? Some musicians prefer an audience to inspire them. Others are more comfortable in the sealed-off atmosphere of a recording studio that is set up to maximize concentration.
- ◆ Are good food and a place to relax accessible? Some studios provide catered food, saunas, and Jacuzzis.
- ◆ At what time do you perform best? Can the environment support your preference? Is the space available to you open-ended or limited to specific hours?

After weighing all of these factors, the important question is—how do you feel? An environment may check out well in all areas and still leave you feeling ill at ease. If so, eliminate it from your list.

Home Studios

Many musicians build their own recording studios. Some are as elaborate as the most expensive commercial studios. They can be fully equipped with used gear for less than $2000, including recorder, mixer, microphones, and speakers. The band's sound reinforcement equipment can be combined with analog or digital recorders and sound processing devices. By adding synthesizers, MIDI control software, and computer interfaces, you can combine recording with composing and arranging.

Having a home studio allows you to gain hands-on experience with recording and acquire useful arranging tools. Tracks can be rehearsed at home and then a commercial studio and engineer can be hired for recording and mixing. Some bands record at home and mix final tracks in a commercial studio; others do their entire project at home.

Having your own studio makes it possible for you to learn techniques at your own speed in a comfortable environment. If you have an idea for a song at 3:00 a.m., you can record it, add a few harmonizing lines, and go back to bed. You can work out complicated arrangements with your band, record, play them back, and analyze to your heart's content. You can train your ears. You can mix and remix tapes and not have to count the dollars whizzing by.

The disadvantages of home studios are they take time and money to build and time to learn the skills. With the money and energy you spend on setting up your home studio, you could make your first recording and learn a great deal about recording in the process. It comes down to being clear about your goals and establishing priorities. How do you want to spend your money? Are you willing to invest the time and hard work building a studio or making and selling your own recording—the two seldom happen simultaneously.

Commercial Studios

For many musicians, a commercial recording studio provides the ideal work environment: a wide selection of microphones, pickups, auxiliary electronic tone generators, and signal processing devices; choice of track format and recording method; adequate recording rooms; and skilled personnel.

The best way to get acquainted with commercial studios is to visit them. In large metropolitan areas, you will find everything from cut-rate studios to beautifully furnished and equipped state-of-the-art complexes, and location recording services.

You should look for a studio that has a reputation for producing good tapes and working with musicians at your level of recording experience. The personnel should be familiar with recording instrumentation that is similar to yours and be able to provide the recording equipment necessary for your project. It must have the space to accommodate your musicians and their instruments, time available when you need it, want your business, fit your budget, and feel right for you.

Call several studios and request rate cards. Then you can eliminate studios that are clearly beyond your means. In addition, a knowledge of rate spreads may help you bargain with a studio you especially like.

Call the studios you are interested in and tell them you are planning to record and are shopping for a studio. Ask when you can meet their

PHOTO BY VINT BLACKBURN

The Brookwood Studio in Ann Arbor, Michigan is owned by David Lau. He specializes in recording jazz, classical chamber music, symphonies, community choruses, and choral and orchestral ensembles.

My goal was to provide an ambience that would help musicians recreate the experience of playing before a live audience. Many jazz and classical musicians feel ill at ease in a traditional pop recording studio. They don't like working in a totally "dead" acoustic space because they can't hear themselves or each other as well as they would in a live concert hall. They may not be used to listening through headphones and not be able to perform to their customary level. Vocalists have a particularly difficult time. They strain to sing louder because they don't hear their voice being reflected as in a concert hall. Even though we can add some reverb in the control room to provide the illusion of a live venue, inexperienced artists still need to hear that as they perform.

To achieve a natural room ambience, I used the golden section ratio for music and art invented by the ancient Greeks, which translates to dimensions of about 18 feet by 30 feet with 11-foot ceilings. Even though some walls are parallel there are no bad resonances to muddy the sound and acoustic instruments sound quite natural. When we had the room tested with a spectrum analyzer, the frequency response was very linear and smooth.

–David Lau

engineers and listen to your music on one of their monitor systems. It is best to bring your own tape (or other storage medium), since you can use it for comparison in other studios.

Provide some general information about your recording plans—the number of songs you plan to record, their instrumentation, and the method of recording you are considering. Bring worksheets that list the instrumentation for each song. (See, Worksheets, in the back of this book).

Here is what to check. How do the monitors sound? Do they have a range of microphones to select from? Do they have isolation rooms for vocals? Check out the cue (headphone) system. It is extremely important that musicians hear clearly through their headphones. Good studios will have cue systems that provide every musician with their own mix. Ask for references and contact them.

You do not have to use the same studio for all stages of your work. You might use one studio for recording basic tracks and another for overdubbing. Mixing can be done in a studio where the engineer is specially skilled or in one with automated mixdown or other appropriate equipment.

Studio Recording Rates

When comparing studio rates, determine what is included and what prices are for extra services. Do basic hourly rates include some free time for set up and breakdown? What instruments and equipment are included in the basic rate? Basic rates rarely include automated mixdown, noise reduction, or special effects, and tape is always extra.

Gentle Warrior

Peg Millett

Singing was part of my environmental activism: it helped lighten the load and keep people awake when we protested for 16- to 24-hour stretches at logging or uranium sites. Singing for the tape recorder was a learning experience: my singing coach, Katie Lee, taught me to pronounce my words clearly; engineer Isaiah Solomon helped teach me to sing for the tape recorder; and producer Walter Rapaport helped keep my spirit together when I had to do take after take to get it right.

—Peg Millett, Gentle Warrior
Hidden Waters Music
Prescott, Arizona

Sometimes studios charge less for morning hours, which are unpopular with musicians. Hourly rates are often cheaper when you contract for a block of time. Ask studios if they have block rates and how much time you have to book to get the special rates. You may get a further discount if you offer to pay cash in advance.

Let the studio owner know you are an independent artist making and selling your own record; you might find a sympathetic owner who is willing to give you a favorable rate.

Location Recording

Location recording captures the feeling and inspiration of a live performance. The sound quality can be excellent, depending on the acoustics of the location, equipment used, and the skills of the engineer/producer.

The best person to help you evaluate the acoustics of any concert location is an engineer experienced with this type of recording. He or she should be familiar with most clubs and concert halls in your area and can advise you as to their suitability. The engineer will look for environments that are not overly resonant (too much reverb), a common problem in halls with many exposed hard surfaces of wood, glass, or concrete. Materials like drapes, curtains, cushioned seats, and pillows help absorb resonance, as do people. The engineer will also look for a "dead" stage—one that is solid and does not produce vibrations when musicians stomp their feet or the drummer hits the drums, and check for outside noises, temperature, humidity, drafts, and radio frequency interferences.

An optimal situation is one in which acoustic musicians, bands, and orchestras use no sound reinforcement equipment. The music can be recorded live to two-track or multitrack with wonderful results.

When sound reinforcement is used, even if the acoustics of the location are optimal, the engineer will have to contend with the sound coming from the main speakers and the musicians' monitors. The sound coming from the monitors will affect the clarity of the overall recording blend, and the level at which any instrument can actually be recorded. Sounds leaking into microphones from other instruments further complicate the situation, and any feedback from the main PA can ruin an otherwise flawless take.

Cooperation between PA and recording personnel is extremely important. Equipment is often shared, particularly microphones, and everyone must take care not to clutter the stage with gear and cables. The most effective recordings are made when the recording company can adjust levels independently of the sound reinforcement system. This is accomplished by the recording company either using their own microphones in addition to the sound reinforcement microphones (double micing); or by splitting the microphone outputs, one output feeds the sound reinforcement system, the other goes to the recorder.

Setup and testing time is at a premium at concerts. Setup and testing of the PA for the audience and the monitors for the performers will take precedence over recording. Under these circumstances, the recording engineer will have to adjust the sound for the first two or three songs and may never get ideal results.

At this point you may be asking why, considering all these difficulties, recording a live concert when sound reinforcement is used is even attempted. First, location concert recording can be less expensive than multitrack recording in a studio. Second, a truly great recording can be achieved if all the conditions are exactly right—a good room, cooperative personnel, musicians that stay in place and maintain pitch and tuning, and especially, an inspired performance.

Location Recording Rates

Location recording services usually charge by the half-day or day. If the equipment and personnel have to travel out of town, they may charge for mileage. Get bids for the work, equipment, and personnel. You may be able to negotiate lower rates by booking consecutive days.

Although a recording studio is the standard place to look for location recording services, sound reinforcement companies, radio stations, and TV stations sometimes offer them.

Look for freelance engineers that are experienced in operating recording equipment and are available for location recording. Other musicians and local recording studios can put you in touch with qualified freelancers. You may find that location recording is a niche specialty in some large urban areas, not attached to any other audio service.

If you are not mixing live to two-track at the event, you will need to make arrangements with a recording studio for mixing.

Two-track location recording is the cheapest: the requirements are a recorder, a pair of microphones and a skilled engineer.

Companies that specialize in producing sound for concerts often offer recording also. Some radio and television stations make the engineers and remote trucks they use for live broadcasting available for hire. The engineers from these operations may be more familiar with this method of recording than their counterparts in studios. Their jobs demand results from the very first take. Thus, they may be more adept at live mixing. Ask to hear a recording that demonstrates the engineer's ability with location recording. Be sure that the recording was mixed simultaneously and is not a multitrack tape that was mixed later.

The next best price will be for multitrack recording with live two-track mixdown. Recording and mixing can usually be done off-stage; microphone splitters will be used to provide an audio signal to the recordist; and there is no requirement for a remote unit. Another option is to record all the signals that go to the sound reinforcement mixing board on ADATs by using mixers that have channel outputs that can be routed to as many ADATs as necessary. The house mixing engineer can oversee the process. This is most effective when a series of shows are to be recorded in a short period of time. The downside is, you must listen to a large number of tapes to choose the best performances.

The most expensive option is a remote unit with 16- to 32-track equipment. You will also have to book studio time for mixing. If you are recording a concert, the price is high and the risk is great, since you stand to lose money if the performance or recording is unsatisfactory. It's not a risk many independents take, unless they are experienced with recording and are reasonably sure the circumstances will be optimal. Some groups hire remote services for recording in their homes.

If you are not recording a concert, venue rental becomes a consideration. The most expensive rentals are concert halls that have union requirements. A cheaper option is a high school auditorium or church. Another good place to look for a rental is a night club that has good acoustics. Even if you cannot get your group booked in such a club, you might be able to rent their facilities for morning or off-day use at a reasonable price.

Payment for Commercial Studio or Location Recording

Payment for studio and location recording is usually COD with advance deposits required as protection against last-minute cancellations. In most cases, you will not be allowed to take your master tape until your bill is completely paid.

When booking time, clarify all costs and payment policies. With studio recording, where rates are usually figured on an hourly basis, you should settle certain questions before sessions begin: Who takes responsibility in case of equipment failure? If you are paying hourly rates to musicians, will the studio pay for their time while they wait for equipment to be repaired? In location recording, technical problems sometimes come up that escape notice until after a session is over. Will the recording company redo the taping for expenses? Resolve issues like these before you sign a contract.

RECORDING PERSONNEL

Recording is a partnership among many different people, each making an important contribution. The recording team may include the artist(s), engineer, producer, arranger, electronic instrument composer, and studio musicians. These people will influence the sound and character of your music and they must be carefully chosen and directed. You will be depending on them to help shape your artistry. Putting together a good recording team is as much of a challenge as finding compatible band members.

How many of these jobs do you want to take on yourself? Do not let your budget or your ego deprive you of the valuable knowledge and objectivity that others can offer. Look for people that can provide the skills you lack. They will shorten the time needed to solve problems.

Putting together teams that work well is one of the skills you should acquire during your career. You can start with just your band and end up with a conglomeration of managers, agents, producers, record companies, song publishers, and promoters. Mutual respect, trust, and your acknowledgment of their contributions and skills will help make the members of your team feel their efforts are worthwhile and will lead to their personal commitment and involvement.

Producer

The producer can facilitate and direct the making of all choices involved in recording. He or she can help focus arrangements toward your intended audience and promotional plan and help choose a recording method and environment appropriate for your music and experience. Your producer should direct sessions so they proceed smoothly and creatively, and generally take responsibility for making decisions regarding the final mix. A producer can help you make a good-sounding recording efficiently and within budget.

Producers must be experienced in working with different arrangements, methods, environments, recording personnel, and musicians. The best producers know how to bring out your talents and can teach you how to choose among the infinite possibilities that recording makes available.

Your producer is also your objective conscience—the one person who can step back from your music and tell you honestly what does and does not work. It is extremely difficult to be impartial about your own music. Objectivity is essential to decide which songs to record, which arrangements work, when you and your musicians are properly rehearsed and ready to begin recording, which takes are satisfactory, what editing needs to be done, and when the mix is complete. Objectivity is also needed for mediating group conflicts and smoothing tensions. This detachment can help avoid mistakes that will hurt your recordings.

When simple methods of recording are used, such as direct to two-track, or when the music has already been arranged by the group or a professional arranger, the leader of the group can often act as a producer. However, in multitrack recording where overdubbing is planned, a professional producer from outside the group can be more useful. Multitrack sessions produced communally often flounder as analysis turns into endless discussion or rearrangements that waste time and money.

Musicians that have worked with good producers swear by them. They will tell you how much they learned about recording, about their music, and about themselves. They may tell you their producer helped them make a recording

Julie Sullivan (guitar and vocals), Keith Gomora (bass fiddle and vocals), and Aaron Tyler (mandolin) of Green Sky.

I heard my vocals in a different way during recording—where I tended to go flat, how I popped my "P's"; what harmonies worked and didn't—and felt relaxed enough to correct them. Recording made me a better singer.

—Julie Sullivan, Green Sky

that excites listeners as much as their live performances—perhaps more!

When looking for a producer, shop the way you would if you were adding a member to your band. First look for the skills that balance those you lack, then consider compatibility. Someone with an agreeable personality and a love for your music may not have the experience necessary to provide the diverse skills you and your group need. The final test is to listen to recordings he or she has produced. Unfortunately, supply and demand rules; there are few really successful producers and many groups need their services.

Many of the best producers are on the payrolls of major labels; others contract their services on a freelance basis exclusively to major label recording groups. Many of the best freelance producers scout for talented groups for whom they produce records and then sell them to major labels for distribution, getting both an advance for their services, a rebate for production expenses (both of which the groups end up paying for), and usually a percentage on every record sold. This type of recording contract, quite common in recent years, is called an "independent production deal." You may be able to hire an independent producer on a freelance basis, but fees are high.

If you desire production help but cannot afford or find a professional producer, what should you do? First, because of their experience in working with diverse groups and instrumentation, engineers can often double as producers, or be hired to provide one or more production skills. They can be extremely talented at organizing and directing sessions. Usually their weakness will be in helping arrange the music. If that skill is needed, hire an experienced arranger, who may also be able to provide direction during rehearsals or sessions.

Musicians that have a great deal of recording experience can also be good producers, particularly if they have worked with good ones themselves.

You might be able to persuade an experienced producer in your community to give you a few hours of time on a consulting basis to help you with particularly thorny problems. Play your rehearsal or demo tapes for the producer. His or her advice about your arrangements, studio, and engineer could save you time and money. Some producers can be hired on an hourly basis to direct rehearsals, conduct complex overdubbing sessions, or direct the mix.

If other resources are not available, one of the members of your group can take on the responsibilities of a producer. If you do this, make sure you select someone whose objectivity you trust. You should also consider prior recording experience and the ability to direct the other musicians in the group.

After you choose a producer, follow his or her directions. Trust in your choice and concentrate on giving your best performance.

Payment for Producer

Some producers charge an hourly fee, others a flat rate for the entire recording. Some also ask for a percentage of sales. The amount depends on the producer's opinion of your sales potential, and their track record. Some producers ask a low flat fee for a talented but destitute group and make a secondary agreement that when the record sells over a certain quantity, or is picked up by a recording label for distribution, they will get a percentage of sales. Expect to pay more for a producer with a reputation for hits. Average producer royalties range from 1% to 3% of the wholesale record price. Hourly rates will seldom be less than $35 an hour.

If you ask your engineer to handle production chores, negotiate price before sessions start.

Engineer

Your recording project needs an engineer to evaluate the recording environment; make the musicians comfortable in it; select, set up, and operate the equipment; execute the final mix; and prepare a master. They are often extreme perfectionists and may want to spend much of your time and money to get the sound just right.

To a large extent, the engineer's skill determines the sound quality and cost of your recording.

If you record direct to two-track and use a simple two-microphone setup in a recording studio, the engineering is uncomplicated. Once the equipment is chosen and the proper sound obtained, the engineer's primary job is to see that everything functions properly.

In a more complex two-track method, where several microphones and a mixer are involved, the engineer will execute the mix "live," simultaneously with the recording of the music.

You definitely need an experienced engineer for multitrack recording. You should choose a studio as much for its engineer as for its equipment or atmosphere. Occasionally, you can find freelance engineers that can use the facilities of recording studios in your community. Some of them can also assist you with production.

An engineer's recording experience is extremely helpful to musicians that are new to studio procedures. In the absence of a producer, your engineer can help organize and direct sessions efficiently, make clear what options are

available, and foster a professional attitude among the musicians. Often, musicians get their first inkling of really good sound quality from their engineer.

It is important that your engineer be willing to work with you at your level of experience and in your musical style. Some engineers are

Flaco Jimenez is king of San Antonio Tex-Mex conjunto music. Ry Cooder, Doug Sahm, and Peter Rowan have played on Flaco's albums; and Flaco has played on several recordings with Bob Dylan and Santana. Today he is an essential part of the Texas Tornados, which records for Warner Brothers.

—Arhoolie Records
El Cerrito, California

not comfortable working with amateurs; some prefer recording jazz or rock to classical or country music. Try to find an engineer who is sensitive to your music and the personalities of your musicians.

An engineer will not try to correct musical errors or make aesthetic judgments about the nontechnical aspects of the recording unless specifically instructed to do so. Engineers are trained to take and follow direction when working with producers and professional musicians.

Payment for Engineer

Most engineers, unless they are hired on a freelance basis, are paid by the studio, and their services are included in the basic hourly rate. If you hire an engineer to operate equipment you provide, it is normal to pay a flat day rate, which depends on the engineer's experience and reputation.

Arranger

An arranger can adapt your regular performance arrangements for recording, simplify your regular arrangements to make room for additional instrumental or vocal parts, score those additional parts, and score arrangements for the entire session.

Some arrangers specialize in particular kinds of music or instrumentation. Most have distinctive styles. Some are able to arrange and play parts on electronic instruments, which can save money.

Recording studio managers and engineers, producers, and musicians that have used arrangers on their records can give you the names of experienced people. College music departments and music conservatories are good places to look for arrangers.

When you hire an arranger, play your music for him or her and explain in general terms what you want to hear. Do you want melodic or abstract lead lines? Do you have preferences for unusual instrumentation? What mood do you want the song to convey? This input will help steer the arranger in the proper direction.

Payment for Arranger

If you hire an arranger to compose music to be played by other musicians, you will pay a fee computed on the length of the arrangements and the number and kinds of instruments involved. If the arranger provides electronic arrangements, you pay by the arrangement.

Most experienced arrangers belong to the American Federation of Musicians (AFM), which sets minimum arrangers' fees. Arrangers that are not affiliated with the AFM may agree to work for less, either to gain experience or to do you a favor. Be sure to credit the arranger on your recording's cover.

Studio Musicians

There are many professional studio musicians in the major recording centers. They can be located through studios, producers, arrangers, the local musicians' union, or local symphony orchestra. You will find that most musicians will want to play with you if they like your music. Professional musicians can save you money in the long run and be helpful in teaching you studio techniques.

Regardless of which studio musicians you use, make sure that there is sufficient rehearsal before you step into the studio.

Payment for Studio Musicians

It can be expensive to use extra musicians on your record if they are members of the AFM or AFTRA.

A common payment method is to agree on an hourly rate. Pay all the musicians at the same rate. You must fix an overall budget and carefully figure out how many musicians you need for each session.

An alternative to an hourly rate is to pay each musician a flat session fee, or fee-per-song (including rehearsals). These options are ideal if you have a tight budget, because it allows you to predict the cost of musicians accurately. Until you have experience recording it is difficult to predict how long a song might take to record.

You might use musicians that are friends of yours and offer to record for free. This is fine if the agreements are clear on both sides. If you are paying some musicians but not others, make sure they all know that fact in advance and feel comfortable about it.

It is unusual to pay session musicians a percentage of the profits, no matter how famous they are. Be skeptical of anyone who demands it. If a record does makes it big, however, it is common to give bonuses to the session musicians.

In addition to whatever money you pay your musicians, you should be sure to credit them, specifying which instruments were played on what songs. It is also customary to give them a few free recordings.

TIME AND MONEY

Throughout your project you will be dealing with your dreams and your finances. Your finances determine how you realize your dreams. You must set limits on the time and money to be spent on recording and stick to them, so you will have money left for promo-tion and distribution. Prepare yourself for the fact that your budget might well limit some of your musical aspirations.

Estimating Time

The cost of recording depends on the method and the time it takes. As a rule, the more complex the method, the longer you will spend recording, unless you are recording a concert. When you estimate time, take into account the recording experience of the musicians, the organization of the sessions, whether you have a producer, whether the music and recording method have been rehearsed, and how much deviation from the planned arrangements might occur during the sessions. No matter how carefully you estimate, add 50% for the unexpected. Recording always takes longer than you think.

Below are guidelines to help you estimate the time you will need, based on actual experiences of groups making recordings for the first time. The guidelines include time for set up and testing, listening to playback, retakes, and final sequencing of the songs. For purposes of standardization, when the word "song" is used, it means a musical composition lasting three to four minutes. No session should last more than six hours.

For direct to two-track, estimate 90 minutes per song.

For two-track with mixer, estimate three hours per song.

If you plan to use multitrack/ensemble to record a single performance in the studio with no overdubbing, estimate five hours per song. If you plan to use one or two tracks for overdubbing

Audio books help teach basic skills and are increasingly being used as textbooks in recording classes taught at colleges and private audio schools.

and an additional vocal or instrument, add an extra hour per song, per track.

For multitrack with extensive overdubbing and a relatively inexperienced band, estimate no less than 15 hours per song. Four hours for basic tracks, five hours for lead instrumentals and vocal overdubs, two hours for vocal harmonies and other instrumental overdubs, and four hours for mixing.

Overdubbing consumes so much time because each track must be worked on with great care. The goal is technical and aesthetic perfection, and that means perfection on each track individually, as well as in the final mix.

If you plan to economize by using ping-ponging or premixing, you should still figure on 15 hours per song. You will save money though on the lower rates for a two-, four-, or eight-track studio.

When you use hard disk editing, you will be charged for real-time downloading and uploading of musical information, as well as its manipulation.

You will save setup time by grouping songs that use similar instrumentation and recording them at one session. If you will be using additional musicians on several cuts, try to book their time for the same sessions.

MAKING SESSIONS WORK

With tight budgets, ingenuity and efficiency must substitute for state-of-the-art equipment, hit-maker personnel, and the luxury of hundreds of hours in the studio. The following are suggestions to help you make the best recording you can.

Visit some actual recording sessions so you can observe and get a sense of the time different procedures take. Make your request to the studio manager or to the manager or leader of a group. Be as unobtrusive as possible when you attend a session. Do not ask questions until afterwards.

Attend courses or seminars on recording. Look for courses given by music stores to encourage the sale of four- or eight-track home studio equipment and for courses offered in music schools, community colleges, universities, or by private organizations. These are often relatively inexpensive. You will gain familiarity with equipment, studio terminology and procedures, and the science of recorded sound. Most classes offer hands-on experience.

If you do not have access to these courses, read magazines like *Mix* and *Home and Studio Recording* that regularly run articles on audio technology and recording techniques.

Plan on recording fewer songs with multi-track methods. Consider which songs will work well with direct to two-track or two-track with mixer.

Use professionals for producing, arranging, and engineering. It can be a temptation to use amateurs that offer to help for cut-rate prices, but it will not save you money. A good engineer or arranger can save you hours and perform a multitude of services.

Make demos of your arrangements so that you know what you are doing before you step into the studio. If you will be recording direct to two-track, a DAT or cassette recorder should be adequate for the demo. If you are planning multitrack recording, do a demo in an inexpensive studio. By trying out different mixes that emphasize different instruments you can check the effectiveness of each part in an arrangement.

Play your demos for as many professional musicians, producers, and arrangers as will listen. Ask their advice about your arrangements. Consider hiring an experienced arranger or producer as a consultant.

Rehearse your songs and studio procedures in a low-cost studio before you begin actual sessions. You should ask the engineer in the rehearsal studio to drill you in studio techniques.

Accustom musicians to listening to music through headphones while playing their parts and to the stop/start techniques used in multi-tracking. The most common editing technique is to record a song or its parts several times and then to splice together the best parts of each. Musicians should be thoroughly comfortable with such instructions as "Let's rerun the first couple of phrases in the second verse" or "Let's take it from the bridge." Musicians should learn to follow these instructions without attaching emotional energy to them or taking them as criticism. This is crucial during sessions, when tension is apt to be high.

If multitrack will be used, rehearse the music in sections (rhythm, lead instrumentals, and vocals) to test precision in pitch and tempo. Check the intonation and phrasing of the vocalists and lead instrumentalists. These are often problems, particularly when parts played through headphones are accompanied. The musicians will be less nervous during sessions if they have learned to perform well in rehearsal.

Practice punching in corrections or alternate arrangements in an inexpensive studio. This is one of the most common multitrack editing techniques and it takes some getting used to.

Book enough continuous studio time to accomplish what you want, but not so much that your musicians will begin to lose their effectiveness. Usually no less than three and no more than six hours per session should be booked by inexperienced groups.

Organize sessions so you work with the same instruments throughout each session. Record all the basic tracks using bass, guitar, and drums for several songs in one session, and the basic tracks requiring brass, keyboards, and woodwinds in another. Check with your engineer to make sure you are not trying to cram too much into any one session.

Learn what pace yields the best results for your band so you can maximize your time and money. Some bands get their best takes in the

first few hours and lose focus after that; others take a few hours to get going.

Leave enough time between sessions for listening to rough mixes, or for further rehearsals.

Buy your own tapes to record rough mixes for use after the session. There is no reason to pay more for them at the studio.

Arrive at sessions on time. Late arrivals waste money.

Have your instruments and amplifiers in excellent working condition. Guitars and basses should have their strings checked and necks aligned; drums should be checked for rattles, amps should be checked for buzzes and loose grounds. Drummers should bring extra sticks; string players should always have extra strings.

Do not bring other people to studio sessions unless they will actually help you. There is little for them to do and they are apt to resent the silence that must be maintained. Moreover, their presence can increase tensions, especially if the musicians are having difficulty during a session.

Relinquish control to the people you have chosen to direct the sessions and follow their leadership. If you have ideas for changes, hold them until after the session or bring them up at rehearsal.

If these are your first recordings, let the producer and engineer do the mix on their own. Directing a successful mix is not a skill musicians new to recording have. Moreover, they usually lack the technical language required to communicate with an engineer.

Stay away from mixing sessions. The fewer people present during mixdown, the better the engineer and producer can concentrate. They will make rough mixes so the band can voice suggestions and air disagreements.

Finally, be prepared to say, "It's done." Naturally, you want your recording to be perfect, but you must recognize the point at which more time spent will not significantly improve it. If you are recording for the first time, do not worry about making your ultimate statement as a musician. Think of this recording as the first of many.

Stony Plain

IN 1974 HOLGER PETERSEN FOUNDED STONY PLAIN (EDMONTON, ALBERTA, Canada) to produce and distribute blues albums of artists he loved—Roosevelt Sykes, Walter Horton (of Willie Dixon's Chicago Blues All Stars), and Johnny Shines, all of whom Holger had interviewed for his radio show, "The Natch'l Blues," on CKUA Radio. (The show is still running.) Today, Stony Plain has released 255 recordings of roots rock, blues, folk, and country music.

Petersen regularly attends MIDEM—the annual international music business convention held each January in the south of France—and large music conferences in the United States and Canada. Contacts made at those gatherings have enabled Stony Plain to release and sell its records in the United States, South America, Europe, Australia, and Japan, and to release recordings of artists from U.S. labels in Canada, such as Emmylou Harris' *Spyboy* and Duke Robillard's *Stretchin' Out—Live*.

It is very important for a small label like ours, which is based well away from major music centers, to attend music conferences and festivals, and to cultivate an international fan base.

Export distributors, foreign record labels, and publishers are interested in doing business with us because a market exists for the type of music we record and because some of our artists tour and receive airplay in several countries. The Internet fuels interest in our artists and has brought responses from the most remote parts of the world. When music evokes a deep, personal response, fans want to know every lyric and every facet of an artist's personality.

What is the main reason for the label's success? I've stayed close to the music I love. I work with exceptional artists and have enough faith in them to allow them to do what they know how to do best, create and perform the music, and not try change that. But, certainly, when the input is welcome, I'm there for that too. I can help bring a project to technical excellence by providing the money for a great studio, mastering, manufacturing, and packaging.

—Holger Petersen
www.stonyplainmusic.com

recording procedures

State-of-the-art equipment and technology do not, by themselves, guarantee a good recording. What ultimately produces a good recording is the operator's skill and experience with the equipment and the type of music being recorded. A person who records grunge rock for manufacturing on vinyl will record differently than someone who records symphonies for manufacturing on CD. The most important question musicians, engineers, or producers can ask in selecting or operating equipment is, "What will work best for the music?" In judging a studio, recording situation, or even an individual piece of equipment, let your ears be your guide. Do you like what you hear?

ANALOG OR DIGITAL?

Engineers, musicians and producers continue to debate whether to record music on analog or digital equipment. The main advantage of digital formats is the inherent quietness of the medium (no hiss), which enables listeners to hear a wider dynamic range. The main disadvantages are digital music sounds less accurate and less warm than analog recordings, to some people.

Which do you prefer? For many, the answer depends on what they are accustomed to hearing and how well they have trained themselves to listen critically.

If you want to make the finest sounding quality recordings at a price you can afford, you must educate yourself about the features and specifications of the equipment available so you can make intelligent choices.

RECORDING EQUIPMENT

Regardless of their size and sophistication, all recording studios are equipped to record (capture and store) sound, play back what was recorded, and improve, alter, and edit sound. Five kinds of equipment provide these capabilities: (1) microphones, pick-ups, direct boxes, and sequencers; (2) recorders; (3) mixing systems; (4) signal processing equipment ("outboard gear"); and (5) speakers.

Equipment Specifications

Analog and digital recording devices can be rated in terms of how accurately they reproduce or transmit information about sound in the form of electronic, magnetic, or digital signals. The important specifications are frequency response, distortion, signal-to-noise ratio, and dynamic range. These specifications apply equally to analog and digital equipment.

The ideal specifications for each piece of equipment are frequency response over the greatest range, with the flattest curve and least distortion; greatest dynamic range, and greatest signal-to-noise ratio.

Frequency Response

The frequency of a sound wave is its number of cycles per second. The basic unit is the Hertz (Hz), which is one cycle per second. Variations in frequency are perceived by the ear in terms of the pitch of the sound. The lowest frequency most humans can hear is around 20 Hz; the highest is around 20,000 Hz, or 20 kilohertz (kHz). Middle A is 440 Hz.

The accuracy with which equipment reproduces frequencies is called frequency response.

Any piece of equipment will be more or less responsive to different frequencies within the extremes of its frequency response range. These

differences are measured in decibels (dB), which are units that compare the relative intensities of audio signals. A 1 dB difference is considered the smallest that can be detected by a human ear; a 3 dB difference can be heard by almost everyone. Thus, frequency response is always expressed in terms of a range of sound intensity, such as "30 to 18,000 Hz plus or minus 3 dB." This means that within that range the intensity of any individual frequency will not vary more than 3 dB from the source.

The relative intensities of all the frequencies within the frequency response range can be expressed as a frequency response curve. The flatter this curve, the more evenly and accurately the equipment will respond to sounds or signals across its entire frequency range.

Distortion

Distortion occurs when the equipment produces audible signals in addition to the input signal which are either multiples of the original signal (harmonic distortion) or the result of interactions among two or more frequencies (intermodulation distortion). Distortion is expressed as a percentage of the original signal, such as ".08% total harmonic distortion."

Signal-to-Noise Ratio

Signal-to-noise ratio expresses, in decibels, the ratio of the maximum audio signal to background noise caused by the equipment itself. For example, a "signal-to-noise ratio of 45 dB" means that the maximum audio signal is 45 decibels louder than the underlying noise.

BASIC RECORDING PATH

Transmission via Cable/Super Cable, Optic Fiber, Radio Frequency, and Infrared

SOURCES

Analog
Acoustic
Electric

Electronic
Tone Generator
MIDI Sequencers
Samples

MONITOR
Control Room
Studio
Musicians

AMPLIFIER
(as per monitor
    needs)
Channel
Mix

INPUT
Microphone
Pickup
Other Transducers

DIGITAL OR ANALOG MIXER
Gain Stages	Equalization (EQ)
Auxiliary Sends	Combining Circuits
Channel Amplifier	Output Matrix
Converters	
(Analog to Digital,	
Digital to Analog)	

PROCESSOR
Limiters
Phase Shifters
Compressors
Graphic EQ
Digital Delays
MIDI
Expanders
Effects
Reverb
Parametric EQ
Filters

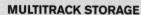

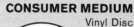

MULTITRACK STORAGE
Analog Tape
Digital Tape
VHS Tape
Computer Hard Disk
CD-R

MASTER STORAGE
Analog Tape   Computer Hard Disk
Digital Tape   CD-R
VHS Tape

CONSUMER MEDIUM
Vinyl Disc
Cassette
CD
CD-R

Dynamic Range

Dynamic range is the difference between the loudest and lowest sound reproducible by a device.

The TASCAM DA-45HR DAT recorder can record 24-bit audio data on a standard DAT tape. It can also record in 16-bit standard mode. Sampling frequencies include 44.1 kHz and 48 kHz. The recorder also features a 24-bit analog-to-digital converter.

Microphones

Microphones convert sound waves into electrical (audio) signals that are processed through the recording equipment. There are three basic types of microphones commonly encountered in recording: dynamic, ribbon, and condenser. These microphones differ in the methods by which they convert sound waves into electrical signals.

Dynamic and ribbon microphones operate on electromagnetic principles. In a dynamic microphone sound waves hit a diaphragm that generates vibrations in a coil suspended in a magnetic field. In a ribbon microphone, sound waves hit a thin metal ribbon suspended between the poles of a magnet and set up vibrations within the magnetic field.

Condenser microphones operate on electrostatic principles. A flexible diaphragm (plate) is placed parallel to a fixed back plate that has a permanent electrical charge. Thus, the area between the plates stores a fixed electrical charge (capacitance). As sound waves hit the flexible first plate, the capacitance alters, a change which is measured electrically and converted to an electrical signal.

All microphones are further classified as either directional—able to capture the sound coming from one or more directions—or omnidirectional—able to capture sounds coming from all directions equally. Directional microphones are classified as cardioid—able to capture sound directly on-axis (in front) and reject sounds from the back or sides—and bidirectional or figure-eight—able to capture sounds from both directly in front and in back while rejecting sounds from the sides. Some microphones give a choice of pickup patterns.

All microphones have an output impedance rating, which is used to match their signal-providing capacity with that of a signal-drawing recipient, such as a mixing console or amplifier, which have input impedance ratings. The unit of measurement is ohms. Low-impedance microphones are commonly rated from 50 to 600 ohms; high-impedance microphones are rated from 20,000 to 50,000 ohms. For the signal to be properly accommodated and transferred the input impedance rating of the signal-drawing equipment should be at least 10 times greater than the output impedance rating of the microphone. Low impedance outputs are preferred because they allow for much longer cable runs.

Microphone choice depends on the instruments and voices being recorded, the kind of music and how it is performed, other recording equipment, acoustics of the recording environment, and the placement of the microphone itself. Two musicians playing the same instrument might have very different microphone setups. Microphones might be changed for different songs.

Practice has established that certain microphones sound better in certain situations. Some display better transient response—the ability to handle sharp attacks, either sung or played, as when a drummer hits a snare drum sharply. Which particular microphone is chosen depends on the judgment of each recording engineer or producer and is based on their experiences working in different recording situations.

Pickups and Direct Boxes

Instead of placing a microphone near or on an acoustic instrument, a pickup can be used. A pickup works like a microphone: it converts vibrations produced from the body of the instrument into an electrical signal. It attaches directly to the instrument. Well-designed pickups have few frequency response peaks, smooth overall sound, and built-in equalization. Pickups are most frequently used with acoustic stringed instruments and some wind instruments. They also provide artists with freedom of movement, which may allow for more creativity.

Pickups are more often used for performing than recording because they generally do not reproduce the timbre of an acoustic instrument as well as a great microphone can in a quiet recording studio.

Magnetic pickups are used with electric or acoustic instruments that have steel strings. They

allow the electrical output of the instrument to be routed directly into the signal path via direct boxes, which can be used with or without an amplifier and speaker. Sometimes a microphone is used in combination with a direct box and their signals are mixed later to obtain a certain quality of sound.

Direct boxes (DI boxes, direct instrument sends, or direct injection devices) convert the high-level, high-impedance unbalanced signals generated from pickups into low-level, low-impedance balanced signals, which are then routed to a mixing board's microphone input channel or to an instrument amplifier.

MIDI Sequencers

MIDI (Musical Instrument Digital Interface) is a standardized control language and hardware specification that enables a musician to create the illusion of a band or orchestra. A MIDI sequencer, which can be a computer program or a stand-alone unit, records, edits, and plays back MIDI data. It allows you to create sounds and rhythms and synchronize them with live instruments and vocals and with other electronic segments. The parts that are created reside as a set of MIDI instruction codes stored in the sequencer's memory. These are called "virtual tracks" they become "real" when the codes tell tone generators which sounds to produce.

Recorders

Sound can be stored on analog or digital audio or video tape, compact disc-recordable (CD-R), or computer disk for transfer to the masters required for the various manufacturing formats.

Magnetic Tape Recorders and Tape

Tape recorders have three main functions: recording electronic signals, playing them back, and erasing them. They convert electrical signals into magnetic ones and imprint those signals as patterns on recording tape. The tape consists of a plastic backing coated with metallic particles that react to the magnetic signals. The recording head on the tape recorder, a small electromagnet, aligns these magnetic particles into patterns that are analogous to the sound being recorded. The

Tom Barabas' graceful melodies have resulted in 12 recordings for the label, Soundings of the Planet, including *Sedona Suite,* which has sold over a quarter million copies.

My home studio has several different synthesizers, including an old Roland D-50 that produces unique sounds I treasure, a Yamaha P 150 electronic piano and a Yamaha conservatory piano. I record the piano directly to my ADAT using two Neumann KM 184 condenser microphones. I use the studio primarily for composing and basic arrangements; then turn my music over to Dave Blackburn, a longtime friend, arranger, and producer. He feels my music; and when we talk over what I hear in my head, he is able to produce it.

—Tom Barabas

playback head converts these stored magnetic patterns into electronic signals, which are amplified and can be heard. The erase function saturates the tape with a very high-frequency signal that destroys the previously recorded patterns and leaves the metallic particles arranged randomly, ready to be rearranged into a new sound pattern.

Magnetic recording tapes differ with regard to the kind of magnetic coating, its thickness, and, to some extent, the kind of backing. Each type displays different abilities to receive and retain the magnetic signal at any given tape recorder speed, and each requires different magnetic strengths to record the signals properly. These characteristics in turn determine each tape's frequency response, signal-to-noise ratio, and saturation levels. (A discussion of the characteristics of cassette tapes appears in the chapter, Manufacturing.)

Two principal variables permit a tape recorder to be adjusted to accommodate the properties of a particular type of tape: bias and equalization. The bias control of the tape recorder adjusts the strength of the magnetic field applied to the tape. All magnetic particles respond nonlinearly (disproportionately) within any magnetic field. By adding the correct amount of a very high frequency signal (100 to 350 kHz), far above the range of hearing, and mixing it with the audio signal, the relative magnetization of the tape particles is changed to react proportionately. Without the proper amount of current, the signal being recorded would be distorted. Different types of tape require different amounts of bias current.

The other adjustment, equalization (EQ), corrects for the fact that tape does not respond equally to all frequencies. The recorder's EQ setting compensates for this during recording and playback and is used *only* to produce a as close to a flat response as possible. It is not used as an effect or a method for "coloring" the signal. That is the role of graphic and parametric equalizers. (See the segment below, Auxiliary Devices.)

Most tape recorders are equipped with bias and equalization controls that optimize performance for each kind of tape. Adjusting these controls is called calibrating the recorder. It is accomplished with the help of test tapes that provide tones at various levels and frequencies for specific recording speeds and types of tape.

Tape Speed and Track Format

Tape recorder speed and tape width affect audio quality. In any given area of tape, the metallic particles can retain only so much magnetic information before becoming saturated. The wider the area of tape exposed to audio signals, the less likelihood the signal will be distorted.

Some engineers use maximum tape widths to achieve the best results. They use half-inch tape for 4-track recording, one-inch tape for 8-track, and two-inch tape for 16- or 24-track. Others feel that improvements in analog technology allow them to achieve similar results with narrower tape.

Professional tape recorders usually operate at speeds of 15 to 30 inches per second (ips). Many home recorders operate at slower speeds. Running tape at high speeds maximizes the area exposed to the recording signal and makes it easier to splice the tape precisely, since musical information is spread over a longer portion of tape.

The accuracy with which a tape recorder maintains its speed affects its overall performance. Variations in speed produce wow and flutter—audible effects that sound much like their respective names. Generally, operating tape recorders at higher speeds mitigates inconsistencies.

Many professional tape recorders offer variable speed. Varying tape speed alters both tempo and pitch. This is especially convenient when a musician or singer cannot perform a song in a particular key or is slightly off pitch, or when an instrument is tuned to other than standard concert pitch, as are some non-Western instruments. Variable speed can also produce special sound effects.

Tape recorder heads come in different configurations. The number of tracks that a head contains identifies the recorder's format.

For standard quarter-inch tape, the formats are—full-track mono, which records one signal over the entire width of the tape; half-track stereo, which records two signals over the width of the tape; quarter-track stereo, which records four tracks (two signals in one direction and two in the other when the tape has been flipped over); and four-track, which records four separate signals over the width of the tape in one direction. This format is the lower threshold of "multitrack" recording.

Multitrack Tape Recorders

Multitracking is the capability of recording four or more synchronized signals on a piece of tape and then mixing them down to a monaural or two-track stereo master tape. Any track can be played back, erased, and rerecorded without affecting the others. Multitrack tape recorders have the ability to record different tracks at different times, and then synchronize those tracks to create the illusion they were recorded simultaneously (overdubbing).

The Sony MDM-X4MkII four-track recorder. Although the original intent was to provide musicians with a portable "scratchpad" on which to lay down their works in progress, many musicians are using MiniDisc recorders in place of DAT and analog cassette recorders for their final master recording. MiniDisc multitrack recorders such as the MDM-X4MkII have built-in mixers and can synch to MIDI time code, which allows users to connect several MiniDisc recorders for additional tracks. The average recording time for four-track usage is 37 minutes per track; two-track usage is 74 minutes per track; mono recording is 148 minutes.

Digital Recorders

In digital recording, the analog signal is converted to binary code that can be stored in various ways.

The advantages of digital formats are no tape noise, no wow or flutter, and digital-to-digital transfers can be made without degradation.

Digital recorders utilize a variety of storage formats. Digital audio tape (DAT) recorders record on two-track quarter-inch digital audio tape; some

eight-track digital recorders, such as the Alesis-ADAT, utilize VHS videotape; others, such as Tascam's DA-88, use Hi-8 eight mm digital cassette tape; compact disc recorders use CD-Rs; MiniDisc systems record on 2 1/2-inch miniature laser discs (MiniDiscs); hard disk recorders (HDRs) record music on computer hard disks.

DAT recorders provide two-track recording or a two-track mix-down master from analog or digital multitrack mediums at sampling rates of 44.1, 48, or 96 kHz. (In a digital audio system, the sampling rate is the times per second that a sample of the analog signal is taken. A sampling rate of 44.1 kHz means that a sample of the analog signal is taken at 44,100 times per second. That rate determines the upper frequency limits of a digital system.)

Editing functions, such as transferring portions of one take of a song to another or resequencing songs, are difficult without using multiple units or transferring the songs to a hard disk recorder or digital workstation. (See segment, Editing DATs, below.)

(There are two major reasons why some music is recorded at 48 kHz. In the early '90s, consumer DATs were developed that only recorded at that rate, to prevent people from pirating commercial products manufactured at 44.1 kHz. Second, some multitrack digital recorders offer the 48 kHz rate [either in addition to or instead of the 44.1 kHz rate], because the higher sampling rate provides a better sounding premix recording. Manufacturers expected users to convert it to 44.1 kHz on a DAT or CD-R. Today, some recorders offer even higher sampling rates to allow more accuracy.)

The eight-track digital formats used by Alesis, Tascam, and others provide multitrack digital recording. Machines can be linked together to provide more tracks.

MiniDisc-based recorders are designed and licensed to many manufacturers by Sony Corporation. These recorders can accommodate mono, two-track, and four-track recording. MiniDisc recorders can be synched to MIDI time code and several recorders can be connected to provide additional tracks. They offer some editing and mixing functions, such as the ability to record a musical segment and move and copy it to another section in a song; and the ability to add a vocal or instrument to a previously recorded track.

During recording, the audio data is compressed so that it can be accommodated on the smaller disk format. Compression in this context means that "unnecessary data" is dropped out of the data stream through an encoded model about how music generally behaves. Some argue that dropping any data means degrading the musical information and a generation of listeners may grow up never knowing what an acoustic piano, guitar, or other instrument can or should sound like, much less the more subtle differences between one brand of instrument and another. Others argue that if you could not hear what data has been dropped anyway, why care. Moreover, musical information has been edited out ever since music was able to be recorded.

What is important? Can you hear differences in sound quality between the same piece of music recorded analog, digital ADAT, or MiniDisc? Which do you prefer?

Hard Disk Recording

Digitized audio signals from digital recorders can be transferred to a computer's hard disk, where they can be manipulated by software programs, such as Digidesign's Pro Tools. The music can then be stored on a variety of other digital mediums, including floppy disks, digital audio tape

The Alesis-ADAT-XT20 24-bit digital 8-track recorder allows you to make copy/paste digital edits between machines or within a single unit, as well as make digital clones of any tracks (or group of tracks) and copy them to any other track (or group of tracks) on the same recorder. Multiple decks can be slaved together to act as one 16-, 24- or 32-track recorder.

(DAT), CD-Rs, MDs, videotape, etc. The preferred storage medium is CD-R and MD, since tape has a greater tendency to deteriorate over time. When the music is ready to be manufactured, the signal is transferred to the required mastering format. (See, Mastering, below.)

Hard disk recorders can be computer based or dedicated stand-alone devices. They offer the advantage of nondestructive editing—the recorder automatically duplicates tracks so you can edit to your heart's and budget's content without destroying the originals. Most systems can store mixer and effects settings, virtual tracks, edits, and different versions of your songs. MIDI controlled tone generators can be programmed to record and play an infinite number of orchestrated virtual tracks in real time. The MIDI information is stored in computer memory where it can be duplicated and edited, which allows musicians to experiment with electronically generated parts.

If you want to repeat a chorus, drum rhythm, or guitar segment, you can instruct the system to play the selected segment multiple times and insert the "loop" anywhere in the desired song.

The Roland VS-1680 24-Bit Digital Studio Workstation is a stand-alone tabletop hard disk system. It enables musicians to record, mix, add stereo effects, and edit. They can burn audio CDs directly from the workstation's SCSI port using an optional compatible CD-R drive.

Computer-based systems are digital workstations that use software to connect, route, and synchronize signals from analog and digital recorders, CD-Recordable devices, keyboards, sequencers, sampling devices, signal processors, and other equipment. The mixing and editing functions enable musicians to access, alter, resynthesize, rearrange and mix recorded sounds in unlimited ways. Operation of these devices requires advanced computer knowledge in addi-

tion to knowledge about sound, music, and methods of recording different instruments.

Stand-alone systems are specifically designed for digital audio recording. Recording and mixing are similar to analog systems. Most offer the equivalent of multitrack analog capability. In stand-alone systems, the music is recorded and stored on digital cartridges, which hold up to 100 minutes of music, depending on recording mode and sampling rate.

Mixing Systems

The ability to manipulate signals from multiple inputs so they can be processed, routed, and combined is the function of a mixing console (mixer). Mixers can be stand-alone consoles or be built into recorders. Their functions can be automated and performed with a computer, MIDI sequencer, and the appropriate software.

Whether mixing functions are part of a stand-alone unit or are in computer memory and software, they are a series of circuits waiting to be told what to do and where to send audio signals. How these functions are used depends on the music and the recording philosophies of the engineer, producer, and musicians. The choices among the many options offered by multichannel consoles and recorders are ultimately resolved in terms of which will allow the best recording and the most flexibility during the mixing process.

Once the music has been recorded on two or more tracks, the mixer can be used to combine them on one channel (mono mix), two channels (stereo mix), or more, each channel then feeding a recorder track. Two or more audio signals can be combined on one tape track (premixing) before being mixed with the information on other recorded tracks; volume, tone, and spatial positioning can be adjusted; and the signal can be simultaneously routed via switching and patching to specific tape tracks, musicians' headphones, or to right or left monitor speakers.

Some of the new features in mixing include automated control and the ability to provide synchronization between tape recorders, mixers, and sequencers.

Dozens of brands of mixers are on the market and there are also custom models. Each can be judged by the number of its inputs and outputs and controls that are available to accommodate microphones and outboard gear, and by their technical specifications, mechanical precision, and ease of operation and maintenance. In the more complex consoles, where multiple inputs can be accommodated, ease of switching and access to circuitry are features to be judged.

Signal Processors (Outboard Gear)

Once the signal has been captured and stored, it can be further modified with a variety of signal processing equipment.

Noise Reduction Systems

Magnetic tape and tape systems (analog systems) produce noise (hiss). Noise reduction systems help reduce this problem. They have become standard features of recorders and recording studios. Commonly, they manipulate the dynamic range of the signal before it reaches the recording head by modifying it (encoding). During playback, the recorded sound of an instrument

or voice is restored to its original sound (decoding) but without the hiss. Hiss builds up as the number of tracks increases, noise reduction on each track reduces this problem. When tracks are decoded and then combined their dynamic range is wider than it would have been without noise reduction.

Must noise reduction be used to make quiet tracks? Not necessarily. Extraordinarily quiet tapes can be made by an engineer who can adjust volume levels ("ride gain") to make soft passages louder and can use fast tape speeds, wide-track high-quality tape with mechanically precise, thoroughly cleaned, perfectly aligned recorders. Another trick is to turn off the tracks that are not being used to prevent hiss buildup.

Analog-to-Digital and Digital-to-Analog Converters

Numerous types of equipment are available to convert analog or electronic signals to binary code and back again. But musical information can be lost and errors can occur even with the best converters. Moreover, the conversions can affect sound as much as preamplifiers and microphones do in analog recording. Producers and engineers must choose converters as carefully as they do microphones.

Auxiliary Processors

Auxiliary pieces of equipment permit further processing or editing of the signal. Some, like compressors, limiters, and expanders decrease or increase the dynamic range of music. Others, like reverbs, phasers, and variable speed oscillators deliberately alter sound. Some are used as accessories to mixing boards, others are accessories to tape recorders or electronic instruments.

Equalizers divide the audio spectrum into separately controllable frequency ranges. They are tone controls that can be used in addition to the equalization controls on the mixing console. They give the engineer creative control over the harmonic balance of the instruments and can be used to make instruments sound different from their actual acoustic output and increase the apparent separation between instruments that are being recorded. Engineers use several different kinds of equalizers.

Graphic equalizers provide control over many frequencies simultaneously; the relative positions of their knobs or levers provide a visual ("graphic") display of the overall frequency response curve.

Parametric equalizers enable engineers to accent or attenuate a particular tone and thus offer more specialized control than graphic equalizers.

Filters are used to cut out frequencies at the extreme ends of the frequency spectrum, like rumble, air conditioning noise, and hiss. (Noise reduction equipment works on all the frequencies.)

Compressors reduce the dynamic range of a signal by automatically lowering the level of the loudest sounds while raising the level of the softer sounds. This allows signals to be recorded louder than the background noise and not distort. The trade-off is diminished dynamics.

Limiters are similar to compressors. They cut off sudden peaks, as when a singer comes in abruptly with a loud note.

Expanders increase dynamic range on playback. They compensate for the work done by compressors. Gates shut off channels at preselected low thresholds to eliminate noise and leakage between tracks.

Echo and reverb devices create discrete, repeating sounds (echo) or combinations of sounds so close together they sound continuous (reverb).

Digital delays can electronically delay signals by adjustable amounts. Digital delay can produce a short echo called slap echo or doubling, which delays a signal so little that a vocal part may sound like one person singing exactly the same part with him- or herself.

Phase shifters delay signals and recombine them, which produces signals that are out of phase, resulting in a whooshing sound.

MIDI-controlled digital signal processors allow extremely fine control over effects.

Speakers

None of the operations described so far produces sound; they merely process electrical impulses or binary code. It is only when those are transformed into physical vibrations of air that music can be heard. That is the function of speakers and headphones.

Recording studio monitor speakers are chosen for their ability to provide a flat response over the widest possible frequency range. However, that response is affected by the acoustics of the room. The same set of speakers can sound entirely different when placed in other environments. Studio engineers, therefore, employ near-field monitors (small speakers set within three feet of the engineer) to minimize the effect of the room's reflective surfaces.

Many recording engineers attempt to reach a mix that sounds good on all types of speakers because they understand that only some people will have sound systems and listening environments equal to those of a recording studio. Therefore, many studios are equipped with one or more additional sets of speakers, including small speakers that simulate those found in car radios, boom boxes, and small hi-fi sets.

Studios provide headphones so musicians can listen to the sounds they are recording or, in the case of multitracking, accompany the previously recorded tracks. Quality headphones are critical, since musicians' performances are greatly influenced by what they hear while singing or playing.

RECORDING PROCEDURES

Recording sessions usually follow procedures designed to maximize quality and help musicians perform effectively. These include, preparing the equipment, setup, testing, recording, playback, mixing, and mastering. The actual performance of music takes only a small amount of total studio time. Many musicians describe their first recording experience as one in which they learned to listen to their music.

Preparing the Equipment

Equipment must be tested before every session and every mix to be sure it is in excellent working condition and will not cause problems. Engineers generally have a routine they perform before every session to ensure that they get the

PHOTO BY BOB SWANSON

Producer and composer David Litwin in his Sausalito, California studio. The studio was used to edit and mix the final master for his recording *Organi Storici d'Italia*, released by Lyrichord Discs Inc. in the spring of 1999. David made live recordings of beautiful and historic pipe organs at five churches in Italy, with resident organists performing music that was composed locally when the organs were new.

To recreate an authentic experience of these wonderful instruments, I paid attention to a trinity of interdependent elements during recording: the organ, the space that surrounds it and into which it is built, and the music itself. I wanted to record in such a way as to place the listener there, in each organ's unique habitat, thus in a sense within the instrument itself, since the reverberant space of these churches is in truth a part of the instrument. I used only one pair of microphones (Bruel & Kjaer type 4006) placed strategically in the best possible listening spots, and used a Panasonic SV-255 portable DAT recorder, which kept the sound as clean as possible, due to its exceptional mic preamps. I did final edits back home in California, using Digidesign's Pro Tools system.

—David Litwin

same sound at the same levels from the mixing board to the tape recorder, a process known as calibrating the equipment. They will also check cables and headsets to make sure they work properly. Periodically, they will also clean and demagnetize the heads of their tape recorders and adjust the bias.

This preparation is usually done when musicians are not present and you should not be charged for this.

Setup

To a great extent, the quality of the final recording is determined by the setup, which is carried out primarily by an engineer who follows directions from a producer or group's leader. In the absence of a producer, the engineer might assume the entire responsibility.

During setup, musicians should tell the engineer how they want to be positioned around one another. A bass player may have to see the guitar player's hands; a drummer may prefer working close to the bass player.

The engineer will assign tracks to specific instruments and voices and decide how to best capture the sounds made by each instrument—whether to use microphones, pickups, or direct boxes.

Setup also involves isolating instruments as much as possible from each other; ideally, the sound of only one instrument will be heard through its microphone. The goal is to minimize sound leakage to other tracks during recording. Maximum sound separation can be achieved by putting each musician in an isolation booth or by recording each instrument individually, but

this usually causes some discomfort to the musicians. Mediating between sound quality and performance ease is one of the challenges encountered in recording.

Engineers use several techniques to maximize separation and still meet the musicians' need to communicate with one another. Instruments can be isolated with separating materials: speaker boxes, a sofa, low flats, baffles or gobos (frames that contain sound absorbent material). A blanket can be draped over the open lid of an acoustic piano to keep other sounds from entering the piano's microphone. This will change the sound of the piano; and when this is a problem the piano should be recorded separately from the other instruments.

Testing

After setup, the equipment and instruments are tested, a process referred to as "getting a sound." First, the musicians tune their instruments precisely to the standard "A" 440 Hz pitch. Then the instruments are adjusted, with the engineer listening, until they have the desired sound quality. Each musician will be asked to play his or her instrument at very low volume to permit adjustment of recording controls to capture soft tones, and at extremely high volume to make sure distortion does not occur. Distortion can occur when an instrumentalist or vocalist exceeds the dynamic range of the recording gear. When the dynamic range is large and distortion is anticipated, limiters can be used. The engineer will listen for buzzes, clicks, pops, rattles, and hiss, and will do what is possible to eliminate them.

Some musicians, with little recording

experience, may feel their sound is not right. They must understand that the sound of each instrument is being considered in the context of the final mix—not individually. Learning how to record for the mix, technically and aesthetically, can take a great deal of recording experience. Effects (echo, delay, etc.) are often added during the mix, and not during recording, which may make musicians uncomfortable because they are used to hearing these effects as they perform.

Each musician will be assigned a headphone set so they can hear the other instruments being recorded or previously recorded tracks and receive instructions from the engineer or producer. The engineer may be able to adjust the sound differently in individual headphones, depending on the sophistication of the equipment.

Once the instruments have been tested, a proper balance must be found when they are all played together. The level at which an engineer records the instruments is as important as how each instrument is played. Not only do instruments sound different at various levels, but musicians play their instruments differently depending on what they hear in their headphones. Setup and testing can take several hours, depending on the number of instruments and voices involved and the complexity of the arrangements.

Recording and Playback

When the instruments sound correct and the musicians feel comfortable, recording will begin. During sessions, the engineer will record a song, or part of a song, and then play it back so everyone can listen to it from aesthetic and technical

I had no idea what I wanted to do with my first recording; I only knew what songs I wanted to record and how long things might take. But it was a hard "birthing." One of the musicians flipped out at the last moment and we had to re-do the tracks. In contrast, recording Blue Angel *was fun. I gathered some of my favorite musicians and had a party. I allotted at least an hour per overdubbed instrumental or vocal per song so there was time to try things. No one ever felt rushed. We recorded and mixed 17 songs in just under 50 hours. Twelve made it onto the album.*

–Lisa Otey

points of view. Sometimes a "take" is brilliantly played, but the recording is marred by a mysterious buzz coming from an amplifier. The buzz has to be eliminated before taping resumes. Conversely, a take might be perfectly recorded but be flawed by inconsistent tempo, out-of-tune instruments, or incorrect notes.

Each microphone and track assignment is noted in a session log kept by the engineer or producer. They keep track of each take with the help of a tape counter or stop watch. Occasionally the producer will write out each part of a score to facilitate tracking every detail, such as a solo that needs three bars redone.

Sessions usually alternate between recording a song and playing it back. There is often more listening and analysis than actual playing, particularly in sessions where multitrack equipment is used. Inexperienced musicians are often frustrated by the long hours of setup and testing and by the start and stop procedures of the actual sessions, but that is necessary to produce good recordings.

Mixing

Mixing blends the recorded signals from all channels and sources into one signal for mono, two for stereo, four for quad, or five for home theater. The mix is made directly onto the mastering format of choice.

In two-track recording, the mix is accomplished at the same time the instruments and voices are recorded; in multitrack recording, the mix usually occurs afterwards, during mixdown sessions. Special attention can be paid to tone, volume, and overall balance, and changes can be made without affecting the performance itself. Special effects can be added or deleted and different parts can be combined from different takes to make one good take.

During a multitrack mix, each track is listened to separately. The engineer and producer listen carefully for leakage from tracks that were rejected, and for extraneous noises that can be edited out. This makes it easier to remember individual lines in the music and to note certain phrases that might be emphasized in the final mix. Then the engineer blends several tracks

together. The most common sequence is basic tracks first, then overdubbed lead instruments, followed by lead vocals and harmonies.

The engineer and producer have two concerns during mixing. Technical details regarding sound quality and mastering requirements are considered, as are the relationships between rhythms, melodies, solos and instrumentation. Too much or too little of even a minor ingredient can mar the result.

No two people will mix a song exactly alike. The engineer relies on the producer to provide guidelines as to what is to be emphasized. It is the engineer's job to translate such general directives as, "it needs more presence," or "the rhythm instruments aren't strong enough," into audible changes. Mixing is a specialty that requires knowing what to choose among the many options available. Different mixes are created for different markets and manufacturing formats. If your intended use is in a dance club, the mix may be very different from that used for FM airplay.

The more tracks used in the recording sessions, and the more complex the arrangements, the more complicated mixing will be. It can take as long as twelve hours for one song to be mixed, since the engineer and producer must make hundreds of decisions—where to bring up the guitar and bring down the piano, when to omit a third harmony, when to add just a little more reverb to the lead vocal, etc.

Once all those decisions are made, a mix will be made in one of two ways. A manual mix is made from beginning to end without interruptions, with all changes ("cues") remembered by the engineer. During the mix, the engineer's fingers are in continual motion on the console. When arrangements are complex both engineer and producer can "play" the console so all the cues will be executed properly. That process will be repeated until a satisfactory mix is achieved.

Automated mixing consoles have built-in computer software and memory, which allow them to remember cues flawlessly and enable their operators to update and make changes easily in subsequent mixes.

Ideally, a separate mix and master should be prepared for each format to be manufactured because of the differences in their dynamic ranges. The dynamic range of digital formats is in excess of 90 dB whereas analog formats (vinyl and cassette) have dynamic ranges of 30 to 40 dB. Ideally, the dynamic range of your mix should not be greater than the range of your manufactured format. If it is, soft sounds can disappear in the inherent hiss (noise floor) of the cassette and vinyl formats. If a separate mix is not made for vinyl and cassettes, the mastering engineer will use compression to reduce the dynamic range of your material.

Selection, Sequencing, and Editing

After the music is recorded and mixed to your satisfaction, the next steps are to select the songs and sequence and edit them. Some recording engineers recommend that sequencing and editing be done by a mastering facility, since this will usually involve loading the mix into a digital workstation, part of the process that will also be involved in the preparation of CD premasters.

Editing will consist of correction for noise, fade-ins, fade-outs, equalization, and dynamics,

songs spaced appropriately, and level adjusted into a single entity that will become the final recording.

Sequence should be considered in terms of tempo and key changes and thematic or musical continuity. Sales and promotional considerations should also play a part. DJs, concert promoters, and store owners will often listen to only the first 30 seconds of the first and last songs on each side of your recording.

Make sure that the entire length of the program can be accommodated in the formats you are manufacturing. This is especially important if you are going to be using two or more formats or are using more material in one than the other.

The amount of music that can be accommodated on a vinyl record depends on its size (7-inch and 12-inch are most common); the playback speed (33 1/3 rpm or 45 rpm); the dynamic range of the music; the amount of low-frequency (bass) information the music contains, and the volume level used for disc-mastering. In general, faster speed, greater dynamic range, and more bass presence increase the mastering levels ("hotter levels") and decrease the amount of program material that can be accommodated. For instance, the optimal length for a 12-inch rock 'n' roll EP may be 18 minutes and the optimal length for a solo acoustic guitar may be 25 minutes a side. Your engineer will know what is best for the music you are manufacturing.

For cassettes, the maximum amount of time that is available is generally 105 minutes for music; and 115 minutes for spoken word.

For CDs, the maximum time that is available is 74 minutes; for CD singles it is five minutes.

HOW MUCH SILENCE SHOULD I LEAVE BETWEEN SONGS?
by Micah Solomon, Oasis CD and Cassette Duplication

If the amount of time between songs seems too long when you are listening intently, it is probably exactly right. Your listeners want extra space between selections when they are listening in an informal setting, i.e., while negotiating traffic on the freeway.

Realize that where the song actually ends on a digital workstation and where it seems to end to the listener are two different things. When you look at a printout of the song from the digital work station, the end is where the decay of the last note finishes. But in reality, nobody hears the end of the note; it is lost in the noise floor of the listening environment.

There are no rules—this is a musical decision. Do not let anyone tell you there is a rule such as three or four seconds between songs.

Some manufacturers experience difficulty in accommodating playing times that approach the maximum limits. Check with them about tolerance limits before mastering begins.

MASTERING

Mastering is the last step before manufacturing. It is the preparation of the final product you give to the manufacturer to produce your recordings. The master should meet the technical requirements of the manufacturer and reflect the artistic views of the musicians and producer.

Because of the variations in technical requirements for vinyl, cassette, and CD manufacturing, many engineers submit final mixes to a mastering house on digital or audio tape to have a mastering engineer sequence and edit the songs and prepare the vinyl and cassette masters and CD premasters required by the manufacturers.

The proper preparation of masters and their accompanying documentation is essential to the manufacturing process. Each manufacturer has particular requirements for equalization, alignment tones, tables of contents, length of program, etc. A separate master should be prepared for each format.

The best audio quality is ensured by delivering a master that is completely finished and needs no adjustments for equalization, noise reduction, compression, editing, resequencing, outtakes, unwanted noise between tracks, etc. Your engineer should make sure the master is free of hold errors and mutes and the tracks and track times are consistent with what is in the documentation. Extra expenses will be incurred to make changes and time will be lost while the results are sent back for your approval. Be sure to request prices and estimates before you contract for corrective work.

Generally, the fewer transfers (generations) between the final mix recording and the mastering process mean fewer errors and better chances of reproducing the sound quality of your mix. Each time information is transferred to a different medium (analog-to-digital or vice versa, tape to disc-mastering lacquer, two-inch tape to quarter-inch tape, one sampling rate to another, etc.) musical information and quality may be lost.

Use a mastering facility that is separate from the firm doing your manufacturing. You will have more control over the work and you and your engineer will have the opportunity to work directly with a mastering engineer who is dedicated to producing quality masters.

Mastering engineers specialize in the creation of masters and CD premasters for replication. They are able to make independent assessments of your mixes and lend a "fresh ear" to a project that may have been worked on for months. They are aware of technical requirements and have the equipment for creating proper masters, premasters, and documentation for all manufacturing processes. Mastering engineers work with high-resolution accurate monitoring systems so they can make accurate judgments about levels and the "sound" of a project. It is possible to hear extraneous sounds in a project, which were missed in recording and mixing, at a mastering studio. The artist, producer, or engineer will be in direct communication with the mastering engineer.

You should listen to every minute of the final masters before approving them.

Ask the advice of engineers, producers, and record label people to find a disc-mastering house that has an excellent reputation. Other

sources are the *Billboard Buyer's Guide, Mix Magazine* and the *Recording Industry Sourcebook.*

Safety Masters

As soon as a satisfactory master has been completed, you should make a copy for insurance against loss or damage. Store it away from your office or studio in a room that is between 65 to

I was lucky enough to have a mentor, my coproducer Bill McGee, who taught me how to learn and do things for myself. He bought the home studio equipment—ADAT, computers, sequencers, samplers—and turned me loose. If I asked a technical question, he'd say, "That's in the manual." When I played him some of my arrangements, he wouldn't say, "That's wrong," but "Here's what you might want to try differently." When I started to design my cover, he took me down to a record store and we looked at what covers jumped out, what colors people in hip-hop were using, how the lettering was placed, how big it was, and we analyzed them together. It made me recognize that just as you can provoke different feelings by the chords, melodies, and raps, you do the same with graphics.

—Danja Mowf

┌───┐

TYPICAL PROCEDURES USED IN SEQUENCING, EDITING, AND MASTERING CDs

1) Digital mixes are loaded from a DAT or CD-R into a digital workstation.

2) Analog mix sources (half-inch or quarter-inch analog tape) are converted from analog to digital (at 24 bits). Analog equalization and dynamics processing may be applied. The resulting digital information is loaded into a digital workstation.

3) The individual songs are arranged in proper sequence in the workstation. The beginnings and ends of each song are trimmed to remove extraneous noise. Fade-ins and fade-outs are applied as needed.

4) The songs are digitally edited. This can be as simple as removing a chorus of a song or substituting alternate versions of mix into portions of the final mix. Or it may be as complicated as using multiple takes and mixes with dozens of edits. Intros, solos, parts of a song, and individual lines can be adjusted in volume.

PHOTO BY TIM MURPHY

David Glasser and Charlie Pilzer, chief mastering engineers, Airshow Mastering, Inc., in Studio A, Boulder, Colorado. They received a 1998 GRAMMY for the mastering and restoration of the *Anthology of American Folk Music*.

5) Each cut can be processed to add equalization, dynamics processing, or reverberation. This is done to match the sound of one song with other songs on the same project and may include the careful conversion of the audio to analog, processing in the analog domain and reconversion back to digital. Mastering houses have specialized highly accurate digital-to-analog and analog-to-digital converters.

6) The volume (gain) of each song is digitally set to an appropriate level relative to the other songs on the project. In determining volume, the mastering engineer takes into consideration the peak levels, the average or "apparent" level, and the ratio between them.

7) The final digital audio is redithered (mathematically bit reduced) into the 44.1 kHz, 16-bit format required for a CD premaster. All digital processing, even gain changes, causes the length of the signal to increase. It is important that digital audio be correctly bit-reduced after ANY digital processing to avoid distortion.

Courtesy Charlie Pilzer,
Co-Owner and Chief Mastering Engineer, Airshow Mastering, Inc.
(www.airshowmastering.com)

└───┘

75 degrees Fahrenheit and no more than 60% relative humidity. Never send your only master to a manufacturer.

CD Masters

Digital master formats for CDs include two-track digital audio tape (DAT) with a sampling frequency of 44.1 kHz, MDs, and CD-Recordables (CD-Rs). If you submit an MD, a compressed digital format, it will be transferred to an uncompressed format, such as DAT or CD-R. Music which has been mixed to a two-track analog tape will be converted to a digital master.

If you are providing a tape master, your engineer should provide at least 10 to 15 seconds of recorded silence at the beginning of the recorded material. This is accomplished by turning the recorder's track inputs off, engaging the record mode, and letting the recorder run for the appropriate length of time over the blank tape. No silence is needed on MDs or CD-Rs.

Some manufacturers accept masters prepared on other digital formats such as JVC half-inch VHS video tape or JVC three-quarter-inch U-Matic video tape. These tapes should include a minimum of two minutes of silence at the beginning of the material and one minute of silence at the end.

Music that has been recorded and edited at a sampling rate different from 44.1 kHz will be converted to that rate during mastering.

Your recording engineer should provide an accurate time log that indicates precisely the beginning and end of all track information on the master. This must include start and stop times (IDs) in minutes and seconds of the peri-

ods of silence (at the beginning and end of the material, as well as between songs) and the sequentially numbered program materials. The log starts at the beginning of the tape in absolute time (00:00:00—hours, minutes, seconds) and is continuous to the end of the program.

Accurate time logs are extremely important because CD manufacturers and mastering engineers use them to make the CD premaster.

You must include your name, address and contact information on every master and documentation sheet and on the box that contains the master.

CD Premasters

The master will be used to make a CD premaster in one of three formats: a Red Book formatted CD-R; a three-quarter-inch U-Matic video tape, prepared in Sony PCM 1610 or 1630 format; or a special high-density 8 mm tape (exebyte) that stores digital information that is formatted to Disc Description Protocol (DDP), similar to Red Book. These premasters will contain the digital subcoding (PQ subcode) for your CD, which conveys such information as total number of selections, start time of the recorded material, and total start and stop times of all the tracks.

Premasters are used to create glass masters, which are the next step in CD manufacturing.

It is entirely possible that a DAT submitted for CD replication, will be transferred from DAT to digital audio workstation to CD-R. And maybe from CD-R to DDP, depending on which format the facility actually uses to make glass masters.

The manufacturing facility should send you a reference CD-R, made from the premaster, to approve.

Enhanced CDs

Enhanced CDs have additional multimedia files along with their music. These files are added after you select, sequence, and prepare the music master. The music master is given to a designer who prepares graphic materials to your specifications and combines them with the music files to make the digital master or CD premaster. Firms that advertise CD-ROM production are your best bet for this service. Your graphic designer or manufacturer should be able to recommend a production company that is skilled in this service. If they cannot, call the largest recording studio or film editing studio in your area for recommendations or look for listings in the *Recording Industry Sourcebook*.

Ask that two reference CDs be made from the CD premaster so you can approve what will be seen and heard once recordings are manufactured and have a backup to facilitate the transfer of content back to the software program used to create the content (authoring program), if any changes are needed.

Play the reference enhanced CDs on Apple Macintosh and PC computers. Not all computers act the same way, even when it appears they have the correct software and memory requirements. If the enhanced CD plays poorly on either type of computer, have the multimedia producer correct the problem.

Cassette Masters

The process used for manufacturing will dictate the requirements for the appropriate cassette masters. Read the processes outlined in the chapter Manufacturing to become conversant with different cassette manufacturing processes before deciding what kind of masters to submit.

If you record your music in the analog domain the best master for analog bin-loop cassette duplication is a two-track half-inch analog tape recorded at 15 or 30 inches per second.

The songs must be placed in the desired sequence with an interval of silence between each song. Alignment (calibration) tones must be inserted by the recording or mastering engineer at the start of the master so the manufacturer's machine can be aligned identically with the machine on which the master was produced.

Ten to 15 seconds of leader tape (paper or plastic) must be provided at the beginning and the end of each tape to provide sufficient length for threading the tape onto another reel. The speed of the master tape translates to feet of leader: 15 inches per second means that 150 inches (12 1/2 feet) will be needed for 10 seconds of leader.

If you recorded and mixed to a DAT, a digital-to-analog transfer will have to be made to accommodate the requirements of the analog bin-loop method. Be aware that three transfers will be necessary and that the first transfer to an analog master requires a digital-to-analog conversion (DAT to analog master; analog master to analog bin-loop master; bin-loop to final analog cassette); all of which will add noise and hiss to the final tape. The DAT should contain a reference tone for 30 seconds, 1 minute 30 seconds of silence, the audio for side A, 1 minute of silence,

DOCUMENTATION FOR CASSETTES AND VINYL MASTERS

The documentation that accompanies vinyl and cassette masters should include the following information:

1. Matrix number (A- and B-side identification).

2. Names of songs in the sequence they occur.

3. Timing of each song.

4. Length of silence between each song.

5. EQ information.

6. Alignment tones used.

7. Type of noise reduction used.

8. Cross-fades used.

9. Where high-frequency boost was used.

10. Any special requests the engineer has, such as resequencing, equalization, etc. Get an estimate of what these requests will cost you.

11. Your name, address, phone number on the tape's box and the tape.

the audio for side B and 1 minute of silence.

A DAT or CD-R is preferable for the digital bin method (see the chapter, Manufacturing), because your material will stay in the digital domain until it is transferred to cassettes, thereby eliminating a generation loss, which ensures a higher quality sounding cassette (DAT to digital bin master; digital bin master to final analog cassette).

Some facilities use a digital audio workstation to prepare the analog bin master and only convert to analog if the bin master needs correction. They prefer the master to be delivered in a digital format.

Vinyl Masters

Before making a master for vinyl, you must contact the manufacturer and ask whether they use an analog or digital method to operate their disc lathes. If analog, the best master is two-track half-inch analog tape recorded at 30 inches per second without noise reduction. Most facilities, however, will accept a two-track half-inch tape at 15 ips with or without noise reduction.

Your engineer will time each song precisely and place it in the desired sequence with an interval of silence between each song. Calibration tones must be inserted at the start of each master so the manufacturer's machines can be aligned identically with the machine on which your master was produced.

As with cassette masters, 10 to 15 seconds of leader tape must be provided at the beginning and the end of each tape.

Five seconds of leader or biased blank tape should separate each song to indicate where each starts and stops.

DATs and CD-Rs are the preferred masters if the manufacturer uses computers to run their disc cutting lathes.

We recorded the latest album at Vintage Studios in Phoenix, Arizona with studio owner and our coproducer Billy Moss, who has made recordings with Stevie Nicks (Fleetwood Mac) and the Gin Blossoms. We picked the songs and trusted Billy to get the sound and balance we wanted. There was a lot of give and take; it wasn't like he came in and told us what to do and squelched our ideas. We recorded the music on digital tracks but mixed to analog to get a warmer sound.

–Michael Bannister
Burning Sky

THE MOST COMMON ERRORS IN SUBMITTING MASTERS TO MANUFACTURERS ◀---

The sequence indicated on written documentation does not correspond with the sequence of songs on

   the master.

The times indicated on the written documentation do not correspond with the times on the master.

DAT masters are supplied with songs at an incorrect sampling frequency or with mixed sampling frequencies.

There are pops, clicks, other extraneous noises, and dropouts on the master.

There is insufficient or incorrect documentation.

In 1975, STEVEN HALPERN RELEASED HIS FIRST ALBUM, *SPECTRUM SUITE.*
Today, after over 50 recordings with sales of 4 million worldwide,
Halpern, who holds a Ph.D. in the psychology of music, is widely
acknowledged as one of the most influential new age recording artists
and contemporary sound healing pioneers. In February 1999, *Spectrum
Suite* was named "the most influential New Age recording of all time"
by *New Age Voice.* Halpern's keyboard-based compositions are used in
homes, hospitals, and business offices to enhance meditation, relax-
ation, and creativity. He is the author of several books and hundreds of
articles on sound, health, and healing, including *Sound Health* (Harper
and Row), *Sound, Stress and Inner Peace,* and *How to Harness the
Healing Powers of Music* (the latter two published by Sound Health
Research Institute, a division of Inner Peace Music).

Steven Halpern
Founder

In 1969 Halpern, who had been playing in jazz/rock bands,
experienced an initiation into the "healing music ministry," and began
composing in a totally unique manner. When he added polyphonic syn-
thesizers and digital samplers, Halpern had the tools to recreate the sounds he was hearing in his
head, and his sophisticated and subtle atmospheric textures have since become a hallmark of the
genre.

Although primarily known as a recording artist, a significant part of Halpern's persona is as a
producer. He has produced and recorded with Paul Horn, Georgia Kelly, Daniel Kobialka, and Nigerian
master drummer Suru Ekeh, among others.

> *In my compositions, I use specific combinations of tone, space, and silence, and create
> dimensionality with reverb, echo, and phasing. This helps people quiet their mind, slow their
> breathing, and balance their electromagnetic energy field (aura). It is like "sonic acupuncture";
> the music induces an immediate shift in brainwaves into an alpha or theta pattern, which is
> associated with relaxation, healing, and feelings of love and joy.*

—Steven Halpern
www.innerpeacemusic.com

manufacturing

manufacturing

You have the choice of making compact discs (CDs), analog cassettes, vinyl records, MiniDiscs (MDs), and Digital Video Discs (DVDs).

Few consumer MiniDisc players have been sold and it is not expected to be a popular consumer format. Because of the data compression methods used, their sound quality is not as good as CDs or vinyl, but is better than analog cassettes. (MD recorders are discussed in the chapter, Recording Equipment.) The future of DVDs as a stand-alone audio format is too unpredictable to include manufacturing information in this book.

COMPACT DISCS

CDs are polycarbonate discs, which are coated with a reflective metal and sealed with plastic. The digital information is arranged in a continuous spiral on one side of the disc. The information is read by a laser beam in the compact disc player. The digital signal is processed and amplified through an audio playback system.

CD manufacturers must meet manufacturing standards (Red Book) established by Sony and Philips to ensure CDs are the same the world over and will play in any CD player or drive.

CD Manufacturing

The manufacture of CDs requires a combination of lasers, robotics, and high standards of quality control and cleanliness. Numerous steps in the manufacturing process occur in cleanrooms, since even the smallest dust particles will affect the final product. Each step of the process is carefully checked for flaws.

The digital information on the premaster controls a laser beam recorder. Its light exposes a layer of photosensitive material that has been applied to a carefully ground and polished glass master disc. When developed, the exposed areas become microscopic pits and flat areas (lands) that are the information bearing formations on the disc. There are close to three billion of these pits on a long-playing CD.

The glass master is coated with a thin layer of metal to render it electroconductive. It is then played on a master player to check for defects like miscoding, phase shifts, and tracking errors.

Stampers, generated from the glass master by electroforming, are used in the CD replication process. The stampers are extremely thin and a particle of dirt under a stamper can cause unplayable errors in the finished CDs.

Injection molding techniques are used to manufacture discs. The stamper is mounted on a mold that is filled with transparent, optical grade polycarbonate. During molding, the resulting CDs are impressed on one side with the pits and lands that carry the digital material.

Each CD is then coated with a thin layer of metal, usually aluminum, to create a reflective surface. In cases where optimum quality is demanded, gold is used. There is little audible difference, but because of the higher cost of gold, the manufacturing facility may spend more time making sure all manufacturing processes are optimal, thereby increasing the chances for a consistently high-quality manufacturing run. Some recording and mastering engineers say gold is a gimmick that allows manufacturers to charge premium prices.

The disc is hermetically sealed with an ultraviolet cured plastic coating to protect it from scratches and oxidation. The label is printed on the protective coating using silk-screen techniques and ultraviolet cured ink.

Most manufacturing facilities do a final quality control check by reading selected discs for defects and either playing them on high-speed test equipment or listening in real time.

Fabrication

The assembling of graphics and recordings, termed fabrication, is generally quoted as an extra charge, so you can select options. Common ones are shrink-wrapping, adding special stickers, and applying top spine stickers with bar codes to CDs earmarked for store sales.

CD-Recordable (CD-R)

Affordable small-quantity CD duplication systems (CD-Recordable or CD-R) are now available as stand-alone systems, integral parts of computers, or as separate CD-R drives for computers. (The latter option costs less than $400.) The advantages to using them are quick turnaround and the opportunity to create smaller runs than most manufacturers will accept.

These systems use lasers to record data on the heat-sensitive dye layers of blank CD-R discs to form the equivalent of the pits and lands in a manufactured compact disc. The discs can be played on any CD player, CD drive, or CD-ROM drive. CD-Rs can duplicate your music in real time or at two, four, or six times the speed at which it was recorded.

Blank discs (called blanks, gold worms, gold discs, and one-offs) are easily recognizable by their colors: gold or silver on one side; and blue-green or bright blue on the other. They are more fragile than manufactured CDs and are susceptible to damage from extremes in light, temperature, and humidity, as well as scratches and dirt.

Care must be taken when labeling because the only labeling surface is the disc itself. The safest methods are to (1) label the nonrecorded surface with a felt-tip pen that has water-based ink (anything else can damage its delicate surface); or (2) use crack-and-peel labels specifically made for CD-R blanks.

Although an Orange Book standard defines the specifications for blank CD-R discs, it does not determine the process by which the discs are manufactured. This means that you should only use those blanks recommended by your CD-R hardware's manufacturer.

Blank CD-Rs cost from $1 to $5. Currently, they come in two sizes: 80 mm and 120 mm. Each offers two different data capacities: 18 or 21 minutes for the 80 mm disc; 63 and 74 minutes for the 120 mm disc.

Some recording studios and mastering facilities offer short-run CD-R replication at costs ranging from $5 to $25 per CD, depending on the quantity.

MANUFACTURING CASSETTES

Analog cassette tape does not reproduce the dynamic range and frequency response of your final studio mix as accurately as CDs or vinyl records. You can, however, ensure optimal quality by choosing high-quality tape, a method of duplication that is compatible with the master you provide, and a manufacturer that has a reputation for delivering quality product.

Cassette Tape

Cassette tape consists of a clear plastic mylar backing and a surface coating. These coatings can be ferric (iron oxide or chrome [iron oxide mixed with chromium dioxide particles]); or metal (all ferric cobalt particles). Each surface has different abilities to receive and retain signals and requires different magnetic strengths within the tape recorder to record signals properly. These characteristics also determine frequency response, dynamic range, signal-to-noise ratio (how much hiss will be present), and saturation levels (how much audio information the tape will hold before distortion or signal loss occurs).

Bias is the process of using an electric current to adjust the strength of the magnetic field that is applied to the tape during recording. Magnetic particles respond to the audio signal · nonlinearly and disproportionately within any magnetic field. The correct amount of an inaudible, high-frequency signal causes the magnetic particles to react proportionately to the audio signal. Without the proper amount of bias, the recording will be distorted. Generally, the higher the bias, the better the ability of the tape to reproduce high-frequency sound and a wide dynamic range.

Ferric tape, the most prevalent, requires normal bias currents. Ferric premium type 1 tapes display excellent response to bass frequencies and good response to midrange frequencies. They can be played on any type of cassette recorder. When sales literature refers to "super" tape, describing it as "super standard bias tape for making serious recordings," it means the highest grade of normal bias type 1 ferric tape available. Ferric type 0 tape has limited high-end response and noticeably more hiss than type 1 tape. It is commonly used for spoken-word recordings.

Type 2 chrome tape (high-bias currents) displays a number of improvements over ferric tape: lower hiss, greater ability to reproduce high-frequency sound, and a wider dynamic range. Chrome tapes are frequently manufactured with a 120-microsecond EQ so they can be played on the ferric or normal settings of consumer tape decks. Chrome tapes can also be manufactured at a 70-microsecond EQ to provide better audio quality, but playback will be limited to tape decks that have "chrome" settings. They will sound muffled or weird when played on decks without this setting.

You will pay a higher price for chrome tape and may have to shop around for it since not all manufacturing firms offer it.

Metal tape is used for digital masters for the digital-bin manufacturing method (described below), demo recording, and copying CDs for personal use on cassette decks that have a "metal" playback setting. Metal tapes will sound harsh and distorted when played on decks without this setting.

Metal tapes are high-bias and have high coercivity. Coercivity is the level of magnetic flux needed to move a particle into its proper position. When all other factors are equal, higher coercivity means this tape will not saturate as easily in the upper midrange and high-frequency levels as do ferric and chrome tapes, which results in better frequency response.

All blank analog cassette tape has a noticeable amount of high-frequency hiss even when no signal is present, which can be heard when music is recorded or played back at low volume. The addition of noise-reduction during manufacturing, most notably Dolby B and C, HX Professional, and dbx, helps quiet hiss, but does not entirely remove it. Less hiss enables listeners to hear a wider dynamic range. Dolby B is widely used because most consumer decks support it. Some duplication facilities do not offer noise reduction.

Real-Time Master Tape Duplication

The master tape is duplicated at the speed it was recorded. Real-time duplication uses tapes that are already in their housings (in-cassette duplication).

Because the frequency response and dynamic range of the master tape are transferred almost exactly, real-time duplication produces the best tapes when high-quality tape is used. It is the most expensive duplication method, often double or triple the price for high-speed duplication.

Every tape deck used for real-time duplication must be properly calibrated to ensure that there are no variations between tapes.

High-Speed Master Tape Duplication

The master tape and the duplicate cassettes are run at speeds up to 64 times the playing speed. The greater the speed, the greater the loss in high-frequency information and the greater the hiss. Cassette manufacturers that reproduce music of wide dynamic range or much high-frequency information will seldom duplicate at such speeds. Most use ratios of 8:1 or 16:1 and claim the audible differences are minimal compared with real-time duplication.

┌───┐
│ ┌───┐   │
│ │ **USING PLAYBACK SETTINGS CORRECTLY**   ◀----   │   │
│ └───┘   │

When noise reduction has been used during manufacturing, it should be used during playback, with the

exception of HX Professional. Cassette tapes with noise reduction that are played without using noise

reduction settings will have a noticeably harsher sound, which can be reduced by turning down the treble.

When no noise reduction has been used in manufacturing, consumers can improve playback quality by

using noise reduction settings to reduce hiss, but doing so will reduce some of the high frequencies,

resulting in a muffled sound.
└───┘

The bin-loop system is used by most high-speed duplicators. First, your master is duplicated several times in sequence on a half-inch four-track analog tape (bin master) at 7 1/2 or 3 3/4 ips. This "running master" is spliced to form a long loop, which is played over and over during duplication to large reels of cassette tape called pancakes. The A and B sides are recorded simultaneously. A 6 Hz tone, which signals the start of each complete section of material, is added to the master. Loading machines read this tone to determine where to cut the pancakes before inserting the tape into cassette housings.

Digital bin methods (DIGalog, DHS, and DAAD) transfer the information on your digital master to a computer's RAM (digital bin master). Copies are duplicated at high-speed from the computer's digital signal to large reels of ferric or chrome tape pancakes. This system produces higher quality cassettes than analog bin-loop technology.

MANUFACTURING VINYL

Manufacturing records involves four processes: disc-mastering, plating (matrixing), pressing, and packaging.

Disc-Mastering

Disc-mastering (disc-cutting), is the process of transferring the music from your master to grooves on a disk. The disks are of two types: one has an aluminum substrate coated with lacquer (master lacquer); the other is a copper disc (direct metal master—DMM). Copper masters look like records and can be played on a record player. Aluminum discs are used to make vinyl acetates (reference copies). Aluminum discs cannot be played on record players because they will ruin the needles; copper will not.

Your master is played through a disc-cutting console (lathe) that converts the music to mechanical motion. The lathes can be operated by analog or digital equipment. If they are operated by digital equipment, a digital master will

Although vinyl is still thriving in this genre, it is becoming more expensive to manufacture, as are covers, inserts, and colored vinyl. These days we are making our music available in as many formats as possible to reach a larger audience. We are currently talking to on-line CD compilation companies, as well as companies working with MP3 and Liquid Audio.

–Uli Elser, General Manager,
Alternative Tentacles Records,
San Francisco, California

be needed. If they are operated by analog equipment, an analog master will be needed. (See the segment, Vinyl Masters, in the chapter, Recording Procedures.)

A stylus cuts grooves, which are analogous to the electrical signals of the music on your tape. A separate master is cut for each side.

Before cutting masters, the engineer will adjust the controls on the disc-mastering console to match the alignment tones indicated at the beginning of your master tape and make accommodations for any noise reduction used.

Your engineer or producer can include special instructions to the disc-masterer as to how to cut the masters, which can be cut as is ("flat") or with equalization to make certain cuts "hotter." The amount of stereo separation can be adjusted also. Monaural lacquers can be cut for singles. If an injection method of pressing will be used for your singles the disc-masterer will be asked to provide more space between the grooves (land) to help compensate for the inherent deficiencies of that method. (See, Pressing, later in this chapter.)

Manufacturers of high-quality audiophile recordings prefer copper masters because they are not as elastic as aluminum. This eliminates high-frequency losses and distortion. The frequency response and dynamic range of the master are transferred almost exactly.

Copper masters have highly detailed grooves, which allow for up to 15% more playing time, and they avoid two of the plating steps required for lacquer. They are more expensive than lacquers and not all manufacturing facilities have the equipment to make them. Copper masters are used for direct-to-disc-recording. (See the chapter, Recording Options.)

No matter how skilled a disc-masterer is, no adjustments can magically improve a poorly engineered tape or mediocre music. The limits of what can be done to make good records are inherent in the master you submit.

To make sure that the disc-transfer is acceptable, reference copies—either vinyl acetates or a copper master—should be requested. Listen to them with your engineer and producer and compare them with your master tape. Acetates are very fragile and are good for only five or six listenings before noticeable sound deterioration. You should save a few plays to verify the quality of subsequent test pressings. Copper masters are not as fragile and can be played more.

You and your engineer will be expected to listen to and approve acetates immediately. Recording engineers feel that for finest results master lacquers should be plated within 48 hours of being cut. This means the manufacturer should begin plating as soon as it receives the master lacquer. You or your engineer should coordinate the scheduling of disc-mastering, references, and plating so this can occur.

If you do not approve the references your producer or engineer will specify what corrections are to be made, a new master lacquer will be cut and a new set of references made. If this happens, you have to reschedule the plating process.

References should be checked for the following problems:

- ◆ Low overall volume level compared with other records
- ◆ Variations in volume levels from song to song
- ◆ Breakup or distortion in the treble at peak loudness levels or towards the end of a side
- ◆ Excessive boominess or airiness in the bass
- ◆ Dullness or lack of presence in the midrange
- ◆ Skips, buzzes, crackling noises, or dull thuds

Your engineer and producer should listen to the references on both large and small speakers to be sure that there is adequate treble and bass response.

Plating

Plating (matrixing) is usually a three-step process to make the stampers (molds) that put the grooves into your records during pressing. The first step, making a "master," or "subfather,"

Quality components (tape, shell, printed material) and quality manufacturing equipment won't result in a quality product unless the equipment is properly maintained. We perform preventive service and maintenance on all our equipment so it will deliver optimum performance and an optimal product. As a result, RTI has one of the lowest return rates for defective goods in the industry. Practically nil....

—Don MacInnis, President, Record Technology Inc., Camarillo, California

involves coating the master lacquer or copper master with a thin film of silver and electroplating it in a tank containing a nickel solution. The nickel plating, an exact negative impression (metal part), is peeled from the silver-plated original lacquer.

The second step, making a "mother," involves electroplating the metal part (subfather) to produce a positive impression exactly like the master lacquer or copper master.

The third step, making a "father," involves electroplating the mother to produce the negative metal stampers (metal molds) which are used to press records.

If you anticipate reordering, request extra metal stampers and file them for future use. These can be stored indefinitely and can be shipped anywhere you want to have records pressed. This avoids the expense of shipping product overseas.

When record manufacturers quote prices for "full protection," it means they will follow the three-step process and make permanent metal stampers.

In the one-step manufacturing process, the subfather is used to press records. (The subfather is also called a "converted master" when it is used to press records.) However, it is extremely fragile and is used only for extremely small runs (under 1500 records). If you are only planning a limited run and do not expect a re-run, choosing the one-step process will save you money.

Pressing

Each stamper can turn out 1500 to 2000 records. Labels are affixed at the time of pressing.

Currently, two different methods and plastics are used in record pressing. The compression method, using polyvinyl chloride, is employed universally for LPs, 45s and EPs. Semi-molten vinyl is inserted into a pressure cavity and then hydraulically forced into the stamper. The temperature of the vinyl and the temperature and humidity of the room, affect the overall quality of the pressing. Improper cooling of finished records can result in warping.

Either virgin vinyl or a combination of virgin vinyl and "regrind" (melted vinyl from defective records, or "flash," the excess edges of records), is used. Insist on virgin vinyl, unless you have dealt previously with your manufacturer and can trust their regrind mixture.

Vinyl comes in different grades. The better the quality, the lower the surface noise. If you want premium vinyl, make sure your manufacturer offers it or can get it. The difference in price can be as much as 100% higher than standard domestic grade.

The injection method is often used for pressing 45 rpm singles. Liquefied polystyrene, a harder more brittle plastic than vinyl, is poured into a mold and quickly baked and cooled. Records are turned out twice as fast as with the compression method and polystyrene is cheaper than vinyl. The records are ready as soon as they come out of the mold. These records wear out faster and tend to register greater background noise. If you care about quality, avoid the injection method.

Test pressings should be made and shipped to you for approval before the final pressing. These will verify the accuracy of both the plating and pressing processes, and tell you how your finished records will sound.

You should listen to the test pressings with your recording engineer and producer and compare them with your references. They should sound the same, or even a little brighter than the acetates, since vinyl is a harder compound, which results in improved high-frequency output. If the sound is duller, if the hole is off-center, if there are pops, skips, or other noises, you should reject

My vision was to start an all-vinyl record label that would become a community of fans, artists, and music business people. I want people to seek out our artists. I want them to buy a turntable to play vinyl. I want them to support our distributors, Fat Beats and Sandbox Automatic (on-line distribution only). People who find out about our label and listen to the music have an incredible bond with us.

—Bobbito Garcia, Founder,
Fondle 'Em Records.

the test pressings and order new ones.

Flawed initial test pressings are not uncommon, and they are usually corrected in subsequent trial runs. To avoid problems, ask your engineer or producer to discuss your complaints. They can be technically specific and have the professional credentials to back up their claims.

If the masters are okay and test pressings repeatedly come back flawed, the problem can be traced to either faulty plating or faulty pressing. The references can prove that the mastering process was satisfactory. Without them, there is no way to prove which process was at fault.

Although plating and pressing services can be done at separate firms, most independents prefer to have both processes done by one company.

Packaging

When the final pressing is completed, your records will be collated with album covers, dust sleeves, and inserts. This is done immediately after the records are pressed and have cooled properly to prevent scratching, warping, or other damage.

CHOOSING A MANUFACTURER

The selection of your manufacturing firm is the final control you have over the quality of your recording. Most firms that advertise they manufacture CDs, cassettes, and vinyl are brokers or middlemen, not actual manufacturing firms. Brokers can sometimes offer you prices that are competitive with or lower than you will get from a manufacturing firm directly because they buy a certain amount of hours annually and have established business relationships.

Good brokers take the time to provide their customers with excellent service (answering questions; providing promotional extras; ensuring quality control), which is the key to their reputation and longevity. Avoid brokers that have been in business for less than two years.

It is extremely important to contact a variety of firms (brokers and manufacturers) for information and estimates. Become comfortable with the language they use, get to know the people involved, discover what is and is not negotiable, and budget appropriately.

Begin your research long before you start recording. Ask for price lists, samples of work, and the names of labels that use their services. Contact those labels and ask what their manufacturing experience has been. Ask manufacturers about the added-value services they offer, such as compilations that are sent to radio stations, Web site listings, etc.

Often, the brochures you receive from manufacturing firms are written in language that assumes you are conversant with all the processes and variables and you will find that each has a unique method for quoting prices. This can make it difficult and confusing when comparing prices.

To estimate manufacturing costs, list the services, quantities, and program length for each manufacturing format you require and request bids from several manufacturers. Manufacturing prices are usually quoted in five-minute variations in tape length per side. Printing and manufacturing costs drop significantly as quantities increase.

In most cases, you will deal with a sales or marketing representative or a customer service representative. Their job is to answer your questions and attract your business. Make it clear that once you receive information and standard prices, you will be soliciting firm price quotations. Let them know they will be competing with other manufacturers. Manufacturers will work harder to satisfy you when they are competing for your business. That is when your negotiating leverage is greatest. Do not hesitate to ask questions. Keep copies of all your letters and makes notes of your phone conversations.

Refrain from making a definite commitment to any firm until all your questions are answered and you have agreed on detailed prices.

No matter which company you select, there is no way to guarantee their work will be perfect or delivered on time. All labels have had problems with defective recordings, flawed test references, or CDs that track improperly. You want to work with a firm that has a reputation for value and service.

REQUEST FOR PRICE QUOTE   ◀----

We would like to obtain a quote on the following project: *Glen Canyon River Journeys.* We want both CDs and cassettes manufactured.

The job will be submitted on DAT masters. Customer will furnish film.

CDs—(program length 70 minutes):

1000   1500   2500

Standard jewel box, assembly, and shrink-wrap.

Two-color disc imprinting.

Four-color, four-panel CD insert and four-color tray card.

Estimated shipping charges to Jerome, Arizona 86331.

Cassettes—(program length 60 minutes). If there is a choice of tape formulations (i.e., chrome vs. ferric) please quote for both:

500   1000   1500

Dolby noise reduction; on-cassette imprinting; Norelco boxes; assembly and shrink wrap.

Four-color, six-panel (three panels, printed both sides) "Z" fold cassette inserts.

Estimated shipping charges to Jerome, Arizona 86331. (Combine with CD order.)

Please call if you have any questions. We look forward to receiving the information.

This request for an estimate was sent to 12 CD and cassette manufacturers. Their estimates varied by as much as 50%.

Check reputations by asking artists, producers, and engineers.

Have all agreements in writing, including final price quotes and delivery times. Make specific agreements about what errors the firms will be responsible for and under what circumstances.

When you place your order, you will be asked for an advance deposit and then payment in full before your order is shipped. First-time customers will not be given credit, unless they have an impeccable financial statement backed with credit references. When you have used a firm several times, you will be able to establish an account, sometimes with a reduction in prices.

Names and addresses of manufacturers can be found in the *Billboard International Buyers' Guide, Mix Magazine,* and the *Recording Industry Sourcebook.*

TIME

The average delivery date for manufactured product is three to six weeks after you have delivered the appropriate master and packaging materials. The plant will generally wait until covers are printed to begin the rest of the manufacturing process. It is important to contract for an estimated delivery date in your final manufacturing contract before you make a down payment. No manufacturer will guarantee a firm delivery date.

August through November is usually the busiest time because all labels are preparing for the Christmas buying season. Records pressed in August and September can be widely distributed in stores by November; records that sell well are usually pressed again in November to meet heavy December buying demands.

PACKAGING AND SHIPPING

Cassette packages will be shrink-wrapped, unless there are instructions to the contrary. EPs and LPs are shrink-wrapped in the United States; in Europe, they are often packaged in loose cellophane. Forty-fives are packed in paper dust sleeves or in plain cardboard covers.

The manufacturer will box your recordings and prepare them for shipping. You will be asked to select the method (mail, truck, rail, UPS). Labels can save money by having their recordings shipped directly to their distributors. Generally, if the weight of an individual shipment is over 100 pounds, the cheapest method is by truck; under 100 pounds, you will find it cheaper via United Parcel Service or parcel post. Insist that the manufacturer insure the shipment.

It is up to you to verify that your shipment has arrived intact. Count the number of boxes carefully and check some samples. Most plants allow 15 days after receipt of your recordings to complain about defective runs, but the sooner you report damage the better.

ROUNDER RECORDS WAS FOUNDED IN 1970 BY KEN IRWIN, MARIAN Leighton Levy, and Bill Nowlin. They operated the record company and did distribution from their communal apartment and used the profits from selling records at music festivals and concerts, and income from their outside jobs to finance new productions. One of their earliest successes was achieving gold record status with sales of over 500,000 albums for George Thorogood and the Destroyers (1978). Today, Rounder is one of the largest and most respected independent labels in the United States, with a catalog of more than 2000 titles of folk, roots music (blues, reggae, zydeco), and bluegrass. Rounder's aim is twofold: to offer recordings dedicated to the preservation of various traditional and ethnic styles, and to provide a creative outlet for contemporary musicians that continue to keep traditional music alive.

Ken Irwin, Marian Leighton Levy, and Bill Nowlin
Cofounders

When we started we didn't have a dream. We wanted to put out a few good records. We shared a mission to find music we liked and believed in and get it to audiences that wanted to hear it. We did have a goal—to make a record that would be considered a classic record in its genre. When we released the Don Stover album, we thought we had achieved it. Then we put out J.D. Crowe and the New South and it became one of the top bluegrass records of the '80s. It's still a highly influential record and one of the best in its field.

We're still putting out music that is real and not aimed at mass markets, music that will hold up over the years. When people get into roots music, they go back and buy the records that have become classics, and, hopefully, a number of ours will be among them.

—Ken Irwin, cofounder, Rounder Records
www.rounder.com

copyrights

Your recording is the best introduction to your original compositions. Although the emphasis of this book is on making and selling recordings, your original compositions may be your greatest asset.

They can produce more income over time than either performing or recording. They can be recorded by other artists and earn mechanical royalties on each record sold and performance royalties from being played on radio and television. They can earn money by being issued as sheet music. Fortunes have been reaped from songs that became popular and were recorded time and again by numerous artists in various countries.

Protect these assets and establish your rights by learning and using the basics of copyright, performance rights, and publishing.

PROTECTING ORIGINAL COMPOSITIONS

Before you put your recording out for sale, you must establish your rights to protect your compositions from unauthorized use.

The U.S. Copyright Law, effective January 1, 1978, grants all composers specific rights regarding the use of their compositions. These include the right to publish the composition, the right to record and distribute copies, the right to perform the composition in public, the right to make "derivative works," such as different arrangements of the composition, and the right to "display" the musical work, as in a printed lyric sheet or picture disc. These rights are termed "Copyrights" and they belong to composers, whether or not they choose to register them with the U.S. Copyright Office. Rights for compositions created or published after January 1, 1978 automatically belong to the composer for his or her lifetime plus 50 years.

Copyright Registration: Compositions

In order to secure your rights, your compositions must be "fixed in a tangible medium of expression." This means they must be reproduced on paper (musical notation and lyrics together) or as a phonorecord (cassette tape, album, CD, videocassette, etc.). Playing your composition in public does not accomplish this.

▶ GETTING YOUR FORMS FROM THE WEB

Forms PA, SR, and other useful circulars, can be downloaded without charge from the U.S. Copyright office Web site at www.loc.gov/copyright.

The next step is to place the proper copyright notice on these mediums. The notice must include the symbol ©, or the word "Copyright," or the abbreviation "Copr.," the year of first publication, and the name of the owner of the copyright; for example, "© 1999 J. Smith." If the copyright owner is a publishing company, the notice could read, "Copyright 1999 J. Smith Publishing Company."

You do not have to register your compositions with the copyright office to put the copyright notice on your works.

Although amendments to the Copyright Act, passed in 1989, specify that you do not necessarily forfeit your rights and lose royalties if you omit the notice, using it serves to inform people that the composition is original to you and in what year.

To insure protection of your copyrights, you must establish proof of authorship, the identity of each composition, and positive proof of the date of creation.

This is accomplished by registering your compositions with an objective third party. The standard method is to register them with the U.S. Copyright Office in Washington, D.C. by using form PA, Application for Copyright Registration for a Musical Recording. The form includes detailed instructions.

Copyright Form PA asks for the name(s) of the composer(s), and, if the composition is a multiple composition, the name and contribution of each composer (music or lyrics). The form has ample space to indicate collaborations by several people and to state the specific contribution of each. The form asks for the name of the "copyright claimant." If the songs have not been assigned to a publishing company, the copyright claimant is you (and any collaborators).

If you have assigned your songs to a publishing company (your own or someone else's), the copyright claimant is the publishing company. In such cases, the Copyright law requires you to add a brief statement on Form PA in the space titled "Transfer" about how the claimant(s) obtained ownership of the copyright. The statement can be as brief as, "Assignment of copyright by author to (name of publishing company)." You would accompany Form PA with two copies of a filled out "Document Cover Sheet" (obtainable from the Copyright Office) and two copies of a typed letter stating that a transfer was made, signed by the author of the copyrighted material. The Copyright Office will then officially record the transfer. For further information, request Circular 12: "Recordation of Transfers and Other Documents."

Compositions that are composed by more than one person are called joint works. All authors co-own the entire work. The copyright form asks that all the people that created the joint work be identified. Information on how earnings are to be divided is not requested.

You must send whatever you have that fixes your composition in a tangible medium. It is best to send sheet music or a tape (or record, CD, etc.). If your composition depends on multiple rhythms and melodies (like choral pieces or symphonies), you should send a score of the music, which indicates all the separate elements involved.

Sheet music and scores should be done by professionals. To find someone who performs this service, call your local musicians' union, the head of the music department at a nearby college or high school, or a member of the local symphony orchestra. Sheet music, scores, and lead sheets can also be made with computers and appropriate software. Charges are figured on an hourly basis, per page, or per song.

For each song you want to register, send form PA, $20, sheet music and a recording to the Register of Copyrights.

It is preferable to copyright each song individually, however, if you have a lot of songs and not much money it is possible to register an unlimited number of songs in an unpublished collection. Just give the collection a title like "The I.B. Cool Songbook #1," and list the songs in the order they appear on the tape. (You no longer need lead sheets though you may submit them instead of a tape.) The copyright claimant for all the songs in the collection must be the same. As of 1996, if you cowrite the songs, you may only copyright a collection in which all songs are written with the same cowriter. (Previously, you could protect a collection with several of your cowriters as long as you were a writer on each of the songs.) Record the name of each song before playing them onto the tape.

Keep a copy of the tape, the list of songs on it, and the registration certificate in a safe place. It usually takes several weeks to get your certificate back from Washington. Your compositions are protected as soon as the Copyright Office receives them. Send everything by registered mail.

The problem with registering a collection is if someone wants to use your song and does not know who wrote it, they will not be able to find it since it will be in a collection, not listed under its own title. Also, if someone wants to publish your song, you must specify that the registration number is for the collection and you are only letting them publish that specific song.

You do not destroy the integrity of the copyrighted collection by removing a song from it. The remaining songs are still protected.

Although you can choose not to register your songs with the Copyright Office, the Copyright Law does require you to deposit two copies of a published recording with them within three months of the time you first offer it for sale. This is absolutely mandatory. Usually this is done at the same time as registering the copyright for the recording. (See, Copyright Registration: Sound Recordings, below.)

Some composers try to establish proof and time of authorship by sending a copy of their composition to themselves by registered mail and not opening the letter. They believe the postmark on the letter is evidence the composition was original as of that date. Variations include the stamping of lead sheets by notaries public or placing compositions in a safety deposit box. These methods, referred to as poor man's copyright or common-law copyright, are considered very risky by most attorneys.

Copyright Registration: Sound Recordings

Legally speaking, the recording you sell is an entity in itself, apart from the songs contained on it, and you must copyright the recording separately to protect against its illegal duplication. The U.S. Copyright Law grants recording companies much the same rights to their creations as composers. The companies are officially referred to as "authors" and their work "sound recordings." According to the law, when a record company issues a new release, it typically involves two distinct "works:" the "musical work" that has been recorded, and the "sound recording" as a separate work in itself. The material objects that the record company sends out are phonorecords, physical reproductions of both the musical work and the sound recording.

This distinction is particularly important in the resolution of copyright infringement due to illegal sampling. A discussion of issues raised by the ability to sample segments from recordings is found in the chapter, Sampling.

Recording companies secure their rights by printing the correct copyright notice on the labels they affix to their recordings and on the covers. This notice includes the symbol ℗; the year of first publication of the sound recording, and the name of the owner of the copyright. For example—"℗ 1999 J. Smith Records."

You can print this copyright notice without registering your recording with the Copyright Office.

To protect your rights as a recording label, however, you should register your recording with the Register of Copyrights in Washington, D.C. by using form SR, Application for Copyright Registration for a Sound Recording. Circulars 56 and 56a provide additional information. The forms and circulars are free.

The copyright will be secured in the name of the "copyright claimant," or "author," generally the recording label.

Form SR can also be used to copyright songs, if the name of the copyright claimant for all the compositions and the recording are the same. In this case, the correct notice would be "© ℗ 1999 J. Smith Music." Usually, the copyright claimant for the recording is your record company while the copyright claimant for the compositions is the author or publishing company.

To register the copyright on your recording, you must send one or two copies, form SR, and $20 to the Register of Copyrights, within three months of the recording's release. If the work is unpublished, you deposit only one complete phonorecord (recording). If the work is for sale to the public, you must deposit two. Include your cover graphics and any special inserts.

PERFORMANCE RIGHTS ORGANIZATIONS

Since one of the rights granted to songwriters by the U.S. Copyright Act is the right to perform their songs publicly, you must give a user, such as a radio or television station, the right (permission) to do so. The American Society of Composers, Authors and Publishers (ASCAP), Broadcast Music, Inc. (BMI), and SESAC, Inc. are organizations that grant performance rights on behalf of their writer and publisher members and collect fees from users of the compositions. (The Society of Composers, Authors, and Music Publishers of Canada—SOCAN—is the performance rights organization of Canada.) By using one of these organizations, you are technically licensing your performance rights to them. In return, they keep track of who is performing your songs, charge licensing fees, and pay you your share of performance royalties.

Yearly licensing fees are charged to radio and television stations, jukebox operators, concert promoters, and on-line (Internet) providers, such as NetRadio Network. These fees vary according to how many people are reached by a particular medium, and how much profit that medium realizes in a year. For example, ASCAP and BMI charge network television stations far more than network radio stations because they reach wider audiences, and earn greater advertising revenues. Fees and terms for Web site licenses are still evolving.

The licensing fees are distributed among member authors and publishing companies according to how frequently their songs were performed. Each organization has different and

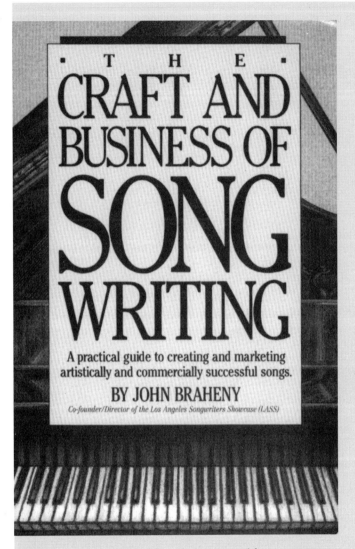

You have to be prepared for whatever good fortune comes your way, and you never know when your time is going to come. Someone who happens on your music and loves it may give it to a DJ who gives it airplay. And if your song happens to get picked up in one of BMI's or ASCAP's samples, you will get more money than you deserve because appearance on that sample leads to the assumption that many more stations are playing your recording.

—John Braheny, author,
The Craft and Business of Songwriting

complicated methods of monitoring ("tracking") television and radio programming to determine what is being performed and how often.

There is no practical way to collect performance royalties or grant permission to users to perform your music publicly without belonging to a performance rights organization. Joining one and placing the name of that organization on your recording gives notice that public users have permission to air your song(s).

Each performing rights society has a different system for monitoring stations. Writers and publishers that have national hits on the radio get the greatest share of the fees collected. (One song could be played as many as 12 times a day for many days running on hundreds of major-format stations throughout the country.) If your record attracts airplay only in your hometown, or even on several major AM or FM stations in your state, you will not receive much income from performance royalties. A song must be a minor national hit before royalties amount to anything substantial. If your song gets radio airplay but is not picked up in a performance rights society survey, you will not receive any performance royalties, but if your songs are picked up in the stations being monitored, the "sampling and projection" system will assume you are being played an equal amount of times in all of that week's unmonitored stations and you may get more than you expect.

You cannot join more than one U.S. performance rights organization in the same year or for the same songs, and you cannot join until you know you will be publishing your songs. (Once you make your recording available for

sale to the public, your songs are considered published.) Both the authors of the songs and the publishing company that administers their copyrights must become members to receive royalties. The exception is BMI. BMI will pay the writer both the writer's and publisher's share of royalties, if there is no publisher involved.

Although you can join ASCAP, BMI, or SESAC after your recording is out, most people choose to do so before, so they can include their affiliation on their recordings' covers and labels. If all the songs are your own or belong to the same publishing company, you can print "All selections from J. Smith Publishing Company, BMI" on the covers. On the recordings' labels, list the affiliation after each song. If some or all of the songs are composed by someone else, or belong to another publishing company, you must print that information on the covers and labels.

ASCAP does not charge a fee to join. Annual dues are $10 for a writer member and $50 for a publisher member. Those people that do not qualify for full writer or publisher membership in ASCAP may join temporarily as associate writer members provided they have had at least one work written and registered with the Copyright Office. There are no annual dues for associate writer members of ASCAP. BMI charges no fees or dues for songwriters and composers, but charges a one-time processing fee of $50 to publishers. SESAC charges no fee to join and no annual dues.

The question of which organization is the most beneficial to join has been widely debated. Each organization's methods of sampling performances and allocating royalties are very different, which makes accurate comparisons difficult. Join the organization that is responsive to your questions and makes you feel comfortable.

SONG EXPLOITATION

In the music industry, the term exploitation refers to the process of making money from original compositions. When other musicians record your compositions you are entitled to mechanical royalties on every recording sold. Sales of sheet music earn you print royalties. Every public performance of your composition entitles you to performance royalties. Your talent as a composer can be sold to movie and television companies and advertising agencies. Music that is recorded for movies, videos, and commercials also earns synchronization (synch) royalties for you.

Once a song is made available for public sale in the form of sheet music, album, cassette, CD, or software, it is legally considered published. The publisher of a song is the person or business entity responsible for making it available for public sale. Therefore, when you offer your recording for sale to the public, you are publishing your songs, whether or not you have formed an actual publishing company or have assigned your songs to a publishing company. You do not have to form a publishing company to publish the songs on a recording you are making or selling.

Once compositions have been published, you have exercised some of your copyrights. Making a recording means that you have exercised the right to reproduce your work. Anyone else who wants to use your composition is now required by the U.S. Copyright Act to give you notice and pay for that use.

Publishing Companies

Businesses that exploit compositions are known as publishing companies. They license songs to recording labels, film producers, musicians, etc. in the medium the songs will be used in (e.g., film, recordings, videos, sheet music). Songs that are well-exploited can earn considerably more in royalties for you than your recordings.

It can be very difficult to sell your songs to producers and established artists, even if your recording proves to be very popular. This is because established publishers that have long-standing relationships with them will be competing with you to sell songs by the "name" and talented new composers in their catalogs. The competition among publishers for the attention of artists and producers makes it difficult for songwriters without long-established publishing companies to get a foot in the door.

Persuading a publishing company to represent your compositions can be more difficult than getting signed to a major label. Even if you are signed, getting them to push your songs over those of more established writers will be difficult.

If a publishing company does approach you, check them out the same way that you would a recording label. Ask for references and a list of the artists that have recorded their writers' songs. An attorney experienced with publishing can negotiate a contract that will protect your rights and provide you with some reversion rights to your songs if the publishing company does not produce results within a stated period of time. Never try to take care of this yourself.

Some independent record labels ask artists to assign some or all of their publishing rights

PHOTO BY ART ROGERS/PT. REYES

treasures left behind:
remembering Kate Wolf

Kathy Mattea ♣ Dave Alvin ♣ Nanci Griffith
John Gorka ♣ Lucinda Williams ♣ Peter Rowan
Cris Williamson & Tret Fure
U. Utah Phillips ♣ Rosalie Sorrels
Greg Brown & Ferron
Nina Gerber ♣ Eric Bogle
Emmylou Harris
Terry Garthwaite

By setting up her own publishing company, Another Sundown Music, Kate Wolf retained the rights to her songs, something she felt very strongly about. When she died of leukemia in 1986, her family was able to keep her music and memory alive by issuing songbooks and videos, licensing her songs to others, and holding an annual festival in Sebastopol, California.

In 1998, Nina Gerber, Kate's good friend and accompanist, paid tribute to her by producing *Treasures Left Behind,* a compilation of some of Kate's songs. Fourteen independent and major label artists, contributed their talents. Emmylou Harris was nominated for a 1999 Grammy for her performance of "Love Still Remains." A portion of the proceeds from the album will be donated to the Seva Foundation.

in their recording contracts. The pros and cons of this are discussed in the chapter, Recording Contracts.

Forming Your Own Publishing Company

Many independents form their own publishing companies under whose name copyrights are filed and performance royalties collected. You can do these tasks yourself. There is no reason to assign your songs to someone else's publishing company and pay them a portion of your earnings until such time as they can effectively exploit your songs.

To form your own publishing company, you must first devise a name that has never been used by another publishing company. This name will be used to conduct all official business. To find out whether a name is original, write or call ASCAP, BMI, or SESAC and ask them to research it for you. You must give them three names at a time in order of preference. (They will also research publishing names in use in the other societies and in other countries.) You may be surprised at how many names you think are unique have already been used. You can use your own name (John Smith Publisher) so long as that name does not conflict with a major composer or performer. For example, you could not use the name "Bob Dylan Publisher" even if that is your given name. Once you select an original name, ask the performance rights society you select to reserve it (for up to six months) until you join. There is no charge for having them research a name.

Use this name every time you copyright a song, make a record, or put out sheet music.

Display it on your recording's cover and label, lyric sheet inserts, and sheet music. This informs others you have officially established your rights as composer and publisher and have complied with the copyright law and makes it easy for those interested in your songs to contact you.

Cocomposers must make written agreements as to how publishing earnings are to be shared. The agreement must show how their publishing company(ies) will control the licensing of the work, the collection of any earnings, the pursuit of infringement, and accounting. Although cocomposers can each make an agreement with a separate publishing company for their portion of the composition, administration of mechanical licenses can become extremely complicated when the licensor has to deal with multiple publishers. You should seek the advice of a lawyer in making these agreements. Oral agreements have resulted in some very expensive lawsuits.

There is no penalty if you elect not to form a publishing company when you release your recording, but if your songs start to get airplay you will have to list your publishing company's name on your recording and affiliate yourself with a performance rights organization.

THE MAJOR REASONS INDEPENDENTS FORM THEIR OWN PUBLISHING COMPANIES ◄ - - -

Airplay is expected; and along with it, performance royalties. Since performance royalties are paid to the composer and the publisher, having a publishing company guarantees the composer receives all the income to which he or she is entitled. You will not be able to collect this income if you do not affiliate your publishing company with a performance rights organization.

It adds a layer of professionalism when a more established publishing company expresses interest in your compositions and it provides you (and your lawyer) with some negotiating leverage to establish a copublishing deal that may decrease the percentage of publishing royalties the new publisher is willing to accept.

It allows the writer to control negotiations with TV and film producers, and others that may demand all or part of the publishing royalties to use the song in a production. A major publishing company will rarely, if ever, make that sacrifice. When you control the publishing you decide whether a flat fee will warrant the loss of publishing royalties.

If you are also the recording artist and the record company, you can negotiate a "Master Use" license for the use of your recording by a film or television producer. This license grants them permission to use the original master of your recording for agreed upon fees and royalties.

PHOTO BY HOWARD BRAINEN

Clifton Chenier took the older Creole music he heard as a child, mixed it with contemporary black music of his era, and in the process helped popularize Zydeco.

When you play in Texas you can't jive...you can't lay back or pretend...you got to just keep on puttin' out that hard music, one song after another.... What I did was to put a little rock and roll into that Zydeco to mix it up a bit. You see people been playing Zydeco for a long time–old style– like French music. But I was the first to put the pep into it....

–Clifton Chenier, Arhoolie Records, El Cerrito, California

Mechanical Licenses

Once you have placed your recording for sale, other artists have the right to record that song and sell it as long as they file a compulsory mechanical license with the copyright office and as long as they do not change the melody

or character of the song. Generally, it is preferred that the publishing company issue a mechanical license directly to the artist. This license states the artist will pay your publishing company mechanical royalties for the right to record your song and will provide a regular accounting of all records sold and returned.

Effective January 1, 1998, the statutory rate set by the U.S. Copyright Act for the use of songs by others on a record is 7.1 cents per song up to five minutes or 1.35 cents per minute, whichever amount is larger, per record sold. For example, if an artist records six of your songs, each of which is three minutes long, the amount of mechanical royalties owed is 42.6 cents per record sold. If the artist records two songs, each nine minutes long, the amount of mechanical royalties owed would be 24.3 cents per record sold.

Effective January 1, 2000, the statutory rate will be 7.55 cents per song or 1.45 cents per minute, whichever amount is larger, per record sold. Effective January 1, 2002, the rate will be 8.0 cents per song or 1.55 cents per minute. Effective January 1, 2004, the rate will be 8.5 cents per song or 1.65 cents per minute. Effective January 1, 2006, the rate will be 9.1 cents per song or 1.75 cents per minute.

A lower rate can be negotiated as long as the songwriter and publishing company agree. Mechanical royalties are divided equally between the publishing company and the songwriter(s).

When another artist records your song with the intent of selling it to the public, that artist's recording label must request a mechanical license from you or your publishing company. On-line businesses that transmit digital copies of individual songs to buyers for downloading to computer hard disks or CD-Rs must also file mechanical licenses. Royalties are payable for each downloaded copy.

Any artist that complies with the legal requirement of filing a mechanical license with you can record your song. You cannot refuse them even if you do not like them or their style of music.

If you have never published a particular song you wrote (released it for sale to the public), you can refuse another artist or group the right to record it for the first time, since that is one of the rights granted to songwriters by the Copyright Law. In some cases, however, it may be advantageous to give up that right, particularly if a famous artist wants to record your song. But make sure that you go through all the steps outlined in this chapter for protecting and exploiting your songs. Consult an attorney before making any contractual agreements.

If your songs begin to be recorded by many artists, dealing with requests for mechanical licenses and keeping track of the number of records sold will become complicated and time consuming. Therefore, many publishing companies use the services of the Harry Fox Agency in New York City or worldwide administration companies such as Bug Music in Los Angeles or Copyright Management Inc. in Nashville. Some major publishing companies have departments that perform administration services for a percentage of the income they collect without actual ownership of the copyright. Publishing companies authorize these companies to issue mechanical licenses to would-be recorders of their songs and collect the mechanical royalties.

The Harry Fox Agency deducts a percentage for its services. Many artists obtain mechanical licenses through this agency, which also handles their reporting and payment obligations under the Copyright Act.

Some recording labels simplify the payment of mechanical royalties by calculating the statutory amount owed on the quantity of recordings manufactured rather than sold, especially when there are less than 3000 units and only a few songs that have not been written by the recording's performer.

USING OTHER COMPOSERS' SONGS

If some or all of the songs on your record have been written by other people you will have to make sure you do not infringe upon their rights.

Once a song has been recorded and distributed, you have a right to record that song and to make your own arrangement of it, provided you obtain a mechanical license from the writer's publishing company. The license states that you will pay the statutory rate or a negotiated fee for the use of the song based on records made and distributed, you will not change the melody or words, and you will make a regular accounting of all records sold and returned. You may want to specify, however, that the obligation to pay is based on records sold, rather than just distributed.

If you do want to make changes, you must ask permission from the publisher who may or may not grant it to you, since that would make it a "derivative work." If you want to write lyrics to previously recorded music or write music to previously published poetry or some other literary work, you are making a "derivative work" and must also request permission from the publisher, which can refuse.

If the publisher grants permission, you should use Form PA to copyright the new portions of the work. Space 6 on the form asks you to fill out information regarding the new additions. The U.S. Copyright Office's Circular 14, "Copyright Registration for Derivative Works" provides complete instructions.

You must also file a mechanical license with the publisher of preexisting music if you add portions of it (sampling) to your record.

If you do not know the address of the publisher of a song you want to use, contact the record company or the performance rights organization listed on the recording.

You must obtain the permission of the songwriter to record a song for the first time. That right can be granted through a contract that specifies the details of your agreement. This agreement should always be written by an attorney who is knowledgeable about song publishing.

SAMPLING

Technically, sampling is the collecting of any aural event in any format for further incorporation into a composition. But it is commonly considered to be the digital acquisition of an aural event—usually of short duration—that will be manipulated before final use.

When sounds are taken from existing recordings and used as part of a new recording, the user may be guilty of copyright infringement, privacy invasion, or unfair competition, if mechanical licenses have not been filed with the

publishers of the original recordings.

A discussion of legal issues that arise from sampling will be found in the chapter, Sampling.

USING SONGS IN THE PUBLIC DOMAIN

Songs and lyrics whose copyrights have expired fall into the "public domain." You are free to use song lyrics, poems, and instrumental music in the public domain in any way you choose. Melodies and lyrics written before 1978 are protected for a total of 75 years from the end of the year the copyright was first secured. From January 1, 1978, music is protected for 50 years after the death of the last surviving writer.

Some works in the public domain, however, have new arrangements, lyrics or melodies that are copyrighted. To be sure that you are using only the original melody or lyrics and not copyrighted material, request a clearance check from the U.S. Copyright Office. It will charge a fee of $20 per hour. You have to supply the original title and either a recording or lead sheet of the version you want to use. Circular 22, "How to Investigate the Copyright Status of a Work" provides more complete information.

The Copyright Office will check your version against any derivative copyrights that have been issued for that title. If you compose lyrics to music in the public domain, or vice versa, you should register your copyright for that portion of the song original to you.

COPYRIGHT INFRINGEMENT

When any of your copyrights are violated, copyright infringement (a federal crime) has occurred and the people that infringed are subject to civil and criminal penalties. Common infringements include unlicensed recordings of compositions; making and selling unauthorized duplications of published recordings (counterfeit or pirate recording); selling recordings made from the illegal copying of a recording or concert (bootlegging); and downloading songs or portions of songs off Internet Web sites and using them on recordings without paying mechanical license fees.

If you find that someone has recorded your song or used a portion of it without filing a mechanical license, your first step should be to write them a certified letter stating that you are the legal owner of that work and you need to issue them a mechanical license so that you can get paid for its use. If you receive no reply (or an unsatisfactory one), contact a lawyer who will send another request for a mechanical license and may threaten to sue.

In order for you to sue for infringement, your work must be registered with the Copyright Office so you can establish proof of authorship and song identity. Infringement, other than pirating or bootlegging, can be difficult and expensive to substantiate because you must demonstrate in court that the infringing song is substantially similar to yours and the infringer had access to your song. Infringement suits are very expensive and time consuming, and may not be worth pursuing unless substantial sums of money are likely to be recovered. Your lawyer can advise you about your options and what they are likely to cost. If infringement occurs after the copyright registration date, you are eligible to receive statutory damages, customarily ranging

from $200 to $100,000 and recover legal fees, if you can prove infringement.

Bootlegging, counterfeiting, and pirate recording are major industry problems. The Recording Industry Association of America (RIAA) estimates that over one billion dollars worth of illegally made recordings are distributed annually to domestic and overseas markets. Federal antibootlegging statutes and some spectacular lawsuits may help curb this problem.

PHOTO BY K. WILCOX

Fugazi–Ian MacKaye, Brendan Canty, Joe Lally, and Guy Picciotto–include their song lyrics on their CD booklets. The band maintains a policy of affordable access to their work through low record and ticket prices and all concerts are for all ages. Their label, Dischord Records, has a policy of selling CDs for $10 or less, postpaid, to their U.S. mail-order customers.

IN 1986, SILVER WAVE RELEASED ITS FIRST RECORDING, *AQUA TOUCH*, BY jazz guitarist Danny Heines. At that time, founder James Marienthal described the label's genre as new age. But the success of *Natives* in 1990, the first collaboration between pianist Peter Kater and flautist R. Carlos Nakai, gradually changed the company's direction to focus on Native American music. Since then, Kater and Nakai have collaborated on many albums, the most successful being *Migration*, which has sold more than 200,000 recordings. Kater also composed, arranged, and performed the original music for *How the West Was Lost*, a 13-hour television miniseries that explores the Native American experience during the mid to late 1800s.

Even though the Kater/Nakai collaboration happened because of our interest in new age music, popular interest was generated because they performed wonderful Native American music. My interest in this genre accelerated when Joanne Shenandoah sang on How the West Was Lost. *Then Peter Kater recorded her haunting and powerful voice on the album* Life Blood. *Her second Silver Wave album* Matriarch: Iroquois Women's Songs *was the AFIM's 1997 Indie Award Winner for best Native American recording. We've also recorded Mary Youngblood (Chugach Aleut/Seminole); the talented poet and lyricist Joy Harjo (Muscogee) who reads her lyrics accompanied by tribal-jazz-reggae music; and flautist Robert Mirabal (Taos Pueblo).*

The biggest challenge facing our label today? Being able to have good music be heard and recognized with the glut of music out there. Fortunately our niche isn't that crowded yet, but we have to maintain our place by finding the best Native American music out there. You can never rest on your laurels and kick back or someone else will take your place.

—James Marienthal
www.silverwave.com

James Marienthal °
Founder

sampling

by Gregory T. Victoroff, Esq.

at its best, sampling benefits society by creating valuable new contributions to modern music literature. At its worst, sampling is vandalism and stealing; chopping up and ripping off songs and recordings by other artists without permission or payment and fraudulently passing off the joint work as the work of a single artist, without giving credit to the sampled work or the unwilling collaborators. The practice is not new. In the 19th century, Rachmaninoff, Brahams, and Liszt "borrowed" material from contemporary Niccolo Paganini's *Caprice* for use in their own compositions.

With the advent of digital technology, MIDI, off-the-shelf samplers, electronic tone generators, and computers, sampling sounds and manipulating them has become relatively easy. As a result, sampling has opened a Pandora's box of old and new sound combinations, and with that, the necessity for new interpretations of issues like copyright infringement, privacy rights, and unfair competition.

COPYRIGHT INFRINGEMENT

One of the many rights included in copyright is the right to copy a copyrighted work. Unauthorized sampling violates this right by copying a portion of a copyrighted work for a new recording.

The music publisher, by itself or together with the songwriter, usually owns the copyright in the song. The recording company usually owns the copyright in the sound recording. These copyright owners are most directly affected by sampling and have the right to sue unauthorized samplers in federal court for copyright infringement. (See also the chapter, Copyrights.)

BREACHES OF CONTRACT
Warranties

Copyright infringement from illegal sampling may also breach warranty provisions in recording contracts. Provisions called "Warranties," "Representations" and "Indemnifications" are almost always found in contracts between musicians and record companies; musicians and producers; producers and record companies; music publishers and record companies; songwriters and music publishers; record companies and distributors; and between distributors and record stores. According to these clauses, the person who provides the product (e.g., the songs, recordings, publishing rights, records, tapes, CDs) promises the person buying or licensing the product (the record company or record store) that the recordings do not infringe anyone's copyrights or other rights.

If a lawsuit for illegal sampling is filed, it could result in lawsuits for "breach of warranty" between each person that sells the illegally sampled product. Claims apply from person to person along the record-making chain, creating a duty of indemnification for each person along the chain. Final legal responsibility may lie with the recording artist. The indemnification rights that exist between each person or company in the process trigger one another like a chain reaction. This can result in hundreds of thousands of dollars in liability to the artist.

Indemnification provisions require the record distributor to pay the record store's damages and attorneys' fees, the record company is required to pay the distributor's fees and damages, the producer pays the record company's fees and damages and the artist may be technically liable for everyone's attorneys' fees and damages.

Unsatisfactory Masters

Another potential problem for musicians that sample is most recording contracts give the record company the right to reject masters that are unsatisfactory. Masters that infringe copyrights of other sound recordings or musical compositions can be so rejected.

Artists are required to obtain copyright licenses ("clearances") from the owners of sampled material or deliver substitute masters, which do not contain samples, to satisfy contract obligations to record companies.

Failure to comply with a record company's master delivery requirements could result in the artist having to repay recording fund advances and possibly defending legal claims for breach of contract.

FAIR USE DEFENSE

The defense of fair use permits reasonable unauthorized copying from a copyrighted work, when the copying does not substantially impair present or potential value of the original work, and in some way advances the public benefit.

One rationale for the so-called fair use defense to copyright infringement is that only a small portion of the copyright work is copied. For many years there was a popular myth among musicians and producers that up to eight bars of a song was fair use and could be copied without constituting copyright infringement. This is not true. The rules controlling which uses are fair uses, and not copyright infringement, are not clear or simple. The fair use standard for sound recordings is, however, generally stricter than for fair uses of musical compositions.

The reason for this difference is that U.S. Copyright law only protects the expression of ideas, not the idea itself. Since there are a limited number of musical notes, copyright law treats single notes like ideas, and does not protect them. For this reason, it is safe to say that borrowing one note from a song will usually be a fair use of the copyright in the song, and not an actionable infringement. Borrowing more than one note, however, could be trouble. Lawsuits have involved copying as few as four notes from "I Love New York" and three words from "I Got Rhythm."

By selecting and arranging several notes in a particular sequence, composers create copyrightable musical compositions, or songs. Songs are the expression of the composer's creativity and are protected by copyright.

But different fair use standards apply to sound recordings. Since there is virtually an unlimited number of sounds that can be recorded, sound recordings are, by definition, comprised of pure, copyrightable expression.

For musicians, engineers and producers, the practical effect of the two different fair use standards is that sampling a small portion of a musical composition may sometimes be fair use because copying a small portion may borrow uncopyrightable single notes like uncopyrightable ideas. But sampling even a fraction of a second of a sound recording is copying of pure, copyrightable expression and is more likely to be an unfair use, constituting copyright infringement.

One way some producers and engineers that sample attempt to reduce the chances of a successful copyright infringement lawsuit is by electronically processing ("camouflaging") portions of the sampled sounds beyond the point of their being easily recognizable. Filtering, synthesizing, or distorting recorded sounds can help conceal the sampled material while still retaining the essence of an instrumental lick or vocal phrase embodied in a few seconds of sound. Adding newly created sounds to the underlying sampling further dilutes the material. This is an attempt to change the sampled materials so that even though material was illegally copied, there is no substantial similarity, thus avoiding a suit for copyright infringement.

UNFAIR COMPETITION

State and federal unfair competition laws apply when the record buying public is misled as to the source or true origin of recordings that contain sampled material.

The Lanham Act is a federal law that punishes deceptive trade practices that mislead consumers about what they are buying or who made the product.

If a customer in a record store is confused by hearing a recording containing sampled vocal tracks of James Brown, or sampled guitar licks by Eddie Van Halen, and mistakenly buys the record only to discover that he or she has bought a recording by a different artist, the customer has been deceived by the sampling. Such confusion and deception is a form of unfair competition, which can give rise to legal claims for Lanham Act violations that can be brought in federal court, or unfair competition claims that may be brought in state court. All of the previous warnings about the costs of litigation apply here as well.

RIGHTS OF PRIVACY VIOLATIONS

When sampled material incorporates a person's voice, statutory, and common-law rights of privacy ("rights of publicity") may be violated. In California, Civil Code section 3344 establishes civil liability for the unauthorized commercial use of any living person's voice. Such a use would include sampling.

Although current federal moral rights legislation does not protect sound recordings or voices, such protection may be available in the near future. Meanwhile, many state laws make unauthorized sampling of voices a violation of state right-of-publicity laws. Further, if the sampled voice was originally recorded without the vocalist's permission, sampling such an unauthorized recording may violate other state privacy laws as well.

FEDERAL ANTIBOOTLEGGING STATUTES

Effective December 8, 1994 the adoption of the Uruguay Round Agreements Act by the U.S. Congress amended U.S. law by adding both civil and criminal penalties for the unauthorized recording or videotaping of live musical performances.

Any person who recorded or sampled in the past, or records or samples in the future, any part of any live musical performance without the performer's consent, can now be sued under the

new federal law for the same statutory damages, actual damages and attorneys' fees that are available in a traditional copyright infringement suit.

Previously, unauthorized recording of live performances was prohibited only under certain state laws.

Federal copyright law (17 U.S.C. §1101 et seq.) can now be used to prosecute so-called bootleggers that secretly record or sample live musical performances, or copy such illegal recordings by including sampled portions in new recordings. This strict new law also prohibits selling or even transporting bootlegged recordings.

Remarkably, the law is retroactive, protecting even pre–1994 recordings if they are currently being sold or distributed, and has no statute of limitations, so that arguably suit can be brought against bootleggers and sellers of bootlegged recordings 10, 20, even 100 years after the unauthorized recording was made, if the unauthorized recordings are sold or distributed after the effective date of the Act. Unlike copyrights, which usually only last for the life of the author plus 50 years, the new federal musical performance rights are perpetual, lasting forever. Moreover, the defense of fair use may not apply to such unauthorized recordings because the fair use defense in section 107 of the Copyright Act was not incorporated into the statute.

Of even greater concern are newly enacted criminal penalties (18 U.S.C. §2319A) of forfeiture, seizure, destruction, and up to ten years imprisonment for knowingly, for profit, making or distributing copies of illegally recorded performances, transmitting an illegally recorded performance, or distributing, selling, renting, or even transporting illegally recorded performances, even if the performance occurred outside the United States!

The serious implications of this new law for outlaw samplers are obvious. Sampling any part of a live performance, or any part of an unauthorized recording of a live musical performance triggers a minefield of federal civil and criminal penalties. Great care should be taken to avoid using such bootlegged recordings in any way.

LANDMARK LAWSUITS

In one of the most publicized sampling cases, the publisher of songwriter Gilbert O'Sullivan's song "Alone Again (Naturally)" successfully sued rap artist Biz Markie, Warner Brothers Records, and others for sampling three words and a small portion of music from O'Sullivan's song without permission for Markie's rap tune "Alone Again."

A lawsuit involving the unauthorized use of drumbeats sought strict enforcement of copyright laws against sampling. Tuff City Records sued Sony Music and Def Jam Records claiming that two singles by rap artist L. L. Cool J ("Around the Way Girl" and "Six Minutes of Pleasure") contained drum track samples from "Impeach the Presidents," a 1973 song by the Honeydrippers and that another Def Jam Record, "Give the People" included vocal samples from the same Honeydrippers song.

The case is important because the common practice of sampling drumbeats is often overlooked as a minor use, too insignificant to bother clearing. This lawsuit reinforces the rule that any sampling of a sound recording may lead to a lawsuit for copyright infringement.

A lawsuit testing the limits of the fair use defense was brought by the Ireland-based rock group U2. The band, its recording company, Island Records, and music publisher Warner–Chappell Music sued the group Negativland for sampling a part of the U2 song, "I Still Haven't Found What I'm Looking For" without the group's permission. While attorneys for U2 claimed that the sampling was consumer fraud, Negativland maintained that the use was parody, satire, and cultural criticism, and was therefore protected under the fair use doctrine. The case was settled out of court. Negativland agreed to recall the single and return copies to Island Records for destruction.

Jarvis v. A&M Records was a lawsuit over the taking of eight words ("Ooh ooh ooh ooh…move…free your body") and a keyboard line. The sampling party argued that the amount of material taken was too insignificant to constitute copyright infringement. The federal district court in New Jersey disagreed and refused to dismiss the suit, ruling that even similarity of fragmented portions of the song could constitute infringement if the portions taken were qualitatively important.

PENALTIES

Attorneys are always expensive. Entertainment attorneys usually charge $100 to $400 per hour. Those that are experienced in federal court copyright litigation charge even more. Court costs and one side's attorneys' fees in a copyright trial average about $150,000. If you lose the trial you will have to pay the judgment against you, which could be as high as $100,000 for a single willful infringement (higher if there are substantial profits involved). An appeal of a judgment against you involves still more attorneys' fees and sometimes requires the posting of a bond.

In some cases a copyright infringer may have to pay the winning party's attorneys' fees. Copyright law also authorizes injunctions against the sale of CDs, tapes, and records containing illegally sampled material, seizure and destruction of infringing matter, and other criminal penalties.

In short, defending a copyright infringement lawsuit is a substantial expense and a risky proposition, exposing you to the possibility of hundreds of thousands of dollars in legal fees and costs.

Even if your particular sampling does not constitute copyright infringement, and is a fair use, it must still avoid violation of state and federal unfair competition laws.

COPYRIGHT CLEARANCES

Obtaining advance "permission," "copyright licenses" or "clearances" from owners of both the musical composition and the sound recording you want to sample is the best way to avoid the problems and expenses that can result from illegal sampling.

Many factors affect whether and when musicians should request and pay for clearances for samples. Although copyright laws and general music industry practices do not give rise to a lawsuit in every sampling situation, the enormous expenses of any sampling dispute should be avoided whenever possible.

In many cases, it is wise to clear samples early in the recording process even if, eventually, they are not used, because when the record is finished

and the sample must be cleared, the artist will have little leverage in negotiating clearance fees.

In some cities, special music clearance firms routinely request, negotiate, prepare, and process clearances for sampled materials for a fee. They know reasonable rates for clearances and will prepare valid copyright licenses for less cost to the requesting party than will most music attorneys.

Clearance Costs: Royalties

The cost of clearances is a major consideration in deciding whether to sample. Generally, record companies will not pay an artist more than the full statutory mechanical license fee for permission to sell recordings of the artist's composition. The current statutory rate is 7.1 cents per unit, for up to five minutes of a recording. However, most record companies and others typically negotiate mechanical license fees of only 50% to 75% of the statutory rate to record an entire composition. Out of that mechanical license fee, the sampling artist must pay the owners of any sampled material. If the clearance fees for the sampled material are too high, none of the mechanical license fee will be left for the sampling artist, and the sampled cut may end up costing the artist more than is earned by the entire composition.

Sampling royalty rates for musical compositions can range from 10% to 25% of the statutory rate. Sampling royalty rates for sound recordings range from .5 cent to 3 cents per unit sold.

Clearance costs double or triple when more than one sampled track is included in a recording. Imagine, for example, a composition containing Phil Collins' snare drum sound, Jimi Hendrix's guitar sound, Phil Lesh's bass, and Little Richard's voice. In this case, combined sampling clearance fees would make the multitrack recording impossibly expensive.

Sampling clearance practices vary widely throughout the music industry. Fees are affected by both the quantity of material being sampled (a second or less is a "minor use," five seconds is a "major use") and the quality of the sampled material (i.e., a highly recognizable lyric sung by a famous artist would be more expensive than an anonymous bass drum track). Certain artists demand exorbitant fees to discourage sampling. On the other hand, some music publishers offer compositions in their catalogs and actively encourage sampling. Prices are affected by the popularity and prestige of the sampling artist and the uniqueness and value of the sampled sounds.

Clearance Costs: Buyouts and Co-Ownership

A percentage of the mechanical license fee (royalty) is one type of clearance fee. Another, is a one-time flat-fee payment (buyout) for the use of sampled material. Buyout fees range from $250 to $10,000, depending on the demands of the copyright owners. Up to $50,000 may be charged for a major use of a famous artist's performance or song. An upper limit on the number of units embodying the sampled material that may be sold may be imposed by some licensors, requiring additional payment at a higher royalty rate or an entirely new license if the maximum is exceeded.

More frequently, music publishers and record companies demand to be co-owners of the new composition as a condition of granting permission

to sample. The option of assigning a share of the publishing (i.e., the copyright) in the song containing the sampled material to a publisher or record company may be helpful to the sampling artist, particularly when a buyout of all rights is not possible. Assigning a portion of the copyright in lieu of a cash advance may be less of a financial burden on an artist, enabling a song to be released where the cost or unavailability of a license would otherwise preclude the record from being distributed legally. If you license the sample for a percentage of the statutory rate, and you later want to license your song with the sample in it for a film, the film producer must obtain separate permission from the publisher who has granted the license. That publisher must always be consulted in new licensing situations. On the other hand, if you negotiate a buyout, you are free from any continuing obligation to the publisher. Similarly, if you negotiate income participation, which is to sell a percentage of your song in return for permission to sample, the publisher becomes a part owner of your song, and may or may not have approval rights in future licensing of the new work depending on the administration terms in the sampling license. Percentage of income participation ranges from 5% for a minimal use within the song to as much as 75% if the sample has been utilized throughout the song and is an integral part of the work.

SOUNDTRACK SAMPLING

Occasionally, artists sample things other than music, such as audio bytes from feature films, television shows, or news footage. In these cases, permission must be obtained from the owner of the footage. Fees range from $1000 to $8000 per minute for buyouts. Sometimes permission is granted for free, or for the Screen Actors Guild minimum scale payment of approximately $600. Private licensing agents such as CMG in Indianapolis, Indiana may charge far more for permission to sample the voice of someone of the caliber of Elvis or Marilyn Monroe. If a film or television program is used, payments may also be due to the writers' and directors' guilds or to the American Federation of Musicians.

CONCLUSION

Throughout history, every new development in music has been greeted with suspicion by the music establishment of the day. Polyphony (playing harmonies) was considered demonic in medieval times, and was punishable by burning at the stake. As modern musicians explore innovative chord progressions, syncopated rhythms, and new electronic instruments, we all learn more about the musical landscape around us. Only time will tell whether samplers will be viewed as musical innovators or plagiarists.

SAMPLE USE AGREEMENTS

The Master Sample Use License Agreement and Mechanical License are short-form examples of licenses to incorporate or sample portions of a recording of a musical composition. Permission to sample the musical composition is granted by the music publisher(s) in the Mechanical License; permission to sample the recording of the musical composition is granted by the record company in the Master Sample Use License Agreement.

Fees for using the master and the musical composition are expressed as a one-time flat fee or buyout, and perpetual, worldwide rights are granted. As discussed above, such extensive rights may not always be granted. Limits on the term, territory or number of units that may be sold, co-ownership and coadministration of the recording and co-ownership of the musical composition embodying the sampled material, or statutory compulsory license fees on every copy sold, may be required by certain record companies or music publishers.

Master Sample Use License Agreement

In consideration of either (the sum of $_____ which covers _____% of the copyright) or (granting _____% of the copyright and publishing right [and coadministration rights]) for the rights and license herein granted thereto, _____ (Record Company), hereinafter referred to as "Licensor," hereby grants to _____ (sampling Artist and/or recording company), hereinafter referred to as "Licensee," the nonexclusive, limited right, license, privilege and authority, but not the obligation, to use a portion of the Master Recording, defined below (hereinafter referred to as the "Master"), as embodied in the tape approved by Licensor, with no greater usage of the Master than is contained in the approved tape (the "Usage"), in the manufacture, distribution, and sale of any phonorecord (as that term is defined in Section 101 of the Copyright Act) entitled " _____ " ("Album"), performed by _____ ("Artist") embodying the recording _____ ("Master") as performed by _____ "Sample Artist"), and produced by _____ ("Producer"). Licensor additionally grants to Licensee the right to exploit, advertise, publicize, and promote such Master, as embodied in the phonorecord, in all media, markets, and formats now known or hereafter devised.

1. The term of this agreement ("Term") will begin on the date hereof and shall continue in perpetuity.

2. The territory covered by this agreement is _____ .

3. It is expressly understood and agreed that any compensation to be paid herein to Licensor is wholly contingent upon the embodiment of the Master within the phonorecord and that nothing herein shall obligate or require Licensee to commit to such usage. However, such compensation shall in no way be reduced by a lesser use of the Recording than the Usage provided for herein.

4. Licensor warrants only that it has the legal right to grant the aforesaid master recording use rights subject to the terms, conditions, limitations, restrictions, and reservations herein contained, and that this license is given and accepted without any other warranty or recourse. In the event said warranty is breached, Licensor's total liability shall not exceed the lesser of the actual damages incurred by Licensee or the total consideration paid hereunder to Licensor.

5. Licensor reserves unto itself all rights and uses of every kind and nature whatsoever in and to the Master other than the limited rights specifically licensed hereunder, including the sole right to exercise and to authorize others to exercise such rights at any and all times and places without limitation.

6. This license is binding upon and shall inure to the benefit of the respective successors and assigns of the parties hereto.

7. This contract is entered into in the State of California and its validity, construction, interpretation, and legal effect shall be governed by the laws of the State of California applicable to contracts entered into and performed entirely therein.

8. This agreement contains the entire understanding of the parties relating to the subject matter herein contained.

IN WITNESS WHEREOF, the parties have caused the foregoing to be executed as of this
_____ day of _____, 199 _____ .

AGREED TO AND ACCEPTED:

_____   _____
LICENSOR (COMPANY NAME)   LICENSEE (COMPANY NAME)

_____   _____
BY (SIGNATURE)   BY (SIGNATURE)

_____   _____
NAME AND TITLE (AN AUTHORIZED SIGNATORY)   NAME AND TITLE (AN AUTHORIZED SIGNATORY)

_____   _____
FEDERAL I.D. / SS#   FEDERAL I.D. / SS#

Mechanical License

In consideration of the sum of $_____ which covers _____% of the copyright and full payment for the rights and license herein granted thereto, _____ ("Licensor") hereby grants to _____ ("Licensee") the nonexclusive right, license, privilege, and authority to use, in whole or in part, the copyrighted musical composition known as_____written by _____ and _____ (hereinafter referred to as the "Composition"):

1. In the recording, making, and distribution of phonorecords (as that term is defined in Section 101 of the Copyright Act) to be made and distributed throughout the world in accordance with the provisions of Section 115 of the Copyright Act of the United States of America of October 19, 1976, as amended (the "Act"), except it is agreed that: (1) Licensee need not serve or file the notices required under the Act; (2) consideration for such license shall be in the form of a one-time flat-fee buyout; (3) Licensee shall have the unlimited right to utilize the Composition, or any portion thereof, as embodied in the phonorecord, in any and all media now known or hereafter devised for the purpose of promoting the sale of the phonorecord which is the subject of this agreement; and (4) this license shall be worldwide.

2. This license permits the use of the Composition or any portion thereof, in the particular recordings made in connection with the sound recording _____ ("Album") by _____ ("Artist"), and permits the use of such recording in any phonorecord in which the recording may be embodied in whatever form now known or hereafter devised. This license includes the privilege of making a musical arrangement of the Composition to the extent necessary to conform it to the style or manner of interpretation of the performance involved.

3. Licensor warrants and represents that it has the right to enter into this agreement and to grant to Licensee all of the rights granted herein, and that the exercise by Licensee of any and all of the rights granted to Licensee in this agreement will not violate or infringe upon any common-law or statutory rights of any person, firm, or corporation including, without limitation, contractual rights, copyrights, and rights of privacy.

4. This license is binding upon and shall inure to the benefit of the respective successors, assigns, and sublicensees of the parties hereto.

5. This agreement sets forth the entire understanding of the parties with respect to the subject matter hereof, and may not be modified or amended except by written agreement executed by the parties.

6. This license may not be terminated for any reason, is entered into in the State of California, and its validity, construction, interpretation, and legal effect shall be governed by the laws of the State of California applicable to contracts entered into and performed entirely therein.

IN WITNESS WHEREOF, the parties have entered into this license agreement as of this _____ day of _____ , 199___ .

AGREED TO AND ACCEPTED:

_____
LICENSOR *(COMPANY NAME)*

_____
BY *(SIGNATURE)*

_____
NAME AND TITLE (AN AUTHORIZED SIGNATORY)

_____
FEDERAL I.D. / SS#

_____
LICENSEE *(COMPANY NAME)*

_____
BY *(SIGNATURE)*

_____
NAME AND TITLE (AN AUTHORIZED SIGNATORY)

_____
FEDERAL I.D. / SS#

Special thanks to Suzy Vaughan, Esq. and Ron McGowan for their generous assistance in the preparation of these agreements.

sampling --→ **187**

Arhoolie Records

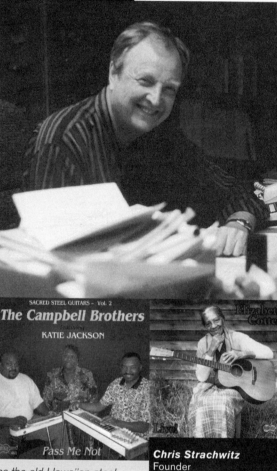

Sᴉɴᴄᴇ ᴛʜᴇ ꜰᴏᴜɴᴅɪɴɢ ᴏꜰ Aʀʜᴏᴏʟɪᴇ ɪɴ 1960, Cʜʀɪꜱ Sᴛʀᴀᴄʜᴡɪᴛᴢ ʜᴀꜱ recorded hundreds of the most interesting and important blues, Cajun, zydeco, Tex-Mex, and sacred steel musicians in America. "Slow selling, long lasting," Strachwitz has often said about sales of his recordings. Since his discovery and recording of Arhoolie's first artist, Mance Lipscomb in 1960, Strachwitz has persistently gone out to discover and record the vernacular musical traditions of ethnic communities. In 1997, he received a Lifetime Achievement Award from the Folk Alliance.

Arhoolie is currently re-editing recordings made over the past 34 years and releasing them on CDs. We continue to record new music. Michael Doucet's Beausoleil recordings are among our best sellers, and a new CD by Michael with the Savoy-Doucet Cajun Band is planned. My newest interest is sacred steel. I have long been an avid admirer of Holiness churches and their philosophy of spreading love and the spirit of God through music. When I received the demo cassette Sacred Steel *from folklorist Bob Stone (now Arhoolie CD 450), I could hardly believe my ears. Here was the old Hawaiian steel guitar tradition brought up to date and played by Afro-Americans in the most emotional and rhythmic manner heard on this planet. I thought I was listening to the late Elmore James playing for a Holiness dance in heaven! That's how I started recording and releasing CDs of individual sacred steel artists.*

Our newest venture is The Arhoolie Foundation, a nonprofit organization we established to educate the public about the history and present state of traditional, vernacular, and regional music, and to acquire and disseminate photographs, song books, records, and other historical documents pertaining to regional music traditions. An example of our projects is the donation of reissues of historic original recordings of Mexican-Texas border corridos (ballads) to about 500 public libraries throughout the Southwest, which was funded by the Rex Foundation.

—Chris Strachwitz
www.arhoolie.com

business

business

Selling recordings is a business and you have all the legal and professional obligations of other businesses.

Your business should start with a plan and a solid legal foundation to help establish your credentials in the industry, protect your financial interests, and satisfy government regulations.

BUSINESS PLANS

Many musicians begin with some idea of how much they want to spend on recording, but few know how many recordings they must sell to recoup that or how to figure in the other expenses they will incur.

A business plan outlines your professional goals, how you intend to achieve those goals, and how and when that achievement will generate income to pay back investments. Even if you are not going to use the business plan to raise money for your project, it will help you identify goals and outline strengths and weaknesses. Your business plan is the map that shows how you will get from the idea stage to project completion and profit. It will help you maintain direction and insure you will have enough money and energy to promote and sell your recording. When your recordings arrive, you will be ready to launch into your sales and promotion plans, rather than be tired and impoverished, wishing someone had convinced you to plan things better.

Business plans are catalysts; they can attract people with skills and show how those skills will be used. You will be calling on friends, family, investors, musicians, engineers, studio owners, producers, arrangers, graphic designers, printers, and manufacturers to help carry out your ideas. A business plan will show them your ideas are grounded in reality.

While on tour with Nanci Griffith in Ireland, we sat in a pub for three hours and began to work out a five-year plan. Since we were a new duo, we knew that we would be starting at the bottom when we returned to the States. The first question we set out to answer was, where do we want to be in five years? The second was, what will make us different from all the other bands in our genre? The first two years were the hardest since we had to have enough paying gigs to pay the rent. Having goals helped us get through some of the worst gigs. We found that having a plan made us more attractive to agents and concert promoters because it helped convince them we were in the business for the long-run.

–Pete and Maura Kennedy
The Kennedys–Rounder/Philo Records

Although there is no guarantee that every aspect of your plan will proceed perfectly, you will save considerable time and money and avoid frustration if you map out a course of action.

Financial Projections

The foundation of any plan is a budget that sets out how much money your project will need and how much it can return. Hopefully, you will plan your budget so that your income exceeds your expenses and you make a profit in less than two years. According to the Small Business Administration, many small businesses take that time to show a profit.

The sum of your efforts in researching sales and performance opportunities is called "market research." It will help you project how many recordings you might sell to your target audience.

TIPS TO A REALISTIC BUDGET ◄- - -

Costs have an uncanny way of spiraling upwards as a project progresses. Many financial experts counsel new business owners to figure expenses carefully—and then double the figures!

Figure sales projections conservatively. Do not plan on selling every last recording and do not be blinded by dollar signs when you compute how much you will make. Start with a realistic sales plan and be pleasantly surprised if you meet with unexpected success.

It is important to work out a preliminary budget for all your expected expenses and income before any money is borrowed or committed to designers, recording studios, printers, and manufacturers. Your budget and market research will help you define your goals by indicating what you can reasonably hope to gain financially from your recording project.

The worksheets in the appendix of this book correlate with the chapters. Using the information you have assembled in your research, estimate the expenses you will incur for each aspect of your project and enter them on the appropriate worksheets. Some of these figures will be based on rates for services quoted by designers, studios, and manufacturers. Others, such as the number of recordings you expect to give away, will be educated guesses.

The final worksheet, Planning, summarizes the figures from the individual sheets, and will give you your first overall picture of the profit (or loss) to be made from your project. This is the time to consider your reasons for making and selling your own recording. Will the project make or lose money, and how much? Is this question the most important to you, or are there other benefits to take into account? For example, are you willing to risk monetary loss to get better bookings, reviews, possible access to major labels, or the chance to learn more about recording or business in general? If so, for how long?

These questions are particularly important if you are borrowing money from others. Your family may be willing to lend you money that cannot be paid back from this project, but most investors will not. Even if it is your own money that may be lost, you should ask yourself whether you want to risk it.

In any case, you should try to revise your estimates so that they show your project breaking even or making a profit. Can you spend less on recording? Is there a way you can bolster sales? Can you save money by manufacturing fewer recordings initially and manufacturing more later? Keep juggling your estimates on the individual sheets until the whole project falls into line. (Caution: resist the temptation to save money by spending less on graphics or promotion.)

Eventually, you will come up with a budget you can justify to yourself and your investors.

BUSINESS PLAN OUTLINE

I. Project summary

A succinct overview of your recording project, how much money is needed to carry the project out, and the income you think it will generate

II. Detailed plan

1. History, background, and management of your recording label (or musical organization of which the label is a part)
2. Background of the company's owner(s)
3. Goals
   a. Short-term sales and promotional goals
   b. Long-term sales and promotional goals
   c. Short- and long-term profits
4. Description of the market for your genre of music and the niche your project will fill
   a. Market size
   b. Market trends
   c. Competition
5. Marketing plan
   a. Estimated sales and market share
   b. Strategy
   c. Pricing
   d. Sales and distribution
   e. Publicity and advertising
6. Operations (how project will be manufactured)
   a. Recording
   b. Design
   c. Manufacturing
7. Project timeline (month-by-month)
8. Critical risks, potential problems, and their solutions
9. Financial information
   a. Financing required
   b. Current financial statements
   c. Budget
   d. Financial projections (three-year profit and loss, month-by-month cash flow, and balance sheet projections)

Make copies of the blank worksheets, as you will be making revisions throughout your project. These worksheets are useful for tracking expenses as your project unfolds, and indicating whether your actual costs are exceeding your earlier estimates. Most importantly, preparing a budget will make you think through the entire project from beginning to end. If you do that, your budget will be one of your strongest selling points for borrowing money, and a reliable guide as you carry out your project.

Do not be tempted to cut short your research and start talking to family and friends about investing money in your recording. If you really hope to get others to lend you money, you will have to demonstrate you are serious enough about your project to have planned it financially. Even if you have money of your own, force yourself to investigate the audience and media outlets for your recording, and prepare a preliminary budget for your entire project before you spend a dime. The time you spend doing research will pay off.

Time Projections

If you have never made a recording before, estimate a year from concept to delivery. Think carefully about all that has to be done before you step into the studio, and about the follow-up work needed to produce a well-made recording and achieve your sales and promotional goals.

Following is a time plan designed to have recordings in hand one year from the start of your project. It is divided into six two-month segments.

ONE-YEAR PLANNING CALENDAR ◀- - -

Months 1-2

Begin to assemble all the information needed to make an initial budget.

Begin assembling mailing list (this will be a continuous process throughout your career).

Research community sales and promotional resources (audience, retailers, distributors, media).

Research promotional opportunities on the Internet. Research artists' Web sites to get ideas about how to start a Web site of your own.

Investigate services and obtain pricing information (recording studios, graphic designers, printers, manufacturers, arrangers, producers, musicians, photographers, artists, lawyers, accountants).

Prepare preliminary sales and promotional plans.

Obtain forms and information (copyright office, performance rights organizations, business organizations).

Months 3-4

Finalize sales and promotional plans. (Include in business plan below)

Finalize time plan and budget. (Include in business plan below)

Set up legal and financial structures (corporation, partnership, sole proprietorship).

Make a business plan.

Contact investors.

Months 5-6

Set up your business and line up commitments from the various people who will play a part in the production of your recording.

Establish your business (office, phone, fax, computer, stationery and supplies, accounting procedures, licenses, organizations).

Make arrangements for an Internet service provider (ISP) for e-mail. Decide whether you will have your own Web site or make arrangements to have pages on a larger music Web site.

Make arrangements for recording (select songs, arrangements, personnel, recording method, recording location; plan rehearsals and sessions).

Obtain mechanical licenses (for recording other people's songs).

Make arrangements for graphics (select graphic designer, determine cover concept, plan copy, photography, and artwork).

Make arrangements for manufacturing and printing.

Protect your songs (form publishing company, copyright songs, join performance rights organization).

Make final arrangements for a recording location.

Make a final session plan.

Months 7-8

Rehearse songs.

Record and mix songs according to session plan.

Create graphics concepts for all promotional materials, write copy, commission photography and illustrations.

Outline the elements you want to have on your Web site and make final arrangements for where this site will be displayed. Make arrangements for Web-site commerce.

Months 9-10

Sequence and prepare master tape.

Produce final artwork for all promotional materials.

Ship artwork and master to manufacturers.

Book performances for the first three months after your recording is released.

Arrange a record release party.

Months 11-12

Manufacture recordings.

Print all promotional materials.

Make final sales arrangements (salespeople, distributors).

Arrange for shipping and storage.

Send out press releases for the record release party.

Most people that make and sell their own recordings for the first time expect things to happen much too quickly. Some pros can record a selection of songs in a week; some major labels can produce and manufacture a recording in three months. But that kind of speed comes only with a great deal of experience. Trying to make things happen too fast is unrealistic and may cause you to foul up some part of your project entirely.

Time is your greatest ally. Most major labels schedule new recording releases every month but only certain ones receive the bulk of their promotional efforts. If a recording doesn't "break" in a month, the majors simply go on to new ones. This formula works for them, often to the detriment of new artists that need more time than the month allotted. Small recording labels can take their time. What will be difficult is believing your plans will work, especially in the first four to six months after your recording is released, when results can be agonizingly slow. Just remember, it took time to learn your instrument and new songs and it takes time to succeed in selling recordings.

Time can also be your greatest enemy. Trying to allocate the time you need for business, creative endeavors, and all too often, a part- or full-time job is difficult, particularly if you have little business experience. One way to deal with this problem is to make a list of priorities—things you want to achieve in any two-month period. List the tasks that will accomplish them and block out specific times to get them done. This takes self-discipline, but the more you do, the better you get at it.

ESTABLISHING YOUR BUSINESS

It is important to separate your personal life from your business life, particularly with regard to finances. And paperwork spreads like wildfire unless you organize and control it from the start.

Giving your business a name other than your own helps establish its separate identity. Having a place where you can conduct business and keep paperwork helps prevent your business from taking over your personal life. This place can be just a room in your house with a desk, computer, stationery, business phone, fax, business checkbook, ledgers, and filing cabinets.

Business Entities

The type of business entity you set up determines accounting methods, forms needed by tax administrators, agreements with people that work with you, and investor relationships. The following is a brief summary about these entities.

A sole proprietorship is a business conducted by one person who is the sole owner. It is the easiest entity to set up and operate. You control the checkbook, hire and fire employees, and make all the decisions about the focus of your business. You are personally responsible for business losses, and your personal assets are on the line should someone sue you and win. You use your social security number on all state and federal tax forms. Many solo performers and composers first set up sole proprietorships and graduate to some other business entity when it is warranted.

General partnerships include two or more people that share decisions about the business. The partnership files a federal partnership return

WHEN THERE ARE NO WRITTEN PARTNERSHIP AGREEMENTS
by Edward R. Hearn

A frequently raised issue is how to structure the business arrangements among the members of a band. Whenever two or more musicians form a band, they have formed a general partnership. While it is important to have a written agreement at some point, most struggling bands cannot afford to hire a lawyer to prepare one for them. If this is the case, it is important for the members of the band to work out answers among themselves. Communicate with each other. Seek professional help from nonprofit legal aid organizations or nonprofit state arts organizations. Follow your instincts on what seems fair and reasonable to you. A good issue on which to focus is to determine at what point your band should make an effort to have a written agreement. It is far less expensive to plan your business properly in the beginning than it is to resolve problems after the fact, especially if the resolution takes the form of expensive litigation. If you cannot reach an agreement, maybe that is a sign you should not be in business together.

LEGAL PRESUMPTIONS

If the members of a band have formed a partnership by working together but do not have a written agreement, state statutes presume that certain conditions apply to the band's arrangements. These conditions are that each partner; (a) has an equal vote in the affairs of the partnership and a majority vote determines the decision of the partners; (b) owns an equal share in the assets of the partnership, which include equipment purchased by the band, the name of the band, and income; (c) shares equally in the profits and losses of the partnership; and (d) is responsible for the acts of all of the other partners performed in pursuing the partnership business. If a partner, for example, delivers the band's independently produced recording to record stores for sale and in the course of making a delivery has a car accident, then all of the partners are liable for any damages.

LEAVING MEMBERS

When there is no written agreement and a partner leaves the partnership, whether willingly or at the demand of the other partners, the partnership terminates automatically. The band has a responsibility to pay all of the debts of the partnership and, if necessary, sell the partnership's assets to do so. If thereafter, the remaining members of the partnership wish to continue performing as a band they may, but in effect they form a new partnership and start over. If the band's creditors cooperate, you may be able to avoid having to liquidate the band's assets so long as the remaining band members continue paying the creditors. You need to work out with the departing members their continuing responsibility to make payments owed or to receive payments due.

TAXES

The partnership does not pay taxes on income earned by the band. Instead, the band files an informational tax return on a federal Partnership Return of Income Form 1065, wherein each partner states his or her distributive share of income or loss. Then each partner lists and adds or subtracts that share of income or loss on his or her individual tax return.

From *The Musician's Business and Legal Guide,* Revised 2nd Edition, compiled and edited by Mark Halloran, © 1996 Beverly Hills Bar Association, reprinted with permission of the publisher, Prentice Hall.

PARTNERSHIPS: CRITICAL WRITTEN AGREEMENT DECISIONS
by Edward R. Hearn

ACQUIRED PROPERTY

When a band acquires expensive property, such as a sound or lighting system, each of its members assumes a share of that system's cost. The partners should be aware of their payment responsibilities and what happens if somebody leaves the band. For example, will the departing member have to continue to make payment? Do the remaining members of the band have any obligation to pay the departing member for the equipment based on its market value or the money paid by the departing member, if the band is going to keep that equipment?

NAME

If the band becomes well known and its name is recognizable to a large audience, who will have the rights in the name if the band breaks up, or individual members leave the band? Partnership agreements generally state that the group, as a whole, owns the name. A provision should be included in the agreement stating that if member(s) leave the group, whether voluntarily or otherwise, they surrender the right to use the band name, which will stay with the remaining members of the group. Any incoming member would have to acknowledge in writing that the name of the band does belong to the partnership and the new member does not own any rights in the band's name greater than the partners' interests.

The partnership agreement could provide that none of the band members may use the name if the group should completely disband, or that any one of the members could buy from the others the right to use the name at a value established by binding arbitration with expert testimony concerning that value, if the members cannot agree among themselves.

LEAVING MEMBERS

Prior to signing long-term contracts such as recording or publishing agreements, the band should determine how to resolve the issues regarding the rights of departing and new band members concerning services already performed or commitments that have to be met under those agreements.

SONG RIGHTS

Can the departing member take his or her songs when they leave the group? If the songs were cowritten with remaining band members, the band can continue to use the songs and record them, as can the departing member, but each will have to report to the other that share of income earned from such usages. If the departing member is the sole author of certain compositions, it could prevent the band from recording them if they had not already been released on commercially distributed phonorecords, and from performing them if they had not been licensed to a performing rights society like BMI or ASCAP. Sometimes bands form a publishing company as part of the assets of the partnership, which controls what happens when a writer member leaves the band. Usually the band will continue to be able to use the songs as will the departing member.

From *The Musician's Business and Legal Guide,* Revised 2nd Edition, compiled and edited by Mark Halloran, © 1996 Beverly Hills Bar Association, reprinted with permission of the publisher, Prentice Hall.

and the individual partners add or subtract their share of income or loss on their individual tax returns.

Many bands start out as partnerships. The bands that are most likely to avoid legal entanglements in the future have written agreements to avoid misunderstandings. The group should discuss such questions as—how will you feel if monthly expenses for running the business eat away at the profits? What should we do with offers from a major label? The situations will differ, but it is important to talk things out at the beginning and hold regular meetings thereafter to go over financial statements and discuss future plans.

Written agreements should set forth how business decisions are made, debt incurred, profit shared, and assets acquired. The most difficult questions to resolve in an agreement are—(1) what happens when one partner puts in much more time and money than what was originally agreed on; (2) what happens to debts and future profits made from recordings when a band member quits; and (3) if the partnership blows up, who keeps the name?

A limited partnership is a two-tiered partnership in which some people control business and financial decisions, while others contribute capital, but have no say in the running of the business, thereby "limiting" the amount of their investment and risk.

A corporation is an artificial, separate legal entity that conducts business and files corporate taxes separate from the individuals that run it. Ownership is obtained by buying shares of stock. The corporation can be owned by one or more

individuals, is governed by a board of directors that are elected by shareholders, and is managed by officers. (In some corporations, the board of directors, shareholders, and officers are the same people.) The personal assets of the individuals that own the corporation generally cannot be touched by legal or financial actions against the corporation. A corporation files tax returns and pays taxes on profits. Receipt of any share of the profits by the individuals (in addition to wages) is reported on their personal tax returns.

Lawyer and Bookkeeper

Two professionals that are essential to setting up your business are a lawyer and a bookkeeper. Both should be consulted in the planning stages of making your recording.

Your lawyer will help you set up your business; write and negotiate contracts; advise you on major business decisions; make sure agreements with band members and cocomposers are properly done; and hopefully, steer you away from trouble. Try to find a lawyer who specializes in entertainment law. He or she will be familiar with standard contracts (recording, publishing, and management) and the acceptable variations. Music industry lawyers frequently know people that work for record companies, agencies, and management companies, and will sometimes put you in contact with people that can further your career. Musicians in your community should be able to refer you to such lawyers.

A bookkeeper will help you keep track of money by setting up ledgers that correspond to your form of business. Ledgers list chronologically all the checks you write and all deposits you make,

Major Lingo's infectious folk/rock rhythms and positive lyrics have made them one of the most popular performing bands in Arizona. They were the first band in Arizona to sponsor "All Ages Dances" (1985). Today, these dances provide a major source of income.

We were raising families ourselves and wanted to provide them and our extended family of friends with a positive, smoke-free, alcohol-free environment to find the joy of movement. The people that come to our dances nurture our souls because the trade of good energy between all of us is unavoidable.

—John Ziegler, guitarist, vocalist and co-founder

by category. They provide accurate and accessible information about the state of your business. Ledgers will tell how much of your income came from performances and how much from the sale of records; how many records your distributors sold; how much you spent on postage and office supplies; and how much you spent on graphics and manufacturing. That information shows which parts of your project were most profitable and where expenses were excessive.

Ledgers make it easy to summarize expenses and income for your tax returns.

Once your books have been set up, you can keep them up-to-date yourself manually or with computer software programs. However, if you can afford it, let your bookkeeper do this and other financial paperwork, such as filing sales tax returns.

Maintaining the ledgers is fairly routine. Your bookkeeper will show you how to list income and expenses, file receipts, and interpret your ledgers. He or she can take care of all federal and state tax returns; and the filing of forms and payments required when you hire employees or have to pay sales tax.

You do not need someone who is specially trained in music business finances; the services of any reliable bookkeeper will do fine.

Accountants and certified public accountants are specialized types of bookkeepers. They are knowledgeable about investments, tax shelters, and pensions. Call upon them when your business starts making more money than you can manage properly with the help of only a lawyer and bookkeeper.

Bank Accounts

Open a business bank account. This provides an easy way to keep track of income and the money spent on business.

You should keep written receipts for your checks and invoices for income, and file them carefully. You can use a credit card that is earmarked for business expenses only, and pay the monthly bill with a business check.

Be sure to collect receipts for everything paid for with cash; at least once a month add up those receipts and pay yourself out of your business account. File these receipts with all other receipts for business expenses.

Sole proprietorships and partnerships provide banks with the social security numbers of the individuals involved and the name of their business. They are not legally required to have an Employer Identification Number (EIN) until they hire employees.

PHOTO BY KARL KORTE

During the 1980s, The McLean Mix, a multimedia electroacoustic duo, began to explore art galleries, museums, and contemporary art centers as potential performing venues, and new ways to involve audiences in their music. In 1989, they presented their first audience-interactive composition, *Rainforest* at an art gallery under the auspices of the music department of the University of Wyoming.

We were intrigued by how institutions such as art galleries, San Francisco's Exploratorium, citywide festivals, and zoos bring in huge masses of audience. What do these venues possess that the recital hall does not? The audience is moving, walking through and relating to an exhibit on its own time frame and terms. If we could duplicate this audience condition in the context of experimental new music, then we just might have a solution to attracting more audience.

In 1989, we took a vacation in Puerto Rico, where we were profoundly inspired by a trip to the El Yunque Rainforest. As we walked down the park's road at night, we entered successive zones of differing sound mixes of insects, birds, and amphibians, which sounded like a walk through an electroacoustic symphony encased in a tropical night ambiance, not unlike a huge electronic music fresco. We, the audience, were walking through the music. Thus our audience-interactive composition Rainforest *was gradually developed.*

–Barton and Priscilla McLean. Condensed from their article, "In Search of an Audience: Outside the Bubble," published in *Seamus Journal*, November, 1995.

Postal Services

You will be a frequent visitor to the post office, mailing out recordings, press packages, business letters, and promotional material. Mail that contains personal correspondence and statements of account must be sent at the First-Class rate.

The U.S. Postal Service's priority mail can be cheaper than other delivery services, such as United Parcel Service, Airborne Express, and Federal Express, depending on the weight. Currently, a recording and press packet that weighs two pounds or less can be sent priority mail for $3.20 to anyplace in the United States in two to three days.

Mail that does not require the First-Class rate or does not need expedited handling can be sent more economically at Standard Mail rates.

Consult with your local post office about the weight, size, content, and number of pieces you plan to mail to determine the cheapest and best way. Factors that can affect mailing costs include the frequency of mailings, quantity of pieces, whether or not they have been bar coded, and the degree to which you have sorted the mail. Preparing your mailing so it requires minimal handling by the post office will save you money.

Padded recording mailers can usually be purchased from discount stores, office supply catalogs, or your manufacturer cheaper than from stationery stores. Envelopes, padded mailers and boxes are also available at the post office.

Business Tools

Here are the business tools start-up recording labels find most indispensable.

Computers—musicians use them most for word processing, e-mail, Internet browsing, and recording and editing music. For Macintosh users, 32 megabytes of RAM are adequate for simultaneously running the operating system, a word processing program, e-mail and Internet applications. For PC users with Windows 95 or later, 72 megabytes of RAM are needed for the same applications. (More RAM is needed if you are running music programs). Five hundred megabytes of hard disk storage is considered adequate for a small business. You can always upgrade RAM or hard disk storage as needed.

Used systems with these configurations, often with monitor, keyboard, and some software can often be found for less than $1000.

You will need a modem for connecting to the Internet and software for faxing. You should have a separate fax machine for faxing documents that are not stored on your computer.

If you plan to send or receive faxes on a regular basis or be on the Internet for long periods, you should get a second phone line, so people that call can reach you.

You will need an answering machine.

PROTECTING YOUR BUSINESS NAME

Choose an original name to assure yourself of the fullest protection for your recording label and your band. According to law, rights to a name for a business or organization belong to the first user in a particular field. If your business name becomes well known and you discover that some other label or band started using it after you did, you can require them to stop and choose a new name—or buy the use of the name from you, in which case you will have to choose a new one.

You should take care not to use a name similar to one being used by another business with an established reputation in the same field since you could be sued for trading on that company's reputation.

A business name belongs to you through use and only by establishing a name through use does it become officially yours. You establish your business name by using it as often as you can—on your checks, letterhead, business card, invoices, recording's cover, label, and advertising—and for anything else you do to sell and promote your recordings.

Once you have done so you are entitled to full protection of the law for the use of that name. You will not lose the rights to your business name even if another band or label that is bigger or more famous uses it after you have established it.

You must research the name to ensure its originality. Sources to check are music industry trade directories, such as the *Billboard International Talent and Touring Directory*, *Recording Industry Sourcebook*, and catalogs that list recordings like the *Schwann Spectrum*.

You cannot copyright a name, but you can trademark the look of your recording label and band name. A trademark can be obtained for the special lettering and logo you use. Until your business becomes well known and has been operating for a number of years, however, there is no reason to go through the paperwork and pay the filing fees required for registration. For further information on trademarks, contact the United States Patent and Trademark Office. (The U.S. Patent and Trademark Office's address is listed in the Directory of Resources.)

Fictitious Name Certificate

If you are not doing business as a corporation and you are using a business name different from your name, you must file a fictitious name certificate, which establishes the name of your business in your county and helps prevent other businesses in the area from using the same name.

To obtain a fictitious name certificate, fill out the form available at the county clerk's office located in your county's administration building or request it from the Secretary of State's office. There is a small filing fee.

Internet Registration

You must register your Web site name (domain name) with the Internet Network Information Center (InterNIC) (rs.internic.net) or the Domain Registry (www.domainregistry.com). InterNIC charges $70 to register for the first two years and $35 per year thereafter; Domain Registry charges $45 per year. You must renew your registration annually. If your registration lapses, the name becomes eligible for registration by someone else. You can research whether your domain name is unique by using the search services provided by either Web site. The domain name does not have to be the same as your business name, but many businesses try to either have them be the same, or find a convenient short-form domain name that is similar. For example, the domain name of Kaleidospace, a popular independent music site, is Kspace.

BE YOUR OWN BEST MANAGER
by Peter Spellman

Successful management is effective, efficient and objective, and it all begins with you.

Identify your values and operate from them
Clarify your purpose, priorities and goals
Design and implement an effective business plan
Create strategic plans of action
Learn to work smarter—not harder
Eliminate time wasters
Plan your days
Set a schedule and keep it
Get feedback from colleagues and experts
Collect information, quotes, articles, statistics
Keep your work space organized
Enhance your telephone skills
Follow through with customers and clients
Market your business consistently
Join at least one professional association
Develop powerful networking abilities
Keep accurate records
Be a calculating risk-taker
Be willing to move on
Make sure your needs are being met
Exercise regularly
Create a support system
Continue your education
Get out of the house/office every day
Remember we are all human and make mistakes
Keep things in perspective
Take responsibility for yourself
Choose appropriate advisors
Delegate or subcontract tasks you hate
Respect your mind's and body's cycles
Balance your personal and professional life
Acknowledge your accomplishments every day

Peter Spellman is Director of Career Development at Berklee College of Music, Boston and founder of Music Business Solutions, a company that provides business and marketing strategies and resources to musicians and music-related companies. (www.mbsolutions.com)

Peter Spellman

GOVERNMENT REGULATIONS

Anyone who operates a business must comply with city, county, state, and federal regulations. These regulations are designed to protect the business and the public and insure that taxes are paid. Regulations, procedures, and fees vary from one geographical area to another. The following provides general information about what types of regulations exist and how you can comply with them.

Resale License

States that assess sales tax on consumer goods sold in the state require businesses to obtain a seller's permit, sometimes referred to as a "resale license." This permit insures that state sales tax will be collected and remitted to the state on a regular basis for every recording sold to the public in your state. Check with your state's Department of Revenue to find out their requirements.

You do not collect sales tax on wholesale sales because you are selling recordings to businesses that will resell them to the public and those businesses will collect and report their own sales tax.

There is usually a fee for this permit. Some states also require you to post a bond or security deposit to guarantee that you will collect sales taxes and remit them. The amount of this deposit is based on the number of recordings you say you will sell directly to the public in your state.

When you acquire the resale license or seller's permit, you will receive the forms needed to prepare sales tax returns. Each month, quarter, or year (depending on your volume of sales) you will file the forms and pay any sales taxes collected during that period. Maintaining and filing sales tax forms is a service commonly provided by bookkeepers.

In most states, your seller's permit allows you to purchase goods at wholesale without paying sales tax—if those goods are going to be resold. That would include record manufacturing and recording cover fabrication costs, but not furniture, instruments, or equipment.

Regulations Concerning Employees

If you have employees, be sure to treat them as such. Withhold taxes, pay the employer's share of Social Security (FICA) and unemployment (FUTA). Be sure to file payroll tax returns on time and pay all payroll taxes due. The penalties for late filing or paying are stiff.

Contact your state's withholding tax department to register your business and get licensed to have employees in that state. Ask for an employer handbook and a copy of state regulations regarding employee/employer regulations.

If your business hires regular employees you will need an Employer Identification Number (EIN), which informs the IRS that you will file quarterly and year-end payroll tax returns. When you have regularly paid employees, the paperwork increases and you must also pay for worker's compensation insurance, Medicare, and social security. To get an EIN, ask your local IRS office (or bookkeeper) for Form SS-4, "Application for Employer Identification Number." The completed form can be faxed to the IRS and the assigned number received back in less than five days. To find out where to fax your completed Form SS-4, call the IRS at 800-829-1040. You will use your EIN when you file tax reports for your business.

Federal laws regulate employment of children under sixteen years of age and the minimum wage payable to employees.

Federal and State Tax Returns

You will have to file federal, state, and possibly city tax returns for your business. If your business is a sole proprietorship, a Schedule C must be included with your personal income tax return (Form 1040). If your business is a partnership, a partnership return must be filled out and a K-1 form that notes the profit or loss made for each partner is sent to each one. That sum is reported on the appropriate line of your personal income tax return. Corporations file their own returns (Form 1120).

It is important to separate your personal and business expenses. This is simplified if you do business under a fictitious name and have a separate business checking account. If you do not, you have to be especially careful to set up ledgers that make these separations.

Keep receipts for absolutely every penny you spend on business. They are necessary to prove every tax-deductible expense you claim on your income tax in case you are audited by the IRS. Check with your bookkeeper to learn what legitimate business expenses are or better yet ask the IRS to send you free informational booklets.

DIRECTORIES

Locating services, key people, specialized manufacturers, touring information, and so on, is facilitated by using the various directories that serve the entertainment industry. There are resource directories for many genres of music

and marketing arenas. Music magazines sometimes provide resource listings also.

A list of directories is provided in the Directory of Resources at the end of this book. Many are available in the business reference section of a large public or university library.

Listings in these directories are usually free and they are as comprehensive and up-to-date as possible. It is, however, the responsibility of each business to inform directories of new listings and changes. The deadlines for information are usually six months preceding publication. To be sure that your recording label or publishing company is listed, request the forms and send the information as soon possible. Remember to include all the services your business offers.

TRADE ORGANIZATIONS

The recording industry is served by several organizations that provide marketing and sales information and trade shows. Becoming a member of these organizations provides you with business contacts and information.

Addresses for the following trade organizations are listed in the Directory of Resources.

Association For Independent Music (AFIM)

The Association For Independent Music (AFIM), formerly the National Association of Independent Record Distributors and Manufacturers (NAIRD), has 1200-plus members that include independent record labels, distributors, retailers, manufacturers, mastering facilities, and recording studios.

The AFIM works to improve communication

among indie music people; identify and promote cooperative activities that benefit the industry; publicize achievements and activities of the industry; and provide educational opportunities for its membership.

The AFIM's annual convention, held in May, includes a full day of crash courses (designed specifically for newcomers to the industry), numerous seminars, workshops, committee meetings, special interest group meetings, and meetings between labels and distributors. Panels cover topics such as "Alternative Marketing," "Distribution," and "New Technologies."

The convention also has a two-day trade show where members have an opportunity to display their services and recordings to other member companies, retailers, and the press.

The convention provides an opportunity for independent labels to meet with distributors and introduce them to their recordings, as well as map out promotional and sales campaigns; visit with successful labels to find out what works and what doesn't; share information about promotional and touring opportunities; and research information about distributors, manufacturers, and other related businesses. Special interest groups within the organization focus on specific genres of music so people can work together to promote their particular genre.

The convention's highlight is the presentation of the "Indie Awards" for the best independent recordings released during the year in more than 40 categories.

The AFIM has several membership categories, but the only one applicable to independent labels and distributors is Classification A. It provides full voting privileges and benefits and is available to independent labels, labels with independent distribution, distributors, mail-order companies, and retailers. In 1999, annual fees are $300 for the first year and $250 thereafter, so long as membership is continuously maintained. Membership runs the calendar year. Members are listed in the annually updated *AFIM Directory*, available in printed form and on-line at their Web site (www.afim.org).

Members get reduced rates for the annual AFIM convention and for renting booth space. They receive the organization's magazine, *Indie Music World,* which contains top 10 indie music sales charts from distributors and one-stops (large wholesale facilities that stock recordings from many labels), feature articles, new release listings organized by genre then street date, and up-to-date information on AFIM programs, services, and events. It is sent to members, retailers, distributors, one-stops, and to a select press list in an effort to assist members in publicizing their recordings and activities. Advertising in *Indie Music World* is discounted to members. The *AFIM Directory,* which includes a resource guide and independent distribution guide, is free to all members and can be purchased by nonmembers as well.

Members can take advantage of discounted advertising rates provided by a number of trade publications, such as *Billboard Magazine, Musician,* and *Pulse.* Other benefits include discounts for broadcast faxing (one fax sent to a large mailing list), long distance telephone services, car rentals, shipping, Web site design and development, and SoundScan usage.

NARM

The big business counterpart of the AFIM is the National Association of Recording Merchandisers, Inc. (NARM). It offers memberships in three categories: general memberships are for music retailers and distributors; associate memberships are for suppliers of recorded entertainment software and related products and services; and free affiliate memberships are for nonprofit organizations in related industries. The NARM annual convention is a music business spectacular. Seminars deal with issues such as "Asset-based Lending in the Music Business," and "Simple Steps to Disaster Recovery." When you find these subjects relevant it is time to join.

NARAS

The National Academy of Recording Arts and Sciences (NARAS) promotes artistic, creative, and technical excellence in the recording industry. Much of the business of this organization centers around its annual Grammy Awards. Chapters hold monthly meetings for informational and social purposes.

Voting memberships are open only to people involved in the creative aspects of recording: musicians, singers, engineers, producers, arrangers, conductors, songwriters, art directors, photographers, artists, and designers. These people nominate and vote for the Grammy winners. Record labels and publishing companies do not belong to NARAS and neither do record promoters, DJs, store owners, or record label executives (unless they qualify under the above mentioned categories).

Nominations for Grammys are conducted solely by NARAS members. Voting members of NARAS receive the *Grammy Awards Guide,* a catalog published monthly by Entertainment Resource Services Inc. It lists newly released recordings members can purchase, at greatly reduced prices, to become familiar with the year's releases.

Manufacturers and record labels can request information from Entertainment Resources Services Inc. about how to have their products listed and made available (at a discount) to NARAS members.

If you feel the awards do not represent independent labels fairly, join and make your voice heard. In 1998, Rounder Records' Alison Krauss and Union Station received three awards, "Best Country Performance by a Duo or Group," "Best Country Instrumental Performance," and "Best Bluegrass Album."

RIAA

The Recording Industry Association of America (RIAA) represents the U.S. sound recording industry. Member companies create, manufacture and market approximately 90% of the recordings produced and sold in the United States. It is a source of marketing information about recordings manufactured and sold worldwide, and provides consumer profiles, and antipiracy statistics.

The RIAA is well known for the administration of its Gold and Platinum Awards Program. These awards are given to recognize the success of recording artists as measured by the number of their recordings that have been sold.

The RIAA surveys the entire music marketplace, including retail outlets, record clubs, rack jobbers, and ancillary markets to track and compile sales data. When a recording has sold the number of units required to qualify, the RIAA issues a Gold, Platinum, or Multiplatinum certificate to mark this achievement. For example, a single must sell 500,000 units to qualify for Gold certification. The requirements for certification vary depending on the configuration and length of the recording.

One of the RIAA's primary missions is to investigate the illegal production and distribution of pirated sound recordings. According to the RIAA, piracy costs the U.S. domestic music industry hundreds of millions of dollars a year. It has an enforcement team of investigators and lawyers, which ferrets out and sues violating companies, and confiscates pirated product. Suspected music piracy can be reported to the RIAA by dialing a toll-free hotline, 1-800-BAD-BEAT or by e-mail to badbeat@riaa.com.

Statistics about domestic and international recordings, and other valuable information, are available on their Web site (www.RIAA.com).

LABOR UNIONS

Two major labor unions serve recording and performing musicians and singers: the American Federation of Musicians (AFM) and the American Federation of Television and Radio Artists (AFTRA). In general, instrumentalists belong to AFM and vocalists to AFTRA. These unions set wages and working standards for their members by entering into agreements with employers, like recording labels, concert promoters, orchestras, and television producers. All major labels (and some independent ones) are signatories to either

the Phonograph Record Labor Agreement, which is regulated by AFM, or the National Code of Fair Practices for Phonograph Recordings, which is regulated by AFTRA. These agreements bind signatory labels to paying union wages to member musicians and vocalists.

Both unions prohibit members from performing or recording with employers that have not signed such agreements, or recording with musicians that are not union members. The goal of these unions is to help their members earn a fair living and provide them with recourse in the event that a contract is not respected. However, neither union acts as an employment agency.

To join either union, musicians and vocalists have to demonstrate their proficiency, agree to abide by all rules and regulations, and pay dues regularly. Most major American cities have a local branch of both AFM and AFTRA.

Not all musicians and singers belong to these unions. In some cases, they do not join because they are just beginning their careers and want to be free to take jobs in nonunion situations, or because it is hard to find union jobs, particularly in communities with high populations of musicians and singers. Some people hesitate to join because they think the unions do not provide enough value or service for the money required to sustain membership.

As long as neither the employee (musician or singer) nor the employer (record label or club) are party to union agreements, the unions cannot step in and regulate wages or working conditions. Many independent labels are not signatories to union wage and working agreements because they do not operate on a large enough

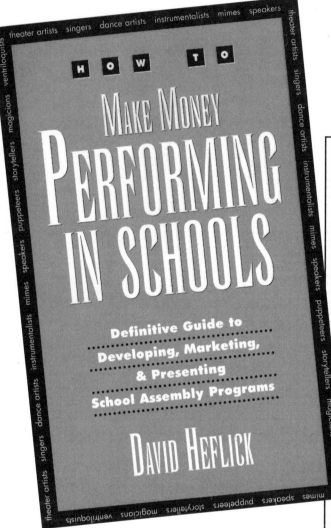

How to Make Money Performing in Schools is a valuable resource for musicians that wish to learn how to develop and present arts-in-education (AIE) programs.

The *Bluegrass Music in the Schools: Implementation Manual,* published by the International Bluegrass Music Association, is a resource for bands and musicians interested in developing school programs and for teachers seeking specific information about bluegrass music. Association members have access to information on more than 900 bluegrass radio programs, record labels, press outlets, and talent buyers for more than 500 annual bluegrass festivals held on four continents.

financial scale. However, a small label will usually sign union agreements when it makes a distribution agreement with a larger label that is a signatory.

CLASSES, SEMINARS, AND WORKSHOPS

Several excellent music business, audio, and songwriter seminars and workshops are sponsored annually in many U.S. and Canadian cities. They are valuable sources of information and are great for meeting people. In the United States, these include the "New Music Seminar" held in New York City during the summer; "South by Southwest," held in the fall in Austin, Texas; the "Folk Alliance Conference" held in a different city each February, and "Songwriters Expo" sponsored by the National Academy of Songwriters (NAS), held in the fall in Hollywood, California. Canadian events include "Canadian Music Week" held in the spring in Toronto, Ontario; and "North by Northeast" held in the summer in Toronto.

Many community colleges, universities, and private schools offer specialized classes in audio production. These classes are invaluable for the equipment they make available to their students. Many first-time recording projects or demos have been made very economically with the use of class time and school equipment.

Tapes and videos of workshops and seminar lectures are often provided by the schools and organizations that sponsor them.

PHOTO BY ROBERT CORWIN

Seminars at the annual Folk Alliance conference are informative and well attended.

Capstone Records

RICHARD BROOKS COFOUNDER AND PRESIDENT OF CAPSTONE RECORDS (founded in 1986), has composed more than 50 classical works in all media, including operas, orchestra, chamber and choral music. His music has been widely performed in the United States and Europe. When he isn't working as head of Capstone, Brooks serves as professor and department chair of the music faculty of Nassau Community College on Long Island, New York.

One afternoon in 1986, my composer/recording engineer friend Reynold Weidenaar—an important multimedia pioneer—and I talked ourselves into doing an album of our own music. We spent an afternoon trying to think up catchy titles. We called the album Music Visions *and the record label Capstone. We thought it was a one-shot thing.*

The next year, we gave a presentation about how to produce your own record at a classical composer's conference. Afterward, a curious thing happened. Several composers approached me and said "It's okay doing it ourselves, but how about doing it on your label?" We produced a second, then a third recording by other composers. The label grew by word of mouth. Now we have nearly 60 titles and are turning out two-to-three records a month.

I have a sense of mission to get some very wonderful music out to where audiences can find it. There are so many good contemporary classical composers and limited exposure opportunities. Many of my peers grew up thinking that if we just wrote the great American symphony, people would knock down our doors. We went to school to be composers and artists. We weren't taught business. Or promotion. Or how to be successful without holding down a teaching job. Today, that's changing. Composers are thinking creatively about promoting themselves.

—Richard Brooks

Richard Brooks
Founder

financing

financing

by Edward R. Hearn, Esq.

there are many approaches to consider when planning the financing of your recording project. The initial decision is whether to handle the financing yourself or to approach an existing record company.

Self-financing can be the most desirable way of funding an independent recording venture. The best way to retain full control of your project is to use your own money. Self-financing allows you to be free of financial obligations to lenders and gives you maximum artistic control. Although you bear all the risk of the project, you also enjoy the benefits.

Frequently, financial control results in artistic control of the recording. Tension can develop between financial backers that want things done in a certain way to insure the project makes a profit, and the artist, who feels pressured to compromise the music.

Self-financing also minimizes the paperwork, record keeping, and other business complications involved in producing a recording.

One technique of self-financing, in addition to drawing on savings, is to presell the record to friends. This technique, however, should be used with extreme caution and only when you are very close to production and are absolutely certain the record will be issued. Limit these sales to sympathetic friends. Failure to deliver can constitute fraud and invite hassles in the form of lawsuits or proceedings by governmental consumer fraud units. It can also destroy your credibility with your most loyal friends.

LOANS

Loans are a fixed sum of money you borrow and agree to repay along with a specified percentage of interest by a certain time. They are usually absolute obligations and must be repaid whether or not the project is successful.

The lender will want you to identify the sources of income from which their investment will be repaid. Will the money be coming from the revenue generated by sales of your recordings, or will it be coming from other sources like live performance, publishing, or merchandising?

Arrangements where the return to the lender depends on the success of the recording will be discussed under the section on profit sharing.

Loan Sources

Commercial sources include banks, finance companies, savings and loan associations, pawn shops, and credit cards with cash advance provisions.

A commercial loan application package usually contains your business plan, profit and loss statements of your business, tax returns for the last two or three years, and a personal financial statement. Banks will check your credit history.

The purpose of the package is to assure the lender you have a sound financial plan and are financially responsible.

Since commercial lenders make money lending money, shop for the most favorable terms, interest and monthly payback amounts. The higher the rate of interest, the longer you have to wait for your project to earn a profit.

Interest on commercial loans secured by such collateral as a home, auto, or the cosignature of a person in whom the bank has confidence will usually be lower than interest on unsecured loans since the risk is lower. No commercial lender will take unproven records or songs as collateral. Loans backed up with collateral or the cosignature of a creditworthy individual are also easier to secure.

A second source for loans is family and friends. Usually they will lend money at a rate lower than commercial lenders. The important thing to consider when borrowing from friends is that strong pressures for timely repayment may be greater than the legal obligation to repay.

When you borrow from friends, the usury laws of most states come into play. These statutes limit the amount of interest that a private lender can charge a borrower. Banks and other commercial lenders are generally exempt from usury limits and charge higher rates.

Loan Repayment

Whether you borrow from friends or from commercial lenders, you should structure a written repayment plan that states the amount loaned, the rate of interest, and the method of repayment.

This can be a simple written promissory note: "On or before June 15, 2001, John Debtor promises to pay Sally Lender the sum of $2,500 plus 9% interest per annum from January 1, 1999, (signed) John Debtor." Interest could be simple or compounded, based on what you negotiate with your lender.

The note from a commercial lender is more complex, but will contain the same elements. Sometimes commercial loans are structured so you pay a smaller monthly amount the first two years and a larger one the next two to three years.

PROFIT SHARING

In profit sharing arrangements, an investor puts funds or time into a project and gets a return based on the success of the recording.

The arrangement can take several forms, depending on whether the investor is "active" or "passive."

Active Investors

Active investors are individuals that put up money to finance a project for another person and become involved in the project (or fail to take adequate action to insulate themselves from responsibility). They assume all of the risks of the business, including financial liability for all losses, even if the losses go beyond the amount invested. Generally, such persons are responsible for the obligations of the business even if they have not given their approval or have not been involved in incurring business debts.

Businesses in which the participants have this financial exposure could be general partnerships, joint ventures, or corporations. The profits or losses of such businesses are shared among the participants according to the terms of their agreements.

A general partnership is co-ownership of an ongoing enterprise in which the partners share both control and profits. A joint venture is a general partnership that either has a very short term or a limited purpose. The production of a single record could be termed a joint venture.

The general partners and the joint venturers are each personally liable for all the debts of the enterprise. This liability is not limited to the amount invested nor to debts incurred with their approval. All personal assets of the general partners or joint venturers are liable for repayment of the debts incurred by the enterprise.

If a corporation is formed, then even if the project is a total failure, only the assets of the corporation are vulnerable to the business creditors. A corporation is a separate entity formed under state laws. Its ownership is divided among its shareholders.

Your local library should have some good books on small business that will provide the information you need to learn more about the structuring of partnerships or corporations.

Passive Investors

A more complex category of investments is that in which backers provide money for a project but take no role in its management and affairs. These backers are passive investors that hope for a return on their money based on the success of the project.

The primary advantage of profit-sharing arrangements, from the point of view of the independent recording artist, is the downside risks are shared. If a recording fails to sell, the artist is not obligated to repay the investors. Offsetting this advantage are several problems that make profit sharing the most complicated form of financing an independent recording.

The foremost problem is security law requirements. Any time one enters into an agreement in which someone gives money for a project with the understanding that part of the profits are to be shared with them, and the investors do not actively participate in the management of the funds or the operation of the business, a "security" has been sold. A security can be a promissory note, stock, points, or any other form of participation in a profit-sharing arrangement, written or oral, where the investor's role in the business is passive. Because general partners and joint venturers are actively involved in the business, their participation is not generally considered a security.

Limited partnerships, promissory notes structured with profit sharing, corporate stock, and contracts that provide for points participation are clearly securities, and the securities laws of state and federal statutes must be satisfied when these types of funding are used. Failure to comply can have serious civil and criminal consequences.

What does this legal talk mean to you? Why should you worry about it if all you want to do is raise money to record some music? The securities laws were enacted to protect investors from being harmed by the fraud of others, by their lack of sophistication, or their inability to afford to lose the money they invest in the project. The legal burden falls on those seeking to raise the money to make certain investors are getting a fair deal and fully understand the risks involved. "Let the seller beware," is the rule that operates.

If you want someone to invest money in your project without allowing them a hand in controlling the project, you should be willing to accept some responsibility to them. And willing or not, state and federal statutes place responsibility on you.

Loan Agreements

Loans structured on profit sharing can take a number of different forms. A promissory note and repayment plan that is conditional on the success of the funded project can be signed. Because such a loan is a security, the note must set out the terms of repayment, including interest rates and payment schedules.

Another common form is a "point" arrangement in which a percentage (points) of the sales of the record are shared with a producer who only puts in time; or some other investor who only puts in money. This arrangement could be provided for in a written contract that simply describes the participation arrangements of the investor, rather than in the more traditional form of a conditional promissory note.

Limited Partnerships

Like a general partnership, a limited partnership has copartnership and shared profits, but only some of the participants are entitled to control or manage the enterprise. These are termed the general partners. The other investors are called limited partners and their only involvement is the passive one of putting funds into the project.

A partner receives that percentage of the business profits or losses set out in the agreement between the partners; for example 10% of the net profits up to $10,000 and 5% of the net profits after the first $10,000. The term of the partnership is often limited to a specified period. If the project has not earned the hoped for return to the investor by the end of the term, the investor has to absorb the loss.

There are rules in the federal law and in several states that apply to limited partnerships and other security investments. If the investments are structured as private offerings, they are easier to qualify for under the law than are public offerings. For example, in California, investments may not be taken from more than 35 persons; there can be no advertising of the investment offering; the investors must represent that they are making the investment for their own keeping with no intent of transferring or selling it to others and, either the people investing the money must have a preexisting business or personal relationship with you, or they or their professional financial advisors, because of their business experience, can reasonably be presumed to have the ability to protect their own interests.

CORPORATE SHARES

A third way to raise investment capital is through the sale of shares in a corporation. Corporate shares are securities and are usually sold for a stated number of dollars per share. That money is used to operate the business or pay for a specific project. A shareholder owns whatever percentage of the corporation his or her shares represent of the total number of shares sold.

Shareholders participate in the profits of the corporation when they are distributed as dividends and vote on shareholder issues according to their percentage of ownership.

Whatever method of financing you choose, it is wise to have your lawyer or accountant set up a good financial record-keeping system.

COMPLYING WITH STATUTES

After reaching a decision on the legal structure to use in raising money for your project, you must make certain your efforts comply with state and federal law. For example, some states require that the party raising and accepting investment capital must file documents with the Corporation Commission explaining in part the proposed investment project, how the money will be used, all the risks in the venture,

the financial ability of the investors, and the background of all persons seeking funding.

Fundamental in any offering of a security, whether public or private, is the disclosure to the potential investors of all the risks involved in the project, including the risk that the project may fail, that no profit may be made, and that the investors may never have their investment returned. You must disclose, in writing, the nature of the project, the risks, the background of the people starting and running the business, the nature of the business, the manner in which the money will be used, and the way the investor will share in any profits or losses. Also, under certain circumstances an offer and sale of securities involving an interstate transaction may require registration of the securities with the United States Securities and Exchange Commission (SEC) in Washington, D.C. Knowledgeable legal counsel should be obtained before seeking to offer any securities.

EVALUATING INVESTORS

If you lack your own money for your project, and do not have the credit necessary to borrow money, then you must face the reality of raising investment capital and complying with the appropriate securities statutes. Probably the most frustrating aspect of this will be your quest to find the person who will give you the money you need. Some investors are attracted by the idea of putting money into an entertainment project because they feel it is a glamorous business, or they have read that the entertainment industry can generate a substantial amount of money and wish to take a risk that they will earn a great return if the project is successful.

For the most part, the money usually comes from family, friends, or interested people that have experienced your talents and wish to be involved in developing your potential. And it is important to keep those finances on a professional business level to preserve the personal relationships.

Unfortunately, there is no magic source of money. It will be up to you to identify who has enough faith in your talents and future to make their money available. Another possible source of money is investment counselors and accountants that are searching for reasonable business opportunities for their clients. In reviewing proposals for investments, financial advisors analyze the possibilities of eventual return on the investment and the tax benefits, if any, available to their investors.

Educating Investors

Once you have identified individuals that are willing to put money into your project, it is very important to examine their expectations and compare them with your own perspective. You must educate your investors about the risks, the rewards, and all the problems and variables that can arise over which you may have little or no control. Investors must know how much money you want them to put into your project in order to evaluate whether they can afford it. If they have any reservations, you should uncover them. If the reservations cannot be resolved, you should not accept the money. Spend time talking with them and make certain you really understand each other and that they are people to whom you want to be committed.

Fair Return

In discussing payback with an investor, you must identify and explore three specific areas. What will be the share of the investor's participation? For how long will the investor participate? And from what sources of income will the investor be repaid?

Investors often negotiate for very healthy returns on their investment. The argument, and it is a good one, is that he or she is taking a substantial risk in putting money into your project that could be invested in other ways for a more certain return.

Evaluating a fair return to the investor is a function of how badly the money is needed and how eager the investor is to put money into your project. These points alone can determine how much either side is willing to offer. Investors that have alternative places to put their money for a good return are not going to be as willing to invest, and if you have no other source of income for a project, you may not be in a position to do a lot of arguing. If you have to give up an amount that you feel will hurt your business or your ability to fund your career, you should not accept the money. Go look for another investor.

Another, perhaps more constructive way of measuring a reasonable return to the investor is to look at the amount of risk assumed by the investor in relation to the amount of money invested: the smaller the number of dollars and the smaller the risk of failure, the smaller the return. For example if your project cost $2,000, it would be hard to justify returning 10% of your income for life to an investor. If, however, the investor put $200,000 into your project, it is easier to justify committing a reasonable percentage of your income to the investor for a substantial period of time.

You can determine the proper percentage to offer to an investor by looking at how much you can afford to give up. Remember, there are only so many slices in the money pie, and there must be something left for you. Consequently, you should identify the parties to whom you have already made commitments, managers, attorneys, other investors, partners, and the like. After you have paid those people, you still need money to run your business and support yourself. You must analyze your income potential and anticipated expenses carefully.

CONCLUSION

There are no simple answers. Deals can be structured in many ways. These decisions require you to analyze your funding sources, the urgency of your need, the risk the investor is taking, and his or her other investment choices, and your other money commitments. Take the time to do your homework, and be very careful about the commitment you are making. When in doubt, seek advice. If the deal doesn't make sense or doesn't feel good to you, walk away from it. Be honest with yourself, identify your goals, your value system, and what you are willing and not willing to give up. Only by taking all these factors into account can you arrive at a financial package that will work for you. However, once you set up such a package, you may be able to accomplish career objectives that would have otherwise remained beyond your reach.

worksheets worksheets

These worksheets will help you estimate income and expenses, and provide guidelines for keeping track of them. Preparing a budget will help you think through your entire recording project and it will be one of your strongest selling points when borrowing money. It will serve as a reliable guide as you carry out your project.

Before making your initial projections, you should make several copies of the worksheets or reproduce them on a computer spreadsheet program and experiment with various quantities of sales in each category. Working out the numbers in advance will help you determine the most profitable and practical sales and promotional plans. The number of recordings you project to manufacture, promote, and sell will provide the boundaries of your expense budget.

Because recording projects vary widely, you may find that some items relating to your project are missing. Be sure to add them when projecting profit/loss probabilities.

These forms may be reproduced solely for private, noncommercial use.

1

promotion promotion

Estimating costs for promoting your record will help you to make some basic decisions regarding your promotional plans. Counting the number of names on your various mailing lists will help you gauge how many promotional recordings you are likely to give away.

The number of names on your lists will serve as a guide for the quantities of various promotional materials that you will be preparing, as well as monthly mailing and phone expenses.

Promotional Giveaways

	Number of Names
Priority Press List	_____
Secondary Press List	_____
Industry List	_____
Fan and Personal List	_____
Purchased Mailing Lists	_____
Total Number of Promotional Giveaways	_____

Initial Mailings

	Quantity	Mailing Cost
Promotional Package (Recording & Press Kit)	_____	
Padded Mailers or Boxes	_____	$ _____
Postage		$ _____
Other (photocopying, secretarial, etc.)		$ _____
Total Initial Mailing Expenses		$ _____

Continuing Mailings

	Quantity	x	No. of Months	x	$Per Month	=	Cost
Padded Mailers or Boxes	_____		_____		$ _____		$ _____
Postage	_____		_____		$ _____		$ _____
Other (photocopying, secretarial, etc.)	_____		_____		$ _____		$ _____
Total Continuing Expenses							$ _____

Enter all items marked with double underline on Worksheet 12, Planning

Advertising

	No. of Months	x $Per Month	= Cost
Display	_____	$ _____	$ _____
Classified	_____	$ _____	$ _____
Radio	_____	$ _____	$ _____
Other (TV, Web, etc.)	_____	$ _____	$ _____
		Total Continuing Expenses	$ _____

Promotional Services

	No. of Months	x $Per Month	= Cost
Record Promoters	_____	$ _____	$ _____
Public Relations Firms	_____	$ _____	$ _____
		Total Continuing Expenses	$ _____

Internet Services

Web developement and design costs are figured on worksheet 4, "Graphic Design."

	No. of Months	x $Per Month	= Cost
Internet ISP Account	_____	$ _____	$ _____
Host Site	_____	$ _____	$ _____
Other Services (advertising, counting services)	_____	$ _____	$ _____
		Total Continuing Expenses	$ _____

Enter all items marked with double underline on Worksheet 12, Planning

sales sales

This worksheet will help you project sales income in each sales category. Using that figure as the multiplier for the number of recordings you plan to sell in each category will provide an annual gross income figure. Subtracting direct sales costs from gross income will give the annual net sales in each category. Adding the number of records you plan to sell to the number you plan to giveaway for promotional purposes will determine the number of recordings to be manufactured.

Price

List Price of Vinyl $ _____

Mail-order Price $ _____

Web Site Price $ _____

Special Performance Price $ _____

Store Discount Price $ _____

Distributors' Discount Price $ _____

List Price of Cassette $ _____

Mail-order Price $ _____

Special Performance Price $ _____

Web Site Price $ _____

Store Discount Price $ _____

Distributors' Discount Price $ _____

List Price of CD $ _____

Mail-order Price $ _____

Special Performance Price $ _____

Web Site Price $ _____

Store Discount Price $ _____

Distributors' Discount Price $ _____

Mail-order Income

Number of Recordings x Mail-order Price = Gross Mail-order Income $ _____

Subtract Sales Tax   - $ _____

Subtract Postage, Packaging, and Handling   - $ _____

Net Income from Mail-order Sales $ _____

Performance Income

Number of Recordings x Performance Price = Gross Performance Income $ _____

Subtract Seller's Commission   - $ _____

Subtract Sales Tax   - $ _____

Net Income from Performance Sales $ _____

Store Income

Number of Recordings x Store Price = Gross Store Sales Income $ _____

Subtract Mailing/Shipping   - $ _____

Net Income from Store Sales $ _____

Distributor Income

Number of Recordings x Distributor Price = Gross Distributor Income $ _____

Subtract Mailing/Shipping   - $ _____

Net Income from Distributor Sales $ _____

Internet Income

Number of Recordings x Distributor Price = Gross Internet Income

From Artist's Web Site $ _____

From Other Internet Stores $ _____

Subtract Mailings/Shipping   - $ _____

Net Income from Web Sales $ _____

Enter all items marked with double underline on Worksheet 12, Planning

recording contracts

If you are dealing with a recording label that is not affiliated with a major label, the recording company that you contract with should be able to provide some estimates of projected sales.

Income projections for a new artist signing with major labels are seldom done. A useful exercise, if you are thinking of signing with a major label, is to figure out what their total advance is going to be and project how many recordings will have to be sold (based on your royalty: net cents per recording sold) for you to pay back your advance.

Distribution Deals

Projected Sales Income $ _____

Pressing and Distribution Deals

Projected Sales Income $ _____

Artist Deals: Independent Label

Projected Sales Income $ _____

Artist Deals: Major Label

Advance divided by net cents artist royalty = Number of recordings that will have to be sold to recoup advance. $ _____

Enter all items marked with double underline on Worksheet 12, Planning

4

graphic design

graphic design

Design expenses will be one-time costs. Plan what you need for the first year. You will find it most economical to design promotional materials and recording covers at the same time since many of the same elements will be used throughout.

It is not unusual, however, for professional photographers and illustrators to require additional fees for reuse of their artwork in different applications, clarify this before commissioning their services.

Logo

Design	$_____
Photography	$_____
Illustration	$_____
Production	$_____
Total Logo	$_____

Stationery Package

Usually includes letterhead, envelopes, mailing labels, business cards.

Design	$_____
Photography	$_____
Illustration	$_____
Production	$_____
Total Stationery Package	$_____

Recording Package

Usually includes cover, booklets, inserts, label imprinting.

Design	$_____
Photography	$_____
Illustration	$_____
Production	$_____
UPC	$_____
Total Recording Package	$_____

Enter all items marked with double underline on Worksheet 12, Planning

Press Kit Covers

Design $ _____

Photography $ _____

Illustration $ _____

Production $ _____

Total Press Kit Covers $ _____

Fliers/Posters

Design $ _____

Photography $ _____

Illustration $ _____

Production $ _____

Total Fliers/Posters $ _____

Mail-order Form

Design $ _____

Photography $ _____

Illustration $ _____

Production $ _____

Total Mail-order Package $ _____

Web Site Development and Design

Organization, Outline, Copy $ _____

Design $ _____

Photography $ _____

Illustration $ _____

Total Web Site Development $ _____

Enter all items marked with double underline on Worksheet 12, Planning

5

printing
printing

Be sure to get quotes, as printing prices vary considerably, and remember that the per unit prices drop as the quantity increases.

 If your printer quotes a package price, or if you are making use of a stock cover, be sure to request a breakdown to note which items are included. Have the printer give you fixed prices on any extras.

Prepress

	Cost
Halftones	$ _____
Duotones	$ _____
Color Separations	$ _____
Stripping	$ _____
Bluelines	$ _____
Chromalins	$ _____
Press Proofs	$ _____

Total Prepress $ _____

CDs and Cassettes

	Quantity	Cost
CD Tray Card + Booklet	_____	$ _____
CD Alternative Packaging	_____	$ _____
CD Labels	_____	$ _____
Cassette J-card	_____	$ _____
Cassette Labels	_____	$ _____
Shipping to Customer	_____	$ _____

Total CD and Cassette Printing $ _____

Vinyl Records

	Quantity	Cost
Cover	_____	$ _____
Label Imprinting	_____	$ _____
Varnishing/Lamination	_____	$ _____
Promotional Inserts	_____	$ _____
Shipping to Customer	_____	$ _____

Total Vinyl Record Printing $ _____

Enter all items marked with double underline on Worksheet 12, Planning

Promotional Materials

	Quantity	Cost
Stationery Package	_____	$ _____
Press Kit Covers	_____	$ _____
Fliers/Posters	_____	$ _____
Photographs	_____	$ _____
Mail-order Form	_____	$ _____
Other Promotional Items	_____	$ _____

Total Printing $ _____

Enter all items marked with double underline on Worksheet 12, Planning

6

recording: songs

recording: songs

This worksheet is the first step in planning your recording sessions. Make a copy for each song you intend to record. List the artists and session musicians for the songs and the instrument (or vocal part) each will play or sing. Then with the help of your arranger, producer, and engineer, assign each part a microphone and track number. Once you have made a worksheet for each song, you can proceed to group the songs and parts into recording sessions on the following worksheet.

TITLE OF SONG _____ **TIME OF SONG** ____ **SESSION DATE** ____

Artist	Instrument/Vocal	Mic No.(s)	Track No.(s)	Session No.
_____	_____	_____	_____	_____
_____	_____	_____	_____	_____
_____	_____	_____	_____	_____
_____	_____	_____	_____	_____
_____	_____	_____	_____	_____
_____	_____	_____	_____	_____
_____	_____	_____	_____	_____
_____	_____	_____	_____	_____
_____	_____	_____	_____	_____
_____	_____	_____	_____	_____

7

recording: sessions
recording: sessions

Use this form to indicate which songs and parts will be covered in each session and what microphones and tracks will be involved.

Make a separate form for each mixing session as well, and plan which songs you will mix in each session to help you estimate mixing times. This information will help you estimate the number of hours needed for all sessions.

Session No._____ **Hours** _____ ☐ **Recording** ☐ **Mixing**

Song Title(s)	Instruments/Vocal	Mic No.(s)	Track Nos.(s)
_____	_____	_____	_____
_____	_____	_____	_____
_____	_____	_____	_____
_____	_____	_____	_____
_____	_____	_____	_____
_____	_____	_____	_____
_____	_____	_____	_____
_____	_____	_____	_____
_____	_____	_____	_____

8

recording: costs
These costs are determined by the number of sessions, and the number of hours. In addition to personnel and studio time, be sure to take into account special equipment or instruments, tape costs, and personal expenses while you are recording.

Personnel

Producer(s)   No. of Hours x Hourly Rate = Cost

Name

Engineer(s)

Name

Arranger(s)

Name

Studio Musicians

Name

Total Recording Costs $

Enter all items marked with double underline on Worksheet 12, Planning

From *How to Make and Sell your Own Recording* by Diane Sward Rapaport. This form may be reproduced solely for private, noncommercial use. Copyright © 1999 Diane Sward Rapaport. All rights reserved.

Studio Time

	No. of Hours x	Hourly Rate =	Cost
Rehearsal	_____	_____	$ _____
Recording	_____	_____	$ _____
Mixing	_____	_____	$ _____
Editing and Tape Copying	_____	_____	$ _____
Location Recording	_____	_____	$ _____
		Total Studio Time	$ _____

Equipment and Instruments

	Items	Cost
Equipment Rental	_____	$ _____
Instrument Rental	_____	$ _____
Other	_____	$ _____
	Total Equipment and Instruments	$ _____

Tape and Disc Supplies

	Cost
Multitrack	$ _____
Half-track	$ _____
Quarter-track	$ _____
Analog Cassettes	$ _____
DAT	$ _____
CD-R	$ _____
Computer Disc	$ _____
Other	$ _____
Total Tape Cost	$ _____

Miscellaneous Expenses

	Cost
Travel	$ _____
Lodging	$ _____
Food	$ _____
Other	$ _____
Total Miscellaneous Expense	$ _____

Enter all items marked with double underline on Worksheet 12, Planning

manufacturing

manufacturing

Be sure to get quotes, as manufacturing prices vary considerably, and remember that the per unit prices drop as the quantity increases.

If your manufacturer quotes a package price for printing and recording duplication, be sure to note which items are included and get fixed prices on any extras.

Vinyl Records   Quantity   Cost

Disc-mastering $_____

References $_____

Three-step Plating Process $_____

One-step Plating Process $_____

Test Pressing $_____

Manufacturing   _____ $_____

Shrink-wrapping $_____

Shipping $_____

                          Total Records $_____

Cassettes   Quantity   Cost

Real-time   _____ $_____

Bin-loop or Digital Bin _____ $_____

Shrink-wrapping $_____

Shipping $_____

                          Total Cassettes $_____

CDs or CD-Rs   Quantity   Cost

Replication   _____ $_____

Shipping $_____   **Total CDs/CD-Rs** $_____

Package Prices   Quantity   Cost

Cassettes/CDs   _____ $_____

Shipping $_____   **Total Packages** $_____

Enter all items marked with double underline on Worksheet 12, Planning

10

copyrights

This worksheet is designed to keep track of income and costs involved in and publishing musical material on your own recording.

Publishing Income

	Title	
Mechanical License Income	_____	$ _____
	_____	_____
Performance Rights Income	_____	_____
	_____	_____
	Total Publishing Income	$ _____

Mechanical License Fees

List each song recorded that is not assigned to your publishing company.

Estimate the cost by multiplying fee by the number of recordings you plan to manufacture (less number recordings you plan to give away).

			$
Title	Publisher	Length (Time)	License Fee
_____	_____	_____	_____
_____	_____	_____	_____
_____	_____	_____	_____
		Total Fees	$ _____

Total Fee x Manufactured Recordings (Less Giveaways) =

Total Mechanical License Fees _____

Song Protection

Copyright Registration (Songs)	$ _____
Copyright Registration (Recordings)	$ _____
Total Song Protection	$ _____

Performance Rights Organizations

ASCAP/BMI/SESAC Songwriter/Publisher Membership	$ _____
Total Performance Rights Organization	$ _____

Enter all items marked with double underline on Worksheet 12, Planning

business
business

This worksheet covers the cost of setting up and running your office, professional services, and governmental fees and licenses, as well as other associated expenses. Although some of these may seem remote when you first start planning your project, be sure to budget some funds for them.

Office Expenses

Annual Cost

Office Equipment		$ _____
Office Supplies		$ _____
Web Site Domain Registry		$ _____
Telephone Installation	**Per Month**	$ _____
Telephone	_____	$ _____
Answering Service	_____	$ _____
Postage	_____	$ _____
Repair and Maintenance	_____	$ _____
Rent/Utilities	_____	$ _____
	Total Office Expenses	$ _____

Professional Services

	Per Month	
Legal	_____	$ _____
Bookkeeping	_____	$ _____
Secretarial	_____	$ _____
	Total Professional Services	$ _____

Fees and Licenses

Incorporation Expenses		$ _____
Seller's Permit/Business License		$ _____
Bulk Mail Permit		$ _____
Trademark Registration		$ _____
	Total Fees and Licenses	$ _____

Enter all items marked with double underline on Worksheet 12, Planning

Industry Expenses

Publications $ _____

Professional Memberships $ _____

Conventions $ _____

   Travel/Lodging/Food $ _____

Seminars/Workshops $ _____

   Travel/Lodging/Food $ _____

Total Industry Expenses   ══════════════

Enter all items marked with double underline on Worksheet 12, Planning

planning

The final worksheet groups all the expenses and income from your recording project into sales income and initial costs, the cost of product, promotional and business expenses. Each of the entries on this worksheet should be taken from the appropriate totals on the preceding worksheets, indicated by double underlines.

Looking at your project from this overall perspective will helpful in figuring your profits.

Income
Sales Income

Net Income from Mail-order Sales	$ _____
Net Income from Performance Sales	$ _____
Net Income from Store Sales	$ _____
Net Income from Distributor Sales	$ _____
Net Income from Internet Sales	$ _____
Total Sales Income	$ _____

Publishing Income

Mechanical License and Performance Rights Income	$ _____
Total Publishing Income	$ _____

Recording Contracts Income

Total Contracts Income	$ _____
Total Income	$ _____

Expenses
Promotional

Mailings —Total Initial Expenses	$ _____
Mailings—Total Continuing Expenses	$ _____
Advertising—Total Continuing Expenses	$ _____
Promotional Services—Total Continuing Expenses	$ _____
Internet Services—Total Continuing Expenses	$ _____
Total Promotional Expenses	$ _____

Design

Total Logo	$ _____
Total Stationery Package	$ _____
Total Recording Package	$ _____
Total Press Kit Covers	$ _____
Total Fliers/Posters	$ _____
Total Mail-order Form	$ _____
Total Web Site Developement and Design	$ _____
Total Design Expenses	$ _____

Printing

Total Prepress $ _____
Total CD Printing $ _____
Total Cassette Printing $ _____
Total Vinyl Printing $ _____
Total Promotional Materials $ _____

Total Printing $ _____

Manufacturing

Total Vinyl $ _____
Total Cassettes $ _____
Total CD/CD-R $ _____
Total Packages $ _____
Total Shrink-wrap $ _____
Total Shipping $ _____

Total Manufactoring $ _____

Recording

Total Recording Personnel Costs $ _____
Total Studio Time $ _____
Total Equipment and Instruments $ _____
Total Tape Costs $ _____
Total Miscellaneous Expenses $ _____

Total Recording $ _____

Copyright

Total Mechanical License Fees $ _____
Total Song Protection $ _____
Total Performance Rights Organization $ _____

Total Copyright $ _____

Business Expenses

Total Office Expenses $ _____
Total Professional Services $ _____
Total Fees and License $ _____
Total Industry Expenses $ _____

Total Business Expenses $ _____

Total Expenses $ _____

Total Income − Total Expenses = NET PROFIT $ _____

resources

resources

TRADE PUBLICATIONS

Acoustic Guitar
PO Box 767
San Anselmo, CA 94979
(415) 485-6946
www.acguitar.com

Acoustic Musician
PO Box 1349
New Market, VA 22844
(540) 740-4005
www.shentel.net/acousticmusician

AES Journal of the Audio Engineering Society
60 East 42nd Street, Room 2520
New York, NY 10165
(212) 661-8528
www.aes.org/journal

The American Organist
475 Riverside Drive, Suite 1260
New York, NY 10115
(212) 870-2310
www.agohq.org/tao/index.html

BAM
3470 Buskirk Avenue
Pleasant Hill, CA 94523
(925) 934-3700
www.musicuniverse.com

Bass Player
411 Borel Avenue, Suite 100
San Mateo, CA 94402
(650) 358-9500
www.bassplayer.com

Billboard
BPI Communications, Inc.
1515 Broadway, 11th Floor
New York, NY 10036
(800) 745-8922 or (212) 764-7300
www.billboard.com

Blaze
104 East 25th Street, 3rd Floor
New York, NY 10016
(212) 375-1825
www.blaze.com

Bluegrass Unlimited
PO Box 111
Broad Run, VA 20137
(800) 258-4727 or (540) 349-8181
www.bluegrassmusic.com

Cadence Magazine:
The Review of Jazz & Blues
Cadence Building
Redwood, NY 13679
(315) 287-2852
www.cadencebuilding.com

Canadian Musician
23 Hannover Drive, Suite 7
St. Catharines, ON L2W 1A3
Canada
(905) 641-3471
www.canadianmusician.com

CCM: Contemporary Christian Music
107 Kenner Avenue
Nashville, TN 37205
(615) 386-3011
www.ccmcom.com

Chamber Music America
305 7th Avenue, 5th Floor
New York, NY 10001
(212) 242-2022
www.chamber-music.org

Christian Musician
4441 South Meridian, Suite 275
Puyallup, WA 98373
(253) 445-1973

Circus
6 West 18th Street, 2nd Floor
New York, NY 10011
(212) 242-4902
www.circusmagazine.com

CMJ New Music Monthly/
CMJ New Music Report
(College Music Journal)
11 Middle Neck Road, Suite 400
Great Neck, NY 11021
(516) 466-6000
www.cmjmusic.com

Crawdaddy!
PO Box 232517
Encinitas, CA 92023
(760) 753-1815
www.cdaddy.com

Dirty Linen
PO Box 66600
Baltimore, MD 21239
(410) 583-7973
www.dirtylinen.com

DJ Times
25 Willowdale Avenue
Port Washington, NY 11050
(516) 767-2500
www.djtimes.com

Down Beat
102 North Haven Road
Elmhurst, IL 60126
(630) 941-2030
www.downbeatjazz.com

Electronic Musician
6400 Hollis Street, Suite 12
Emeryville, CA 94608
510-653-3307
www.emusician.com

EQ
6 Manhasset Avenue
Port Washington, NY 11050
(516) 944-5940
www.eqmag.com

Fingerstyle Guitar
3645 Jeannine Drive, Suite 201
Colorado Springs, CO 80917
(719) 637-3395
www.fingerstyleguitar.com

Gig
460 Park Avenue South, 9th Floor
New York, NY 10016
(212) 378-0400
www.gigmag.com

The Gospel Voice
8122 Wren Road
Goodlettsville, TN 37070
(615) 851-1841
www.gospelvoice.com

Guitar
10 Midland Avenue
Port Chester, NY 10573
(914) 935-5200
www.guitarmag.com

Guitar Player
411 Borel Avenue, Suite 100
San Mateo, CA 94402
(650) 358-9500
www.guitarplayer.com

Guitar World/Guitar World Acoustic
1115 Broadway, 8th Floor
New York, NY 10010
(212) 807-7100
www.guitarworld.com

Hollywood Reporter
5055 Wilshire Boulevard, 6th Floor
Los Angeles, CA 90036
(213) 525-2000
www.hollywoodreporter.com

Indie Music World
Association For Independent Music
147 East Main Street
PO Box 988
Whitesburg, KY 41858
(606) 633-0946
www.afim.org

International Musician
American Federation of Musicians
1501 Broadway, Suite 600
Paramount Building
New York, NY 10036
(212) 869-1330
www.afm.org

Jazziz
3620 N.W. 43rd Street
Gainsville, FL 32606
(352) 375-3705
www.jazziz.com

JazzTimes
8737 Colesville Road, 5th Floor
Silver Spring, MD 20910
(301) 588-4114
www.jazztimes.com

Keyboard
411 Borel Avenue, Suite 100
San Mateo, CA 94402
(650) 358-9500
www.keyboardmag.com

Live Sound! International
4741 Central Avenue, Suite 222
Kansas City, MO 64112
(913) 677-8688
www.livesoundint.com

Metal Edge Magazine
233 Park Avenue South, 6th Floor
New York, NY 10003
(212) 780-3500
www.mtledge.com

Mix
6400 Hollis Street, Suite 12
Emeryville, CA 94608
(510) 653-3307
www.mixonline.com

Mobile Beat
L.A. Communications, Inc.
PO Box 309
East Rochester, NY 14445
(716) 385-9920
www.mobilebeat.com

Modern Drummer
12 Old Bridge Road
Cedar Grove, NJ 07009
(973) 239-4140
www.moderndrummer.com

Music City News
PO Box 22975
Nashville, TN 37202
(615) 329-2200
mcnonline.com

Music Connection
4731 Laurel Canyon Boulevard
North Hollywood, CA 91607
(818) 755-0101
www.musicconnection.com

Music Educators Journal
Music Educators National
Conference (MENC)
1806 Robert Fulton Drive
Reston, VA 20191
(703) 860-4000
www.menc.org

Music Inc.
102 North Haven Road
Elmhurst, IL 60126
(630) 941-2030

The Music Trades
80 West Street
PO Box 432
Englewood, NJ 07631
(201) 871-1965
www.musictrades.com

Musician
BPI Communications, Inc.
1515 Broadway, 11th Floor
New York, NY 10036
(800) 745-8922 or (212) 764-7300
www.musicianmag.com

*The National Academy of
Songwriters Musepaper*
6255 Sunset Boulevard, Suite 1023
Hollywood, CA 90028
(323) 463-7178
www.nassong.org

OffBeat
421 Frenchmen Street, Suite 200
New Orleans, LA 70116
(504) 944-4300
www.offbeat.com

Overture
Professional Musicians, Local 47
AFM
817 North Vine Street
Hollywood, CA 90028
(213) 462-2162
www.promusic47.org

The Performing Songwriter
6620 McCall Drive
Longmont, CO 80503
(800) 883-7664 or (303) 682-1442
www.performingsongwriter.com

Piano and Keyboard
PO Box 2626
San Anselmo, CA 94979
(415) 458-8672
www.pianoandkeyboard.com

Pro Sound News
460 Park Avenue South, 9th Floor
New York, NY 10016
(212) 378-0400
www.prosoundnews.com

Pulse!
MTS Inc.
2500 Del Monte Street, Building C
West Sacramento, CA 95691
(916) 373-2450
www.towerrecords.com/pulse

Radio And Records
10100 Santa Monica Boulevard
5th Floor
Los Angeles, CA 90067
(310) 553-4330
www.rronline.com

Rap Sheet
2270 Centinela Avenue, Suite B-4
Santa Monica, CA 90064
(310) 412-0639
www.rapsheet.com

Recording
Music Maker Publications, Inc.
5412 Idylwild Trail, Suite 100
Boulder, CO 80301
(303) 516-9118
www.recordingmag.com

Request
10400 Yellow Circle Drive
Minnetonka, MN 55343
(612) 931-8740
www.requestline.com

Rolling Stone
1290 Avenue of the Americas
2nd Floor
New York, NY 10104
(212) 484-1616
www.rollingstone.com

RPM Weekly
6 Brentcliffe Road
Toronto, Ontario M4G 3Y2
Canada
(416) 425-0257

Sing Out!
PO Box 5253
Bethlehem, PA 18015
(610) 865-5366
www.singout.org

Sound & Communications
25 Willowdale Avenue
Port Washington, NY 11050
(516) 767-2500
www.soundandcommunications.com

The Source
215 Park Avenue South, 11th Floor
New York, NY 10003
(212) 253-3700
www.thesource.com

Strings
PO Box 767
San Anselmo, CA 94979
(415) 485-6946
www.strings.com

*Tapeless Studio Computer Audio
Magazine*
(Online only)
www.nctweb.com/studio

Up Beat Daily
102 North Haven Road
Elmhurst, IL 60126
(630) 941-2030

Variety
5700 Wilshire Boulevard, Suite 120
Los Angeles, CA 90036
(213) 857-6600
www.variety.com

Vibe
215 Lexington Avenue, 6th Floor
New York, NY 10016
(212) 448-7300
www.vibe.com

Victory Review
PO Box 2254
Tacoma, WA 98401
(253) 428-0832
www.victorymusic.org

INDUSTRY DIRECTORIES

AFIM Directory
Association For Independent Music
147 East Main Street
PO Box 988
Whitesburg, KY 41858
(606) 633-0946
www.afim.org

*The Album Network's Yellow
Pages of Rock*
The Album Network, Inc.
120 North Victory Boulevard
Burbank, CA 91502
(800) 222-4382
(818) 955-4000
www.yprock.com

Billboard Directories
1695 Oak Street
PO Box 2016
Lakewood, NJ 08701
(800) 344-7119 or (732) 363-4156
All Billboard directories are updated
annually.

*Billboard Nashville 615/Country
Music Sourcebook*

*Billboard International Buyer's
Guide Directory*

*Billboard International Latin
Music Buyer's Guide*

*Billboard International Talent and
Touring Directory*

*Billboard International Tape/Disc
Directory*

*Billboard Radio Power Book:
Directory of Music Radio and
Record Promotion*

*Billboard Record Retailing
Directory*

Festivals Northwest Quarterly
Festivals Northwest
PO Box 7515
Bonney Lake, WA 98390
(253) 863-6617
E-mail—festivalsnw@wolfenet.com
(Lists over 800 festivals, fairs, camps,
and conferences in the Northwest.)

Grammy® Awards Guide
Entertainment Resource Services, Inc.
PO Box 1469
Tucker, GA 30085
(770) 934-0906

*Mix Master Directory of the
Professional Audio Industry*
6400 Hollis, Suite 12
Emeryville, CA 94608
(510) 653-3307

The Music Business Registry
7510 Sunset Boulevard, Suite 1041
Los Angeles, CA 90046
(800) 377-7411 or (818) 769-2722

   A&R Registry

   Film/TV Music Guide

   *Music Business Attorney, Legal and
   Business Affairs Registry*

   Music Publisher Registry

Music Directory Canada
CM Books
23 Hannover Drive, Unit 7
St. Catharines, Ontario L2W 1A3
Canada
(416) 641-3471

The Music Yellow Pages
National Music & Entertainment Inc.
184 Hempstead Avenue
West Hempstead, NY 11552
(800) 357-8776 or (516) 489-6514
www.musicyellowpages.com

Performance International Touring
Talent Publications
1101 University, Suite 108
Fort Worth, TX 76107
(817) 338-9444
Updated annually. All directories
contain international listings.

   Talent Management

   *Equipment Manufacturers and
   Production Personnel*

   Black Book

   Talent Buyers

   Talent Agencies

   Concert Production

   Talent—Country and Christian

   Transportation/Accommodations

   Facilities

The Recording Industry Sourcebook
c/o Intertec Publishing
PO Box 12901
Overland Park, KS 66282
(800) 543-7771 or (913) 967-1719

RECORDING CATALOGS

Muze for Music/Phonolog
Muze Inc.
Manager, Label Relations
Music Department
304 Hudson Street
New York, NY 10013
Listings are free and open to all
recordings on sale and generally
available in record stores. To obtain
a listing, send a copy of your recording including packaging, production
notes, and promotional materials.

Schwann Artist and Schwann Opus
(classical listings)
Schwann Spectrum
(nonclassical listings)
Schwann Publications
1807 2nd Street, Suite 101
Santa Fe, NM 87505
(505) 988-2045
Listings are free and open to recordings that are available through a U.S.
telephone number and address or
distributed nationally to stores. To
obtain a listing, send a copy of the
recording, along with record company information (name, address,
phone number, and contact person).

FEDERAL AGENCIES

United States Copyright Office
Register of Copyrights
Library Of Congress
101 Independence Avenue, S.E.
Washington, DC 20559
(202) 707-3000 (Information)
(202) 707-9100 (Forms hotline—
use this number if you know which
form(s) you need.)
www.loc.gov/copyright

United States Patent and
Trademark Office
2021 Jefferson Davis Highway
Arlington, VA 22202
(800) 786-9199 or (703) 308-4357
www.uspto.gov

United States Securities and
Exchange Commission (SEC)
450 Fifth Street, N.W.
Washington, DC 20549
(202) 942-7040
www.sec.gov

ORGANIZATIONS AND TRADE ASSOCIATIONS

Academy of Country Music
6255 Sunset Boulevard
Suite 923
Hollywood, CA 90028
(213) 462-2351
www.acmcountry.com

American Federation of Musicians
(AFM)
www.afm.org

   1501 Broadway
   Paramount Building, Suite 600
   New York, NY 10036
   (212) 869-1330

   7080 Hollywood Boulevard
   Suite 1020
   Hollywood, CA 90028
   (213) 461-3441

American Federation of Television
& Radio Artists (AFTRA)
(Offices nationwide)
www.aftra.com

   260 Madison Avenue, 7th Floor
   New York, NY 10016
   (212) 532-0800

   5757 Wilshire Boulevard, Suite 900
   Los Angeles, CA 90036
   (323) 634-8100

   1108 17th Avenue South
   PO Box 121087
   Nashville, TN 37212
   (615) 327-2944

   One East Erie, Suite 650
   Chicago, IL 60611
   (312) 573-8081

American Institute of Graphic Arts
(AIGA)
164 Fifth Avenue
New York, NY 10010
(212) 807-1990
www.aiga.org

American Society of Composers,
Authors, and Publishers (ASCAP)
www.ascap.com

One Lincoln Plaza
New York, NY 10023
(212) 621-6000

7920 Sunset Boulevard, Suite 300
Los Angeles, CA 90046
(323) 883-1000

Two Music Square West
Nashville, TN 37203
(615) 742-5000

844 Alton Road, Suite 1
Miami Beach, FL 33139
(305) 673-3446

1608 West Belmont Avenue
Suite 200
Chicago, IL 60657
(773) 472-1157

Association For Independent Music
(AFIM)
147 East Main Street
PO Box 988
Whitesburg, KY 41858
(606) 633-0946
www.afim.org

Association of Independent Music
Publishers (AIMP)
PO Box 1561
Burbank, CA 91507
(818) 842-6257

Broadcast Music Incorporated (BMI)
www.bmi.com

320 West 57th Street
New York, NY 10019
(212) 586-2000

8730 Sunset Boulevard
3rd Floor West
Los Angeles, CA 90069
(310) 659-9109

5201 Blue Lagoon Drive, Suite 310
Miami, FL 33126
(305) 266-3636

10 Music Square East
Nashville, TN 37203
(615) 401-2000

California Lawyers for the Arts (CLA)
www.sirius.com/~cla

1641 18th Street
Santa Monica, CA 90404
(310) 998-5590

1212 Broadway Street, Suite 834
Oakland, CA 94612
(510) 444-6351

Fort Mason Center
Building C, Room 255
San Francisco, CA 94123
(415) 775-7200

Country Music Association (CMA)
1 Music Circle South
Nashville, TN 37203
(615) 244-2840
www.countrymusic.org

Electronic Industries Association
(EIA)
2500 Wilson Boulevard
Arlington, VA 22201
(703) 907-7500
www.eia.org

Folk Alliance
North American Folk Music and
Dance Alliance
1001 Connecticut Avenue, N.W.
Suite 501
Washington, DC 20036
(202) 835-3655
www.folk.org

Gospel Music Association
1205 Division Street
Nashville, TN 37203
(615) 242-0303
www.gospelmusic.org

The Harry Fox Agency
711 3rd Avenue, 8th Floor
New York, NY 10017
(212) 370-5330
www.nmpa.org/hfa.html

Home Recording Rights Coalition
PO Box 14267
1145 19th Street, N.W.
Washington, DC 20044
(800) 282-8273
www.hrrc.org

International Bluegrass Music
Association
207 East 2nd Street
Owensboro, KY 42303
(502) 684-9025
www.banjo.com/IBMA/ibmahome.htm

Los Angeles Women in Music
8489 West Third Street
Los Angeles, CA 90048
(213) 653-3662

Music and Entertainment Industry
Educator's Association (MEIEA)
Department of Music Business
Belmont University
1900 Belmont Boulevard
Nashville, TN 37212
www.ecnet.net/users/mimusba/meiea

National Academy of Recording Arts
and Sciences (NARAS)
(Offices nationwide)
3402 Pico Boulevard
Santa Monica, CA 90405
(310) 392-3777
www.grammy.com

National Academy of Songwriters
(NAS)
6255 Sunset Boulevard, Suite 1023
Hollywood, CA 90028
(323) 463-7178
www.nassong.org

National Association of Recording
Merchandisers (NARM)
9 Eves Drive, Suite 120
Marlton, NJ 08053
(609) 596-2221
www.narm.com

National Music Publishers
Association
711 Third Avenue, 8th Floor
New York, NY 10017
(212) 370-5330
www.nmpa.org

The PAN Network
PO Box 162
Skippack, PA 19474
(215) 661-1100
www.pan.com
(Computer network that provides
communication and information
services to music professionals.)

Recording Industry Association of
America, Inc. (RIAA)
1020 19th Street, N.W., Suite 200
Washington, DC 20036
(202) 775-0101
www.riaa.com

SESAC, Inc.
www.sesac.com

421 West 54th Street
New York, NY 10019
(212) 586-3450

55 Music Square East
Nashville, TN 37203
(615) 320-0055

Society of Composers, Authors and
Music Publishers of Canada
(SOCAN)
41 Valley Brook Drive
Don Mills, Ontario M3B 2S6
Canada
(416) 445-8700
www.socan.com

Society of Professional Audio
Recording Services (SPARS)
4300 10th Avenue North
Lake Worth, FL 33461
(561) 641-6648
www.xensei.com/spars

The Songwriter's Guild of America
(SGA)
www.songwriters.org

1560 Broadway, Suite 1306
New York, NY 10036
(212) 768-7902

6430 Sunset Boulevard, Suite 705
Hollywood, CA 90028
(323) 462-1108

1222 16th Avenue South, Suite 25
Nashville, TN 37212
(615) 329-1782

1500 Harbor Boulevard
Weehawken, NJ 07087
(201) 867-7603

Uniform Code Council, Inc.
8163 Old Yankee Road, Suite J
Dayton, OH 45458
(513) 435-3870
www.uc-council.org
(Bar code information)

ANNUAL CONFERENCES AND SEMINARS

Folk Alliance
1001 Connecticut Avenue, N.W.
Suite 501
Washington, DC 20036
(202) 835-3655

New Music Seminar
632 Broadway, 9th Floor
New York, NY 100132
(212) 473-4343

North by Northeast
185A Danforth Avenue, 2nd Floor
Toronto, Ontario M4K 1N2
Canada
(416) 469-0986

Songwriter's Expo
National Academy of Songwriters
6255 Sunset Boulevard, Suite 1023
Hollywood, CA 90028
(213) 463-7178

South by Southwest
PO Box 4999
Austin, TX 78765
(512) 467-7979

BOOKS

This is the author's selected list of
books on particular aspects of
recording and business.

*The Acoustic Musician's Guide to
Sound Reinforcement and Live
Recording*
Mike Sokol
Prentice-Hall, Inc.
Upper Saddle River, NJ (1998)
Teaches how to set up and operate
a sound system and describes the
techniques that must be learned to
provide good performance experi-
ences for musicians and audiences.

*All You Need to Know About The
Music Business* (2nd. Ed.)
Donald S. Passman
Simon & Schuster Trade
New York, NY (1994)
A music business primer.

*The Billboard Guide to Home
Recording*
Ray Baragary
Billboard Books
New York, NY (1996)
A comprehensive reference and
step-by-step approach to recording
techniques and equipment options.

*The Billboard Guide to Music
Publicity*
Jim Pettigrew, Jr.
Billboard Books
New York, NY (1997)
Covers preparing an effective press
kit; producing press releases, public
service announcements, and pitch
letters; staging a publicity campaign;
using technology; and more.

*CD-ROM Professional's CD-
Recordable Handbook: The Complete
Guide to Practical Desktop CD
Recording*
Dana J. Parker and Robert A. Starrett
Pemberton Press, c/o Online Inc.
462 Danbury Road
Wilton, CT 06897 (1996)
A comprehensive guide to CD-R
technology. Provides information
about how to publish, distribute, and
archive information, images, audio,
software, and multimedia with CD-R.

*The Craft and Business of
Songwriting*
John Braheny
Writer's Digest Books
Cincinnati, OH (1995)
A practical guide for songwriters.

*Creating Internet Entertainment: A
Complete Guide for Web Developers
and Entertainment Professionals*
Jeannie Novak and Pete Markiewicz
Wiley Computer Publishing
New York, NY (1997)
A complete guide to planning,
creating, operating, and marketing
entertainment-based sites on the
World Wide Web.

Cutting Edge Web Audio
Ron Simpson
Prentice Hall PTR
Upper Saddle River, NJ (1998)
A comprehensive guide to creating
and deploying audio for the Web.
Includes a CD with demo versions of
several Web audio tools, along with
Web audio shareware and freeware.

Getting It Printed (Rev. Ed.)
Mark Beach
North Light Books
Cincinnati, OH (1993)
A guide to working with graphic
arts services and printers to assure
quality, stay on schedule, and con-
trol costs.

*Grateful Dead: The Official Book of
the Deadheads*
Editor: Paul Grushkin
Quill
New York, NY (1983)
A history of a great fan club.

Hard Disk Recording for Musicians
David Miles Huber
Amsco Publications
New York, NY (1995)
A guide to the equipment, tech-
niques, and processes of digital audio.
Includes information on computer-
based sound editing, digital audio
workstations, digital signal processing
techniques, etc.

Hit Men
Fredric Dannen
Vintage Books
New York, NY (1991)
An exposé of the darker side of the
music business.

How to Be Your Own Booking Agent
Jeri Goldstein
The New Music Times, Inc.
PO Box 1105
Charlottesville, VA 22902 (1998)
(804) 977-8979
www.nmtinc.com
An in-depth guide that will teach
you how to book tours creatively,
make efficient cold calls, develop
an effective press kit, sharpen your
negotiation skills, find funding
resources, access the media, maximize

record company relationships, and
expand your audience. Contains
information about where to find
gigs, what to include in your contract, which conferences to attend,
etc. Also includes hot tips and advice
from industry professionals.

*How to Make Money Performing
in Schools*
David Heflick
Silcox Productions
PO Box 1407
Orient, WA 99160 (1996)
(509) 684-8287
A complete guide to developing,
marketing, and presenting school
assembly programs.

How to Run a Recording Session
Jayce De Santis
Mix Books
6400 Hollis Street, Suite 12
Emeryville, CA 94608 (1997)
(510) 653-3307
Explains the duties of the engineer,
producer, and artist. Provides advice
on choosing songs, selecting a studio, planning a session, etc.

*Internet World Guide to Maintaining
and Updating Dynamic Web Sites*
Jeannie Novak and Pete Markiewicz
Wiley Computer Publishing
New York, NY (1998)
Provides proven methods for keeping your Web site interesting to
visitors and operating at maximum
efficiency.

Making Money Making Music
(Rev. Ed.)
James W. Dearing
Writer's Digest Books
Cincinnati, OH (1990)
Practical tips for increasing your
earnings by diversifying, examining
potential markets, and focusing on
building a local following.

*Making a Living in Your Local Music
Market*
Dick Weissman
Hal Leonard Publishing Corporation
Milwaukee, WI (1989)
A guide to regional music markets;
includes a comprehensive regional
resource list.

MIDI for Musicians
Craig Anderton
Music Sales Corporation
New York, NY (1987)
An introduction to how MIDI
works; setup and operation of
MIDI-based studios.

MIDI for the Professional
Paul D. Lehrman and Tim Tully
Amsco Publications
New York, NY (1993)
A complete technical guide to MIDI
devices and applications.

The MiniDisc
Jan Maes
Focal Press
Oxford, United Kingdom (1996)
A guide to the MiniDisc for audio
engineers, electronics students, and
hi-fi enthusiasts.

*Music Biz Know-How: Do-It-Yourself
Strategies for Independent Music
Success*
Peter Spellman
MBS Business Media
PO Box 230266
Boston, MA 02123 (1997)
(617) 639-1971
A wealth of information to help
boost your career, get better gigs,
network successfully, get airplay and
press, etc. Includes a comprehensive
resource list.

Music in Video Production
Roseanne Soifer
Knowledge Industry Publications
White Plains, NY (1992)
A business book for video producers.

*Music Publishing: A Songwriter's
Guide*
Randy Poe
Writer's Digest Books
Cincinnati, OH (1997)
Explains how songwriters and music
publishers earn royalties; and covers
publishing options—from single-
song contracts to starting your own
publishing company.

*Music Publishing: The Real Road to
Music Business Success*
Tim Whitsett
Mix Books
6400 Hollis Street, Suite 12
Emeryville, CA 94608 (1997)
(510) 653-3307
A guide to starting and operating a
music publishing company.

*The Musician's Business and Legal
Guide,* (Rev. 2nd Ed.)
Editor: Mark Halloran
Prentice-Hall, Inc.
Upper Saddle River, NJ (1996)
Prominent lawyers and business
people provide expert information
on key legal and business issues.
Clause-by-clause analyses of key
industry contracts are a real plus.

Musician's Guide to Home Recording
Peter McIan and Larry Wichman
Amsco Publications
New York, NY (1994)
Recording fundamentals, including
advice on how to set microphones
and record various instruments.

*The Musician's Guide to Making and
Selling Your Own CDs and Cassettes*
Jana Stanfield
Writer's Digest Books
Cincinnati, OH (1997)
A practical guide written by a triple-
platinum singer/songwriter on how
to produce your own recording and
build a successful career.

Networking in the Music Business
Dan Kimpel
Writer's Digest Books
Cincinnati, OH (1993)
Explains all the vital steps of net-
working.

*Off the Charts: Ruthless Days and
Reckless Nights Inside the Music
Industry*
Bruce Haring
Carol Publishing Group
Secaucus, NJ (1996)
A behind-the-scenes look at the
music industry and the shift of
emphasis from music to marketing.
The title says it all!

Rap: This Game of Exposure
a company called W
PO Box 618
Church Street Station
New York, NY 10008 (1992)
A guide to starting your own rap
record label and doing your own
promotion. Includes lists of "rap
friendly" radio stations, retail stores,
video shows, magazines, distributors, etc.

*The Songwriters Guide to
Collaboration* (Rev. 2nd Ed.)
Walter Carter
Mix Books
6400 Hollis Street, Suite 12
Emeryville, CA 94608 (1997)
(510) 653-3307
Discusses how to find a collaborator,
legal issues, the mechanics of writ-
ing, etc.

*Sound Check: The Basics of Sound
and Sound Systems*
Tony Moscal
Hal Leonard Corporation
Milwaukee, WI (1994)
A primer for musicians, students,
and aspiring audio engineers.

*Tim Sweeney's Guide to Releasing
Independent Records*
Tim Sweeney and Mark Geller
TSA Books
21213-B Hawthorne Boulevard
Suite 5255
Torrance, CA 90503 (1996)
(310) 542-6430
Teaches you how to set up an independent record label, make a
great-sounding record on a budget,
obtain distribution into major retail
chains and indie record stores.
Discusses successful promotion techniques, how to obtain airplay, etc.

You Can Hype Anything
Raleigh Pinskey
Citadel Press
Secaucus, New Jersey (1991)
Creative tactics and advice for anyone
with a product, business, or talent to
promote.

VIDEOS

Think Like A Producer
Tutt and Babe Music
950 2nd Street, Suite 304
Santa Monica, CA 90403
(310) 395-4835
Teaches multitrack recording techniques with a focus on the dynamics
and language of music production,
regardless of the type of equipment,
recording format, or number of
tracks being utilized. The video
provides step-by-step, track-by-
track demonstrations on how to
transform rough song ideas into
high-quality professional recordings.

SOFTWARE

*StarMaker, The Office Suite for
Musicians and Indie Labels*
Stringfellow Technologies
4392 Proctor Place
San Diego, CA 92116
e-mail: questions@stringfellow.com
www.stringfellow.com
Features include contact manager;
Digital Napkins; album release
planning and budgeting; record
sales (direct, distributors, and
stores); major record deal analyzer;
complete word processor; easy mail
labels and mail merge; to do lists
and calendar; accounting with royalty
calculations; bank account balancer
and check writer; complete spreadsheet; and tips, guidance, and useful
Web sites. Available for Windows.

about the author and contributors

about the author and contributors

diane Sward Rapaport began offering courses for musicians in music business management and publishing in 1974, after working for seven years as an artist's manager for Bill Graham's Fillmore Management.

Her dream was to help musicians overcome the conditioning that had many of them convinced they should starve for the sake of their art.

In 1976, she cofounded, edited, and published *Music Works—A Manual for Musicians,* a magazine hailed as a "bible for musicians" by the San Francisco Chronicle.

In 1979, her book *How to Make and Sell Your Own Record* was published. It has sold more than 150,000 copies since it was first published in 1979.

In 1988, she founded Jerome Headlands Press, a company which produces, designs, and copublishes books for musicians and artists. Its current catalog includes *How to Make and Sell Your Own Recording; The Musician's Business and Legal Guide; The Visual Artist's Business and Legal Guide* and *The Acoustic Musician's Guide to Sound Reinforcement and Live Recording.* The books are published by Prentice Hall.

Her company also provides public relations services for companies that sell pollution prevention and environmental remediation technologies.

edward (Ned) R. Hearn is in private law practice. He has offices in San Jose and San Francisco. Mr Hearn's practice concentrates on entertainment, Internet, and computer software businesses. He is a director of the California Lawyers for the Arts, an organization that provides legal assistance to musicians and other artists, board president of the Northern California Songwriters' Association, and coauthor of The Musician's Guide to Copyright and The Musician's Business and Legal Guide. Mr. Hearn also lectures on music business and related legal issues.

• • •

gregory T. Victoroff has been an entertainment litigation attorney since 1979, representing clients in the music, film, and fine art businesses in Los Angeles. He is a frequent author and lecturer on copyright and art law. Mr. Victoroff is editor and coauthor of The Visual Artist's Business and Legal Guide and coauthor of The Musician's Business and Legal Guide. As an orchestral musician, he has backed such artists as Huey Lewis and the News, Santana, and Bobby McFerrin.

index